THE HISTORY OF JAPANESE ECONOMIC DEVELOPMENT

This is an easy-to-read book that explains how and why Japan industrialized rapidly. It traces historical development from the feudal Edo period to high income and technology in the current period. Catch-up industrialization is analyzed from a broad perspective including social, economic and political aspects. Historical data, research and contesting arguments are amply supplied. Japan's unique experience is contrasted with the practices of today's developing countries. Negative aspects such as social ills, policy failures, military movements and war years are also covered.

Nineteenth-century Japan already had a happy combination of strong entrepreneurship and relatively wise government, which was the result of Japan's long evolutionary history. Measured contacts with high civilizations of China, India and the West allowed cumulative growth without being destroyed by them. Imported ideas and technology were absorbed with adjustments to fit the local context.

The book grew out of a graduate course for government officials from developing countries. It offers a comprehensive look and new insights at Japan's industrial path that are often missing in standard historical chronicles. Written in an accessible and lively form, the book engages scholars as well as novices with no prior knowledge of Japan.

Kenichi Ohno is Professor at the National Graduate Institute for Policy Studies, Tokyo. He was born in Kobe, Japan and holds a PhD in Economics from Stanford University, California. He worked at the International Monetary Fund and taught at the University of Tsukuba and Saitama University before assuming his current position.

THE HISTORY OF JAPANESE ECONOMIC DEVELOPMENT

Origins of Private Dynamism and Policy Competence

Kenichi Ohno

Routledge
Taylor & Francis Group
LONDON AND NEW YORK

First published 2018
by Routledge
2 Park Square, Milton Park, Abingdon, Oxon OX14 4RN

and by Routledge
711 Third Avenue, New York, NY 10017

Routledge is an imprint of the Taylor & Francis Group, an informa business

British Library Cataloguing in Publication Data
A catalogue record for this book is available from the British Library

Library of Congress Cataloging in Publication Data
Names: Ono, Ken'ichi, 1957- author.
Title: The history of Japanese economic development : origins of private dynamism and policy competence / by Kenichi Ohno.
Description: First Edition. | New York : Routledge, [2017] | Includes bibliographical references and index.
Identifiers: LCCN 2017018249| ISBN 9781138215399 (hardback) | ISBN 9781138215429 (pbk.) | ISBN 9781315444048 (ebook)
Subjects: LCSH: Economic development—Japan—History. | Japan—Economic policy. | Banks and banking—Japan—History.
Classification: LCC HC462.95 .O626 2017 | DDC 338.952—dc23
LC record available at https://lccn.loc.gov/2017018249

ISBN: 978-1-138-21539-9 (hbk)
ISBN: 978-1-138-21542-9 (pbk)
ISBN: 978-1-315-44404-8 (ebk)

DOI: 10.4324/9781315444048

Visit the companion website: www.routledge.com/cw/ohno

CONTENTS

FIGURES

TABLES

BOXES

INTRODUCTION

This book offers a historical tour of Japan's socio-economic changes over the last few centuries paying particular attention to industrialization. It is not intended to be a monotonous chronology or a collection of specialized academic research. Rather, it explains why Japan developed so fast among all latecomers by presenting a broad and coherent picture of its steps from a comparative perspective. While the writing style of this book may seem plain and not overly technical, it nonetheless introduces the reader to a large amount of facts and data as well as advanced—and sometimes highly controversial—research on the modern history of Japan. As such, the book is suitable for those who have little prior knowledge of Japanese society or economy but want to take a quick look at how Japan industrialized. But those who already know much about Japan will also benefit greatly from the rich information and arguments concisely presented in this volume. In this sense, the book is introductory and professional at the same time.

Materials contained in this book were originally made available to master-level students who took my course, Economic Development of Japan, from 1999 at the National Graduate Institute for Policy Studies (GRIPS), Tokyo. The majority of my students were young government officials from developing countries. In 2006, course materials were printed in textbook form and began to be distributed free of charge to enrolled students. Soon, it became clear that the book was very much wanted beyond the classroom by policy makers and advisors in different countries who were eager to learn about Japanese development experience. I was approached variously by my former students, a Chinese publisher, the Japan Foundation and researchers abroad specializing in Japan, for permission to translate my English textbook into several other languages. As a result, Japanese, Vietnamese, Chinese, Arabic, Russian and Persian editions are now available. I have also frequently been asked to give a condensed lecture on the subject to various audiences in Japan, Vietnam and Ethiopia. Meanwhile, my course kept evolving and expanding as I discovered new studies and as my students raised stimulating questions and comments.

The popularity of this textbook convinced me that the time was ripe for significant revision and commercial publication—the original printing was financed by a research fund that required noncommercial circulation—to incorporate new findings as well as to reach larger readership. All chapters, sections and boxes have been revised considerably or entirely rewritten, new information and diagrams have been added, and the final chapter was extended with recent developments. The present publication should thus be regarded as a new production rather than a slightly updated second edition.

I am not an economic historian but a practitioner of economic development. My main research interest is why some economies industrialize rapidly while others stagnate at low to

DOI: 10.4324/9781315444048-1

middle income and never attain great prosperity. My hypothesis is that divergent growth performance can be explained mainly by the amount of initial private dynamism and the quality of industrial policy. In close cooperation with the Japanese government, I regularly conduct industrial policy dialogue with the leaders and policy makers of Vietnam and Ethiopia. I advise them and train young people from these countries as well as other countries in Asia and Africa. I also teach Policy Design and Implementation in Developing Countries at GRIPS with other instructors. Through these activities, I am acutely aware of practical difficulties these countries face in executing development policies. The central topic of this book, how and why Japan industrialized rapidly from the mid-nineteenth century onward, may seem a little worn-out to Japanese scholars who have already spilled a huge amount of ink on the issue. But I still take it up, in the hope that we may see the road traveled by past Japan in a new light shed by the standards and common sense of today's developing countries.

This book contains no original research or new primary data. It is just a careful rearrangement of facts and analyses extracted from a large amount of existing literature mostly written in Japanese. But this can be the strength of the book. It portrays Japanese history not as random details specialists like to investigate, but as a comprehensive and continuing story that compares Japan with other latecomers. Japanese experience is told not as a past tale to be reminisced about but as a contemporary message to foreign elites who are at this very moment struggling to develop their national economies. We recognize ourselves by the existence of others. International comparison is essential to understand the characteristics of any society in both its uniqueness and commonality. My lectures at GRIPS are meant to be a mirror in which foreign students discover their own societies and their strengths and missing elements. At the same time, they can also serve as a mirror for Japanese people to re-discover themselves. I myself encountered numerous surprises in preparing and delivering these lectures. Domestic research closed to the rest of the world cannot uncover Japan's true position in world history.

History proceeds as endless interaction between domestic factors and foreign influences, with the relative strength of each changing over time. In this process, domestic society is the solid foundation into which foreign elements are selectively introduced—or so it should be if foreign impact is to energize the existing society rather than destroy it. Japanese history is unique in that the alternation of domestic and foreign forces went on for over two millennia without serious disruption or eradication of any previous major achievements. This imparted evolutionary and cumulative quality to Japanese history, unlike societies where foreign influences often came in the form of violent invaders who wiped out existing political structure and rewrote state and ethnic boundaries, which made social continuity hardly possible. In contrast, Japan's evolutionary history generated resilience, flexibility and long memory in both the rulers and the ruled. Japanese society developed organically from centralized monarchy to its gradual disintegration, which brought a rise of local powers, and private commerce and industry under feudalism. By the end of the Edo period (1603–1867), from which this book starts its journey, Japanese society was mature enough to be able to quickly absorb and internalize new systems and technology imported from the West.

After the general framework is presented in Chapter 1, the rest of the book sequentially explains concrete cases of interaction between domestic and foreign forces, as well as between public and private sectors, from the Edo period to present. Japanese industrialization, which progressed very fast in the Meiji period and the post-WW2 period, is depicted as social transformation driven by strong private dynamism supported by appropriate policies from the sideline. The main engine of growth was active private players while the government, on average, also played a useful role as a coach and promoter. The strength of both sectors, in turn, was the result of Japan's evolutionary history mentioned above. The reader should be duly amazed at such dual strength, which is rarely seen in today's developing and emerging economies. Few latecomer societies combine globally competitive entrepreneurship with wise government, with the possible exceptions of Singapore, Taiwan and Korea. My students from developing country governments are often impressed with how effectively Meiji leaders and Showa businessmen worked, competed and cooperated. This also leads to the conclusion that Japanese experience cannot be transplanted to a different soil without prior adjustment and serious additional learning.

Another feature of this book is ample discussion of the socio-political elements behind economic growth. Economics cannot be separated from politics and social change as they arise mutually to shape national development. Negative events such as wars, social unrest, environmental damage and political uncertainty are also taken up so far as they defined and influenced the path of industrialization. The question of why Japan became an aggressive invader and colonizer of neighboring Asia, ultimately leading to the Pacific War, which is often skipped in the teaching of Japanese history, is squarely addressed to the extent that this can be regarded as another main theme of this book apart from the reasons for rapid industrialization.

I would like to thank my students at GRIPS over the last eighteen years for giving me an opportunity and reason to write and continuously revise this book, and Ms. Yuka Akiyama for her proficient support in preparing the current edition. The result looks quite different from the original textbook, not just because the text and diagrams have been greatly modified and added, and the front cover has been redesigned, but also because photographs generously used in the previous edition were all eliminated for reasons of space and cost. Additional lecture slides and data available to my students cannot be included for the same reasons. Nevertheless, the book is sufficiently rich to serve as the first textbook for newcomers in Japanese history as well as a compact guidebook on ongoing issues and debates for specialists. Missing photos of political and business leaders, major historical events and early factories and structures can be viewed easily in the internet age. I hope the readers will enjoy the book.

Kenichi Ohno

1

AN OVERVIEW

Evolutionary history and translative adaptation

Domestic society and external forces

In any country, history proceeds as an interaction between domestic and foreign forces. In the discussion of Japanese development that follows, this aspect of systemic interaction will be highlighted. Japan's modernization began with its encounter with the powerful West in the nineteenth century. The path of Japanese industrialization thereafter can be interpreted as the process of various domestic actors, including the government, businesses, communities and individuals, responding to shocks and influences coming from abroad. This perspective is very useful even today, since developing countries are now required to develop in the strong presence of globalizing pressure. The development process of such countries can also be understood as two systems, local and foreign, in dynamic interaction. Today, new ideas and systems often come with such names as the market mechanism, democracy, conditionality, international best practice, MDGs and SDGs, bilateral and regional free trade agreements, and so on.

Domestic society is the base into which new foreign systems are introduced. Each society has unique characteristics reflecting its geography, ecology and history. Existing institutions in any society are mutually dependent and form a coherent whole (this is called "institutional complementarity"). Domestic societies have their own logic and mechanisms of internal evolution and, for certain periods, can evolve mainly through internal forces. This evolution is usually slow and continuous. But when exposed to strong foreign impacts, social equilibrium is suddenly disturbed and the country is dislodged from its previous course. If the domestic response to foreign elements is resilient and appropriate, the society will begin a new dynamic path of evolution. But if the response is weak or inconsistent, the society may be destabilized or even destroyed under foreign dominance.

In the twentieth century, isolation and self-sufficiency were pursued under socialist planning in some countries, but the effort failed miserably to produce economic dynamism. Since the disappearance of the Soviet Union, refusal to integrate into the global economy has been totally discredited as a national development strategy. While the policies of the World Trade Organization (WTO), the International Monetary Fund (IMF) and the World Bank contain many shortcomings, latecomer countries have no option but to join these international organizations and receive their policy advice. Now the question is not whether to integrate but how

DOI: 10.4324/9781315444048-2

to integrate better. International integration is the necessary condition for development, but it is not sufficient (UNCTAD, 2004).

The term *development* does not necessarily imply the existence of external influence. Theoretically, development can be either internally motivated or externally driven. In our age, however, it has become almost impossible to achieve sound and sustainable development without effectively coping with and integrating into the global system. Development now carries almost the same meaning as "catching up with industrial countries" or "modernization through trade, FDI, and industrialization." From a long historical viewpoint, this is a very special type of development. But we can hardly think of any other way. Whether desirable or not, this is the reality we face today.[1]

Throughout its history, Japan also experienced periods of relatively tranquil internal evolution and periods of dynamic change under strong external influence. These periods alternated to create Japanese society in a multi-layered fashion (Figure 1.1). Major external impacts on Japan included the following:

- Rice cultivation—introduced from the Eurasian Continent around the third century BC (recent evidence shows that arrival of rice cultivation may have been earlier).
- Buddhism—brought from China via Korean Peninsula in the sixth century AD.
- Chinese culture and political system—imported vigorously from the seventh to the early tenth century AD.

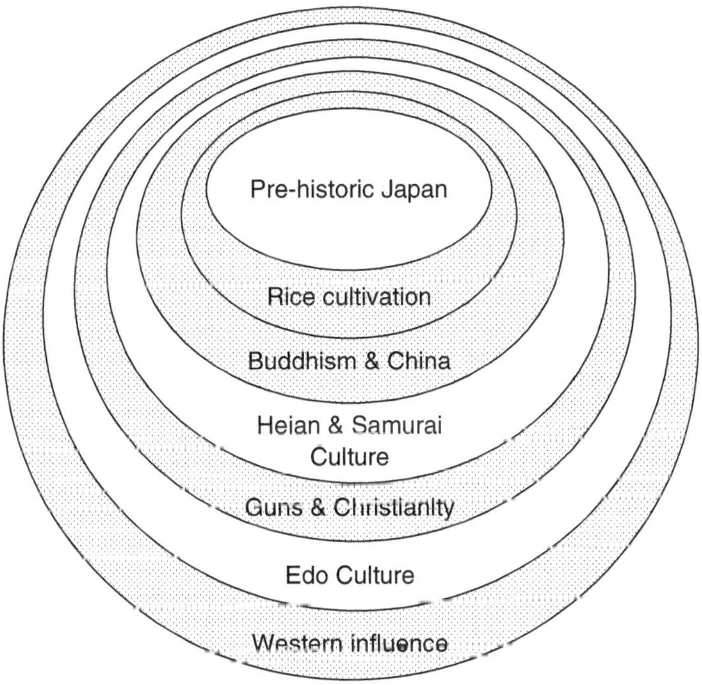

Figure 1.1 Japan's multi-layered identity

Note: shaded areas indicate external impacts.

- First direct contact with Europeans (Spaniards and Portuguese)—guns and Christianity arrived in the sixteenth century AD.
- Modernization—second contact with the industrialized West in the nineteenth century.
- Post-WW2 reforms—under US occupation, defeated Japan was transformed into a non-warring capitalist nation.

The Mongolians also tried to invade Japan twice in the thirteenth century, but their military attempts failed. On each occasion, Japanese resistance, combined with a huge storm, destroyed their fleet off the coast of Kyushu Island. Had the Mongolian invasion been successful, Japan would have received another big foreign impact.

Compared with the history of other countries in the non-Western world, it can be said that Japan absorbed successive external shocks rather well, and used them positively for change and new growth. Japan also retained its national identity throughout this process, although Japan today and Japan in the past look entirely different in their appearance. Japanese society exhibits a multi-layered, onion-like structure as shown above, where old and new elements coexist flexibly and different characteristics can surface depending on the circumstance. Meanwhile, one Chinese social scientist has remarked that China is like a hard stone ball that cannot change unless it is exploded and replaced by another hard ball (called "revolution"), maybe of a different color.

The Japanese people happily absorb a large number of potentially conflicting elements and use them interchangeably as occasions require. This is a unique feature of the Japanese people not often seen in other societies. To put it positively, the Japanese are flexible, generous and pragmatic. But to put it critically, they are without principle, fidelity or consistency. In his book *Japanese Thought* (1961), Maruyama Masao lamented that the Japanese had no tradition of thinking logically though they were full of emotion and experience. This criticism may be legitimate from the viewpoint of Western rationalism. But from another aspect, the seemingly principle-less way of the Japanese may have value if we are to coexist peacefully among different ethnicities, religions and ideologies in an integrated world. At any rate, the point to be stressed here is that Japanese attitude is quite different from Western attitude, without asserting which is superior.

This book focuses on Japan's last great transformations driven by external shocks, namely the process of Westernization and industrialization under the strong pressure of the West during the nineteenth and twentieth centuries.

Translative adaptation

The idea of translative adaptation is proposed by Maegawa Keiji (1998), an economic anthropologist at Tsukuba University.

When a country in the periphery joins the world system, it may look as if the country (say, Ethiopia) is being absorbed in the dominant international order (say, the global trade system). It looks as if the country is forced to abandon its traditional culture, systems, social structure and so on, which are considered "backward," in order to embrace the "international best practice." Viewed from inside the country in the process of "being absorbed," however, the situation is not always passive. In a proper integration process, Maegawa argues that the country should take initiative in deciding the scope and speed of integration, making sure that it can retain ownership (national autonomy), social continuity and national identity.

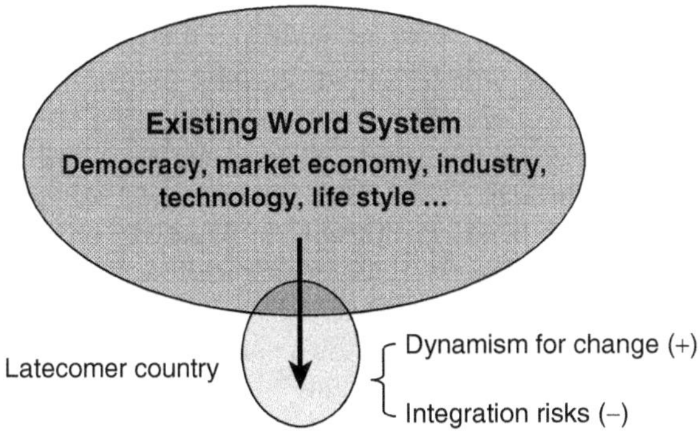

Figure 1.2 Integration viewed from outside

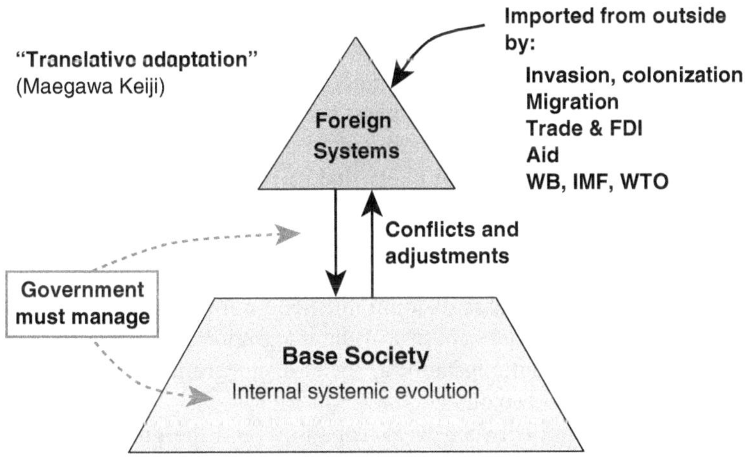

Figure 1.3 Integration viewed from inside

The country surely changes, but the change is managed by its government and people and not by foreign firms or international organizations. Foreign ideas and systems are introduced not in the original form but with modifications to fit local needs and context. If this is achieved, the transformed country is not really so weak or passive. It is taking advantage of external stimuli to change and grow. This is called "translative adaptation." Maegawa says that Japan since the Meiji period did just that.

> When a non-Western society encounters a powerful representative of Western civilization, it is hardly possible to escape from its influences. Some ethnic groups have been eradicated in short periods after contact with the West. At the same time, many nations and societies have adopted Western institutions and objects from without in order to survive (or by their own choice). However, it is important to recognize that

> they did not accept Western inventions in their original forms. Any item in one culture will change its meaning when transplanted to another culture, as seen widely in ethnography around the world. Not only cosmology, religious doctrine, rituals, but also the family system, the institution of exchange, and even socio-economic organizations like the firm exhibit the property of adapting to external institutions and principles with the existing cultural system maintaining its form of structure. The essence of what has been called "modernization" is the adaptive acceptance of Western civilization under the persistent form of the existing culture. That is, actors in the existing system have adapted to the new system by reinterpreting each element of Western culture (i.e. "civilization") in their own value structure, modifying yet maintaining the existing institutions. I shall call this "translative adaptation."
>
> (Maegawa, 1998, pp. 174–175)

However, international integration is a risky process and not all countries can perform translative adaptation successfully. A developing country exposed to strong external pressure faces a great challenge. This is a critical moment in the history of that country. Compared with the more predictable days of internal evolution, the fate of the society and its people now hinges critically on how they react to this challenge. Domestic capability is still weak, while the demands of globalization are high. Suddenly, the country is required to make a great leap forward or fall into an abyss. It is as if an average student is told by his teacher to participate in an international math competition. With enormous effort, he may improve his skill and win. But it is more likely that he will fail miserably. The problem is that the challenge is too big for his current ability. If the goal is unreachable, the effort is not fruitful.

While there is no doubt that the effort of domestic businesses and communities is important, the most crucial response to globalization must come from the policies of the central government. If the government loses control of the integration process, dire consequences may occur, such as macroeconomic instability, social disintegration, political crises, ethnic conflict, foreign dominance, and so on.

When caught in a dilemma between weak capability and the great challenges of globalization, some governments refuse to deal with the external world and revert to isolation, economic control and the rejection of Western ideas. Other governments rush to embrace the imported principles of free trade and Western democracy uncritically, without considering the effects this brings to the domestic society. Both reaction patterns are shallow, extreme and unadvisable. Translative adaptation requires much deeper knowledge of the top policy makers. It is indeed a very difficult task.

Japan too faced great challenges when it opened up to the Western world in the middle of the nineteenth century. It also experienced similar hardship after the war defeat of 1945. In both cases, Japan eventually emerged as a brilliantly successful latecomer, at least economically.

Why Japan could succeed

Traditionally, we consider Japan in the nineteenth century as a weak, agricultural and backward country with low technology suddenly exposed to influences from the powerful West. Japan struggled to industrialize and somehow succeeded. But why did only Japan succeed so early, among all non-Western countries? This is the biggest question for whoever studies

Japan's modern history. However, Umesao Tadao, a distinguished scholar in comparative civilization, says that there is no mystery here. According to him, Japan emerged as a non-Western industrial country very naturally.

Until 1993, Umesao was the director general of the National Museum of Ethnology in Osaka, which he founded in 1974. In his earlier days, he traveled extensively in Mongolia, Afghanistan, Southeast Asia, Africa and Europe undertaking anthropological fieldwork. In 1957, he proposed a new theory of Japanese history and national identity.

Umesao (1986, 2003) says that the traditional view of Japan as a backward country is wrong. He argues that Japan and Western Europe are two very unique societies in the world. Both enjoy temperate climate. More importantly, both are located on the periphery of the huge Eurasian continent. Thus, they are relatively insulated from violent invasions by nomadic peoples residing in the central dry areas of the continent. He argues that this locational advantage is crucial for the spontaneous and continuous development of society. Japan and the United Kingdom are particularly similar in that they are island nations just off the Eurasian Continent.

Japan and Western Europe were situated at an appropriate distance (not too far, not too close) from the great civilizations of Eurasia—namely, China, India and the Middle East (Islam). Both could absorb the cultural achievements of these civilizations easily by sending official envoys or commercial traders while the chance of being invaded and destroyed is much smaller than that of societies located in the middle of the continent. According to what Umesao calls an ecological view of history, this geographical advantage permitted both societies to evolve cumulatively and organically. They mixed domestic culture and foreign impact properly, without being wiped out every few centuries and having to start over again from scratch. The right distance from superior civilizations had the double advantage of managing cultural inflow and defending against invaders.

Under these similar historical conditions, Japan and Western Europe developed independently and in parallel—from centralized imperialism to power decentralization, feudalism, absolutism, emergence of strong local private sectors, and finally capitalism. It is no accident that the Industrial Revolution originated in the United Kingdom, and that Japan

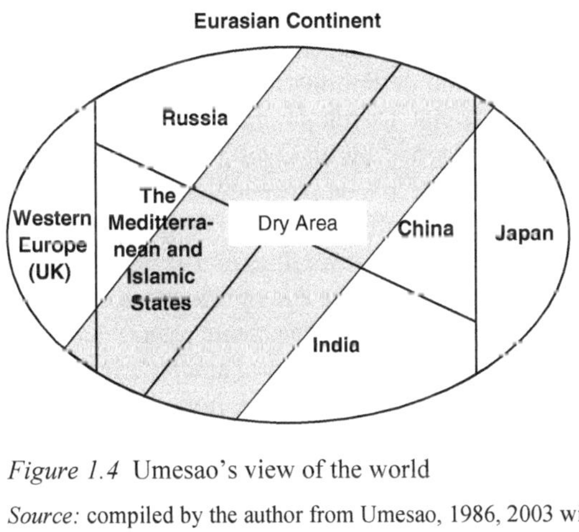

Figure 1.4 Umesao's view of the world

Source: compiled by the author from Umesao, 1986, 2003 with comments and approval by Umesao.

was the only non-Western country to industrialize as thoroughly as the West by the twentieth century. In no other areas did history evolve so sequentially. According to Umesao, Japan got behind the United Kingdom because it adopted the bizarre policy of external isolation from 1639 to 1854 (Chapter 2). Had this deviation not occurred, Umesao asserts, the two nations would have achieved the Industrial Revolution at about the same time.[2]

What do repeated impacts from the outside world, without eradicating the core of the receiving society, produce? Umesao seems to suggest that frequent merger of domestic and foreign elements makes the society resilient to external shocks and at the same time flexible enough to change, producing dynamism under continuity. This is plausible, but exactly how this is done is still in the black box. One possible explanation is that the mind-sets of both the ruler (policy maker) and the ruled (farmers, workers and entrepreneurs) are transformed by institutional memory that leads to the formation of dominant social ethos that preserves the society against shocks. That is to say, the history of turbulent times and forced change is told and re-told through books, poems, songs and theatrical arts in which the hero or heroine laments the cruel fate but chooses or accepts the action that best serves the interests of the society and not of self. Such stories are never forgotten. Spiritual values such as hard work, high aspiration, honesty, patience, sacrifice and broad vision become esteemed and reinforced.

Chinese, Indian and Islamic civilizations produced great cultural achievements, but their social structures were fundamentally static; only empire and dictatorship (and later, colonialism) ruled. From one dynasty to another, there was no clear progress from the viewpoint of social and political evolution. For thousands of years, emperors and kings were basically the same though some were wiser than others and policies differed from one dynasty to another. According to Umesao, only Western Europe and Japan satisfied the historical conditions necessary to industrialize. Japan did not imitate the West as the two areas developed spontaneously and independently (North America can be regarded as an offshoot of Western Europe). He is pessimistic about the possibility of industrialization in the rest of the world, including all the developing countries today.

This chapter has introduced Umesao's view not because the author agrees with him completely, but because it contains something that is interesting and stimulating. His interpretation of Japanese history is unique and in the minority. In fact, his view is not very well known even among Japanese, as he himself admits. Many would feel uneasy with the assertion that industrialization takes place only under certain strict historical conditions and nowhere else, which seems too simplistic and deterministic. If the path to industrialization cannot be crafted but only inherited, Official Development Assistance (ODA), Foreign Direct Investment (FDI), development assistance by bilateral and multilateral donors, and all studies in economic development (including this one) are in vain. Can we really say that China or India will never become a fully industrialized country? Does Africa have no hope?

Industrialization is more dynamic and flexible today. Umesao's explanation may be valid up to the recent past. However, we are now living in the age of internet, air travel and global exchange of information. Physical distance from the center country should no longer matter very much. Even though history is ingrained deeply in the characteristics of each people, ethnic traits are also dynamic and changeable. There should be more than one path to development in response to different initial conditions and shifting historical circumstances. With great leadership and ideas, a new way of development suitable for each country should be found. Additionally, Umesao does not discuss the role of technology, entrepreneurship and investment very much. Being a specialist in comparative civilization, he emphasizes the evolution of social structure rather than the technical absorptive capacity of each nation. But the latter is also crucial in determining the success or failure of development.

Having said this, however, Umesao may be quite right in certain points. In particular, his theory can explain why Japan had a unique social structure suitable for industrialization that is not observable in other countries, even before its encounter with the industrialized West. This was forged by the uninterrupted organic evolution of the Japanese society over the two millennia. This permitted Japan to absorb new foreign influences flexibly in the translative adaptation of Western thought and technology. Japan's industrialization was driven by private dynamism, which was the primary force, supplemented by mostly appropriate policy support, which was secondary. Both of these conditions were generated through Japan's long evolutionary history. This, at least partly, should be an answer to the question of why Japan was able to achieve success so early.

In a series of historical essays entitled *The Shape of This Nation* (1986–1996), writer Shiba Ryotaro asked "What shaped Japanese people". The two key elements extracted by him as shapers of Japanese characters are an island nation and the samurai spirit. The former made Japanese curious about foreign ideas and technology, and willing to import them after adjusting them to local tastes and mindset (i.e., translative adaptation). For the latter, the highest value of samurai is honor, not personal gain or family prosperity. This sentiment has permeated Japanese life. Japanese people want to live and die honorably, avoiding shame even without the commandment of God or government.

A brief history of Japan

While this book focuses on modern Japan, it is useful to take a brief look at the entire Japanese history at the outset. The summary given below is not meant to be an academically respectable discourse but a very rough sketch for those who know little about Japanese history. For beginners, Japanese history can be divided into four major periods: (i) the period in which emperors held real power, (ii) the period of samurai (warrior) leaders, (iii) the period of modernization and military invasion, and (iv) the period of post-WW2 growth and slowdown. Figure 1.5 shows this graphically while a concise table of Japanese history is provided in Table 1.1 at the end of this chapter.

Ethnically, the Japanese are a mixture of various people who came from the South and the North and inhabited the archipelago first, and the people who later came via the Korean Peninsula. The precise origins of these people are still debated. In the pre-historic period, the Japanese people were hunter-gatherers with limited agricultural activity. They lived separately in small villages with family as the basic unit but there was also trade through long-distance maritime traffic. They lived relatively peacefully.

When rice cultivation was introduced from the continent (third century BC or earlier), life changed significantly and history started. Rice cultivation on Japanese soil required collective effort by all villagers under effective leadership. Village size grew and social order was established. Religious and military leaders emerged to form mini states. Wars among mini states became common, and after a few centuries of fighting (details of which is not known due to the shortage of written evidence), Japan was politically unified for the first time, around the fourth century AD. But many powerful clans existed to influence the ruler and policies, including the acceptance or rejection of imported Buddhism.

After a few more centuries, the imperial family grasped real power by slaying the most powerful clan leaders and subordinating others (Reform of Taika, 645 AD). Under a series

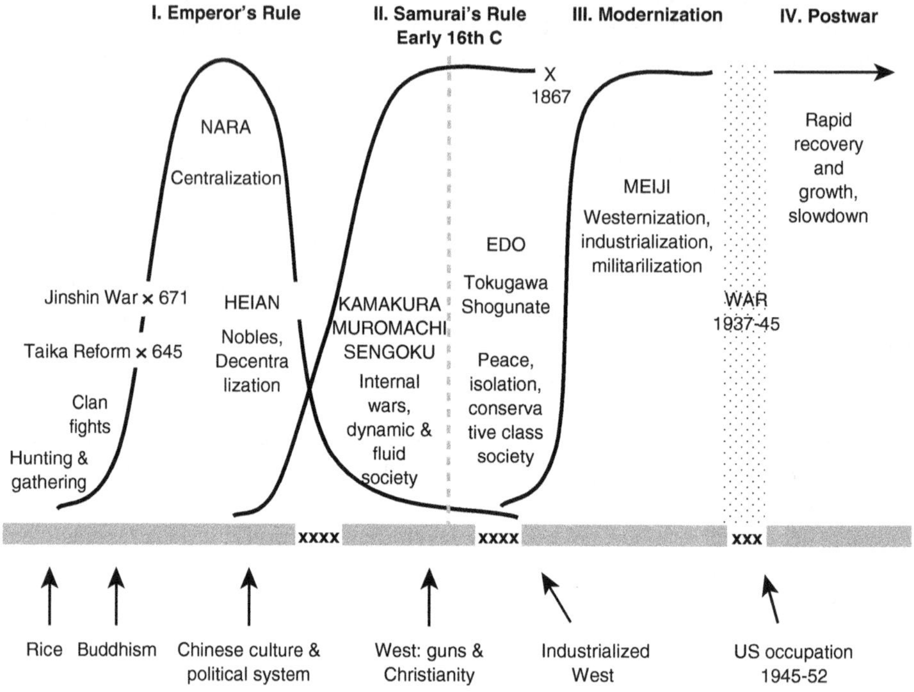

Figure 1.5 Four periods of Japanese history

Note: the bar at the bottom illustrates vigorous importation of foreign ideas and objects while xxx indicates interruption or reduction of such imports. Major occasions of foreign imports are also shown.

of strong emperors, a centralized government modeled after Chinese bureaucracy and tax system was created. Many capital cities were built and abandoned one after another (consider how much resource was wasted in doing this!), but finally, in 794, the nation's capital was settled permanently in Kyoto.[3] Military conquests of minority peoples were conducted. Buddhism was used for the political purpose of demonstrating the emperor's power and ruling the country. This was the only period in Japanese history in which the emperor had real political and military power.

The age of samurai

But power concentration did not last very long. Soon, local leaders, landlords and temples became more independent from the central government and stopped paying taxes or obeying official orders. They established *shoen* (manors) and employed people to cultivate it. To protect their land from invaders, the warrior class (samurai) emerged. For samurai, land was the most precious asset to be defended with their lives. Meanwhile, the political power of the imperial family and surrounding nobles gradually declined. They composed poems, performed countless rituals and ceremonies, and played *kemari* (garden football) in Kyoto. To suppress uprisings or solve conflicts, they had to rely on the military might of the competing samurai groups.

From the end of the twelfth century onward, samurai leaders began to form government with the permission of the emperor.[4] The age of samurai went through two distinct periods. The first period saw constant fighting for land and power among samurai leaders while the second, after national reunification was attained in the early seventeenth century, featured a peaceful but highly conservative and bureaucratic rule by the Tokugawa family.

The first samurai government was established in Kamakura, 350km east of Kyoto, in 1192 (Kyoto was still the capital—where the emperor resided—but real power rested with samurai in Kamakura). The top samurai was called *shogun*. The Kamakura government guaranteed follower samurai their right to possess land and also distributed new land to those with distinguished service in war. However, Japan was greatly shaken by two invasion attempts by the Mongolians in 1274 and 1281. Each time, the great Mongolian fleet attacked the coast of Kyushu but was repelled by a combination of Japanese resistance and a huge storm. While unsuccessful, the Mongolian attacks led to the eventual collapse of the Kamakura government in 1333. It ran out of land to distribute to samurai who bravely fought Mongolians.

After this, long fights among *daimyo* (regional samurai leaders) ensued for nearly three hundred years. It was a dynamic but very dangerous age. The Kamakura government was replaced by another military government, based in Kyoto, of the Ashikaga family, but the latter failed to restore order. The imperial family split into two lines (later merged), and samurai fighting for family leadership or local land sided with the one or the other to justify their private cause. Daimyos were initially appointed by the central government, but later became autonomous from it. Private fights, some lasting for decades, became common, devastating Kyoto and other cities, burning temples and weakening the central authority. Internal wars culminated in the seventeenth century, called the Sengoku (Warring) Period, where daimyos mobilized any means, military or otherwise, to eradicate others in a competition to emerge as the ultimate ruler to reunify Japan and end all wars.

Oda Nobunaga, the merciless fighter, and Toyotomi Hideyoshi, the witty manager, came close. But they did not finish the job. Finally, Tokugawa Ieyasu, the old and patient, emerged as the winner and established the Edo government in 1603 (in what is now called Tokyo). He burned the Osaka Castle and eliminated the Toyotomi family. The Warring period came to an end and the Tokugawa family ruled Japan for two-and-half centuries, with fifteen shoguns in all.

The Edo samurai government was politically conservative. It imposed rigid social order and severely limited and monopolized foreign contact and trade, with a few exceptions.[5] Under the feudal system, the central government allocated land to rule (called Han) to daimyos. Peace was restored under a strict bureaucratic rule. Nevertheless, in recent historical research, the Edo period is viewed as a dynamically evolving period rather than a stagnant dark age. Under international isolation that lasted more than two centuries (1639–1854), land cultivation expanded, agricultural productivity rose, and commercial crops, trade, industry and finance grew. Rich merchant families emerged and Japan's unique culture developed. Conditions for industrialization were ripe.

Meiji and modernization

Several Western powers wanted to open up Japan from its self-imposed isolation. First, the Russians came. Then the British, the Americans, and the French knocked on the door. But the Edo government refused to deal with them. Finally, in 1853, the American troops led by Commodore Perry came with four "Black Ships" loaded with powerful guns to open Japanese ports. The Edo government—and the entire nation—was thrown into confusion. In the following year, the government yielded to the American pressure and signed the Japan–US Friendship Treaty. Other Western powers followed the American move. The Americans further demanded a full commercial treaty with Japan. A strong anti-foreigner movement emerged all over Japan while others argued for actively trading with the West and importing modern military technology. In 1858, in the midst of a heated national debate, the Edo government suppressed the opposition and concluded commercial treaties with the West without the consent of the emperor. These commercial treaties were later found out to be defective, with Japan having no right to judge foreign criminals or set its own import tariffs (Chapter 3). Criticism against the Edo government rose sharply and internal political fights over foreign trade as well as the legitimacy of the Tokugawa rule ensued for about a decade, finally toppling the Edo government militarily in 1867–1868.

The new Meiji government restored the emperor (who for a long time had no real power) as the nation's supreme ruler and adopted a policy of rapid Westernization, modernization and militarization. In the political area, the first constitution modeled after German constitutional monarchy was promulgated in 1889 and parliamentary election and sessions began in the following year. In the economic area, the adoption of Western technology and the creation of modern industries became the top national goal. The textile industry gradually emerged as an internationally competitive industry. In the military area, Japan won a war against China (Qing Dynasty) in 1894–95 and began to invade Korea (it was later colonized in 1910). Japan also fought a victorious war against the Russian Empire in 1904–5. In the early twentieth century, about a half century after opening ports under American military threat, Japan was admitted as a member of Big Five, the group of powerful nations, along with the US, the UK, France and Italy.

The Japanese economy experienced an enormous export-led boom during WW1. But a period of mediocre growth ensued after the export boom ended. During the 1920s, heavy industrialization proceeded despite frequent recessions, the Great Kanto Earthquake of 1923, and banking crises. The 1920s also witnessed the party cabinet system featuring competition between the two major political parties, and foreign diplomacy couched on the spirit of international cooperation (especially with the US). However, Japan turned decisively to militarism in the 1930s. In the 1931 Manchurian Incident, Northeast China was occupied by Japanese army stationed in China that acted independently from the Tokyo government. Effort to fight militarism by politicians, academic and press eventually failed to stop army aggression. Political terrorism was rampant. A full-scale war with China was initiated in 1937 and the Pacific War began in 1941. Wartime economic planning was adopted. People were mobilized for war effort, and production of food and clothing was curtailed for military production.

Postwar growth and slowdown

Japan was defeated in 1945 and the country's economic base was lost by American bombing and sinking of ships. Under the US military occupation of 1945–1951, a production recovery strategy based on material planning was successfully conducted in 1947–1948 and postwar inflation was terminated in 1949. From the mid-1950s through the early 1970s, Japan enjoyed very rapid growth and industrialization. The manufacturing sector expanded

Table 1.1 Outline of Japanese history

	Period	*Domestic events*	*External events*
Rise and Fall of Emperor	**Jomon** (–3c. BC)	Hunting and gathering, limited agriculture	
	Yayoi / Kofun (3c. BC–5c. AD)	Internal wars → **Unification of Japan**	←**Rice production** introduced →Diplomacy with China (tributary) →Intervention in Korea (failed)
	Asuka / Hakuho (5–7c. AD)	Clan politics *Tenno* (emperor) family consolidates power	←**Buddhism** introduced (via Korea)
	Nara (710–794) Capital: Nara	**Ritsuryo System**—emperor's direct rule based on laws and centralized government; Buddhism promoted as state religion	←**Chinese political system and culture** imported
	Heian (794–1192) Capital: Kyoto	Court politics and rituals by nobles Manorial system (power decentralization) Rise of samurai (warrior) class	× Diplomacy with China terminated
The Age of Samurai	**Kamakura** (1192–1333) Cap: Kamakura	**First samurai government** New Buddhist sects for people emerge	←**Two Mongolian invasions (failed)**
	Muromachi (1338–1573) Capital: Kyoto	Samurai government Two emperor lines compete (north and south) Internal wars and rebellions	→Trade with China resumes →Japanese pirates attack Chinese coast →**Active trade with Southeast Asia**

(continued)

Table 1.1 (continued)

	Period	*Domestic events*	*External events*
The Age of Samurai	**Sengoku** (–1603)	Fierce wars among *daimyo* (regional leaders) Oda and Toyotomi gain power →Reunification by Tokugawa Ieyasu	←**First contact with Europeans** – guns and Christianity introduced →Invasion of Korea by Toyotomi army
	Edo (1603–1867) Cap: Edo (Tokyo)	**Tokugawa Shogun Government** (samurai rule, agricultural tax, class system) • Stability under strong government • Hans' promotion of local industries • Agriculture and handicrafts develop • Transport, finance, commerce, education develop, unified national market emerges • Rich merchant families emerge • Unique popular culture develops Fight over "open door" vs. "anti-foreigner campaign" Han samurai topple Shogun Government	× **Closed door policy**—diplomacy and trade severely restricted (except China, Holland, Korea, Ryukyu); bakufu monopoly of controlled trade; Christianity banned ←**America opens Japan by military threat** (1853–54); commercial treaties Danger of colonization by West
Modernization	**Meiji** (1868–1912) (Capital: Tokyo to present)	**Strong government under emperor** adopts open door policy and rapid Westernization ***Fukoku kyohei*** (strong economy and army) **Industrialization** (private dynamism supported by government policy)	National desire to catch up with West →**War with China** (Qing Dynasty, 1894) →**War with Russia** (1904) →**Annexation of Korea** (1910)

Modernization	**Taisho** (1912–26)	Democracy movement (short-lived) • Recessions and economic crises (1920s–30s)	→Pursuit of Chinese economic interest; conflicts with US and Europe mount
	Early Showa (1926–45)	Fight among political parties, right-wing and military; political terrorism; coup attempts Military takes over government Mobilization of people and resources for war	→Invasion of Manchuria (Northeast China, 1931) →**Full-scale war with China** (1937) →**Pacific War** (1941); **invasion of Southeast Asia**
Postwar	**Late Showa** (1945–88)	**Democratization and demilitarization Economic recovery from postwar crisis** Priority production system **Rapid industrialization** (1950s–60s) • Strong private initiative • MITI's industrial policy Economic slowdown (1970s–80s) Heisei bubble economy	**War defeat** (1945) ←US occupation (1945–51) →Multilateral open door policy →Membership of IMF, World Bank, OECD World's No. 2 economy (around 1970)
	Heisei (1988–)	**Bursting of the bubble** causes economic stagnation (1990s–) Fiscal and monetary stimuli fail to activate economy; Abenomics	Top ODA donor (1990–99) Rise of China and other emerging economies Conflicts with China, Korea accelerate

strongly and Japan became the second largest economy in the world after the US by the end of the 1960s. National security under the US military umbrella, global trade expansion and a stable exchange rate contributed to the miracle growth.

As the Japanese economy matured, growth slowed down. In the 1970s, oil shocks and floating exchange rates reduced Japan's growth to about 4 percent per annum. An asset bubble in land and stocks occurred in the late 1980s which burst in 1990–1991. Since the early 1990s and even to this day, the Japanese economy has virtually stopped growing. Fiscal and monetary stimuli have been tried repeatedly in increasing doses, but growth did not pick up. Under Abenomics, even more aggressive monetary policy was started in 2013, improving the short-term prospects and popular psychology. But growth strategy remained as ineffective as ever.

The rest of the book will chronologically discuss circumstances and conditions surrounding each age, as well as concrete cases of strong private dynamism and proper official support which are the hallmark of Japanese industrialization. Alongside achievements, failures will also be reported in economics, politics and diplomacy. The next chapter will focus on the Edo period (1603–1867), which preceded the amazing Meiji period and prepared preconditions for rapid catching up with the West in the late nineteenth to the early twentieth century.

Box 1.1 The gap between economic and social achievements

In the book entitled *Japan's Modernization and Social Change*, sociologist Tominaga Kenichi proposes a general framework to understand the various aspects of Japan's modernization and industrialization. Traditionally, there have been two opposing interpretations of Japan's modern history. The first view positively considers Japan's economic performance, especially its brilliant success as a latecomer. The second view castigates past Japan as the oppressor of its own people and a military invader of the neighboring countries. Is Japan a model for all developing countries, or a negative case to be avoided at all cost? Tominaga cautions that a debate over such simplistic dualism yields little result. According to him, modernization is a complex phenomenon that must be analyzed with scientific concepts and models.

Tominaga first emphasizes that the modernization process of a non-Western country does not trace the same path experienced by the West.

> To be successful, the modernization of a non-Western country must be a creative process in which comparison between indigenous and foreign culture is made, the superior aspects of the latter are selectively introduced, imported and indigenous elements are combined to breed something new, and conflict between the two is mitigated. Japan's modernization was precisely such a process. Modernization currently proceeding in the societies of Asia's newly industrializing economies also conforms to this description.
>
> (Tominaga, 1990, pp. 38–39)

As the reader will surely notice, Tominaga's assertion is essentially the same as Maegawa's translative adaptation explained in the main text. From this perspective, Tominaga's method divides society into the following four subsystems and describes the evolution of each in detail:

(i) economic modernization (growth through industrialization);
(ii) political modernization (democratization);
(iii) social modernization in the narrow sense (transition from *gemeinschaft* [land- and lineage-based groups] to *gesellschaft* [functional groups] as well as a shift from closed rural communities to open urban communities);
(iv) cultural modernization in the narrow sense (transition from superstition and irrational customs to scientific and rational thinking).

Tominaga's main argument can be summarized as follows. The modernization of Europe started with the internal development of political and social subsystems followed by the Industrial Revolution. But latecomer countries cannot follow this sequence. For them, economic modernization is "easier" than political modernization. Social and cultural modernization is even harder. This is because much more time and energy are required to transform a structure that dominates and permeates every detail of people's lives than to copy new technology and industries. This naturally leads to a gap between fast economic growth and slow progress in all other aspects. However, since the economic subsystem and the non-economic subsystems are interdependent, this gap generates tension and conflict that distorts the modernization process of that country. Prewar Japan, which boasted high technology and modern industries on the one hand while imposing the concept of the holy nation ruled by the emperor family lasting for millennia and the feudal family system on the other, is a typical example. While expressed in sociological terms, Tominaga's assertion belongs to one of the very popular views on the merits and demerits of Japan's modernization process.

Tominaga also argues thus:

- Before the Edo period, Japan did not generate any ideas or systems that could support modernization. For this reason, modernization beginning from the subsequent Meiji period called for a total negation of traditional systems and a switch to foreign systems.
- Modernization cannot succeed in a society where *gemeinschaft*, closed rural communities and irrational thinking remain. If modernization is pursued in the presence of these elements, dilemma and friction become inevitable.
- The serious modernization gap in prewar Japan was largely removed as a result of bold postwar reforms, but some traditional elements still remain even today. Japan's modernization will not be complete unless these cultural remnants are finally eliminated.

It is clear that Tominaga views Japan's indigenous elements very negatively. He regards them as nothing but obstacles to modernization rather than a basis on which imported elements are to be grafted. This is in sharp contrast to Umesao's high evaluation of the continuity of Japanese history which prompted him to say that Japan, as Britain, evolved naturally and autonomously as a modern nation. It is also at odds with Maegawa's concept of translative adaptation and his assertion that Japan successfully mixed domestic systems with foreign ones with the former serving as the more fundamental base. Which interpretation is more reasonable? It is up to the reader to decide.

Notes

1 Among development strategies, the promoters of endogenous development argue for restricting external integration and letting local systems within each society become the growth engine. This includes, for example, agricultural production for local consumption rather than commercial sales, and communal development based on traditional religion, values and customs. This approach may activate communities and provide a risk sharing mechanism in certain stages of development. But its validity as a long-term universal development strategy is not confirmed.

2 In the historical discourse of Umesao Tadao, perhaps the most shocking passage is his view on Japan's invasion of neighboring Asian countries from the late nineteenth century to 1945. He argues that, without the strange isolationism adopted in the seventeenth century, Japan would have reached Southeast Asia much sooner and fought the British and French forces there. In his words, "Japan's role in international power politics was similar to that of Britain, France and the Netherlands. Japan's later behavior as a regional power was not solely the result of a surge of militarism after the Meiji Restoration (1868). It grew from the gap between Japan and Southeast Asia in terms of their situation in the history of civilization, and from the similarity of circumstances between Japan and Western Europe" (Umesao, 2003, p. 110).

3 Kyoto literally means capital city. If the capital is defined to be the location of the emperor's official residence, Kyoto remained the capital of Japan until 1868.

4 Even after the emperor lost real power, samurai leaders still sought imperial approval to set up a new government and legitimize their power. All subsequent governments (even today) have used the symbolic authority of the emperor instead of terminating the imperial family and themselves establishing a new kingdom or dynasty. The benefit of receiving a formal imperial sanction to rule must have been greater than the cost of keeping the emperor who rarely intervened in politics (there were a few exceptions, however). Once this practice was established, deviation from it became politically too costly as it would surely invite a severe accusation of demeaning the divine family.

5 The central government monopolized trade with China and Holland at Dejima, a tiny artificial island in Nagasaki. All other Western nationals were expelled from Japan. Meanwhile, diplomatic and commercial exchange with Korea was conducted via Tsushima Han, the Ryukyu (Okinawa) was under the control of Satsuma Han, and Matsumae Han traded with the Ainu people in Ezo (Hokkaido).

2

THE EDO SOCIETY

Preparing conditions for industrialization

The Edo period: 1603–1867

Japan was ruled by the governments of samurai (military leaders) from the end of the twelfth century to the middle of the nineteenth century. Nominally, the emperor was the supreme ruler who granted the authority to govern to the samurai leader, but the real power rested with the latter. There were a few emperors who tried to restrain samurai power but they did not succeed very much.

The first half of the samurai period (Kamakura 1192–1333, Muromachi 1338–1573 and Sengoku 1573–1603) was dynamic, dangerous and open to foreign trade, where samurai were fierce fighters vying for land and power. The second half of the samurai period (Edo 1603–1867) saw the nation reunified by the Tokugawa family restoring peace and order under a conservative, bureaucratic and class-based government. Samurai continued to practice sword but there was no more fighting.

Transition from the first to the second period of samurai, which occurred at the end of the sixteenth century and the beginning of the seventeenth century, was a turbulent one. Oda Nobunaga (1534–1582) and Toyotomi Hideyoshi (1537–1598) almost emerged as final winners but their control slipped. The real winner was Tokugawa Ieyasu who won the decisive Battle of Sekigahara (located between Nagoya and Kyoto, and visible today from the Shinkansen) in 1600 and attacked Osaka Castle in 1614–1615 where the rival Toyotomi family perished. The remaining daimyo (warlords) were reorganized as subordinates with different ranks based on the degree of allegiance to the Tokugawa family. Ieyasu created a new capital city in Edo and became the first shogun of the Edo Bakufu in 1603. Edo, a sleepy little fishing village until then, was transformed into a huge political city by aggressive public works including land reclamation, artificial canals and water supply networks. The Tokugawa family ruled Japan for the next 264 years (fifteen shoguns in all). After the death of Ieyasu, he was deified as the founder of the Tokugawa shogunate and is still worshiped at Nikko Toshogu Shrine.

A particularly important development during the transition (the Sengoku period and the early Edo period) was the removal of various middle-layer organizations such as Buddhist temples and sects, manorial owners and regional landlords that had existed from the ancient times. Power decentralization and indirect rule were now replaced by direct and unified rule by the newly emerged daimyo (warlord) in each region. This was achieved by a number of policies and brutal actions taken by Sengoku daimyos, especially Oda Nobunaga and Toyotomi Hideyoshi mentioned above, who were the two most powerful military leaders

 DOI: 10.4324/9781315444048-3

Table 2.1 Some basic terms of the Edo period

Bakufu	Residence of a military ruler. Later it meant the central government established by a military leader.
Shogun	Originally, the supreme commander of a dispatched army. But it usually means the top ruler of a central military government.
Han	A local government unit (such as province or regional state); domain given to daimyo to rule under the feudal system.
Daimyo	Regional samurai ruler. In the Edo period, daimyo meant the head samurai of a local government (han).
Edo	The old name for Tokyo. Edo literally means the mouth of a bay. Incidentally, Tokyo means the eastern capital (the western, or the traditional, capital is Kyoto).
Gosho	Rich merchant families (Mitsui, Sumitomo, Konoike, Tennojiya, etc.)
Terakoya	Private elementary school.
Shi-No-Ko-Sho	Samurai–Farmers–Craftsmen–Merchants; the four classes of Edo period from high to low.
Sat-Cho-Do-Hi	Satsuma, Choshu, Tosa and Hizen; four powerful hans toward the end of the Edo period that eventually ended the Bakufu and established the Meiji government; now called Kagoshima, Yamaguchi, Kochi, Saga.

before Ieyasu finally took power. Their policies included military annihilation of opponents, liberalization of commercial activities in newly occupied land, abolition of inter-regional custom duties, official land survey and farmer registration (*kenchi*), confiscation of all arms from non-samurai population (*katanagari*), construction of only one castle town in every region, residential requirement of all samurai in castle towns, relocation of markets and craftsmen to castle towns, and so on. Daimyos began to directly rule land, farmers and samurai retainers. From this time onward, samurai and farmers were strictly separated in profession and residence. Samurai who no longer protected their land became urban officials receiving rice salary. This movement which started in the Sengoku period was continued and completed by the Edo government.

If we define feudalism as the leader–follower relationship based on the granting of the right to govern assigned land, the Edo society was a feudal system (there are academic debates as to what exactly is feudalism but we will not go into that). The Bakufu had the absolute authority to increase, reduce, relocate or even eliminate han, the land provided to each daimyo for governing, depending on the degree of allegiance and the behavior of each daimyo. Any violation of central order or regulation was severely dealt with, but as long as this condition is cleared, each daimyo was free to conduct his policies within his domain as explained below. At the end of the Edo period there were about 300 hans in all sizes. The Bakufu itself occupied about 20 percent of the total nation, as if it were the largest han. The Bakufu's domain included major cities such as Edo, Osaka and Kyoto, strategic ports, and gold, silver and copper mines.

We start the story of Japan's economic development from the Edo period because the preconditions for later industrialization and modernization were created internally during this period. Let us list these pre-conditions at the outset:

1 political unity and stability;
2 agricultural development in terms of both cultivated area and land productivity;
3 the development of transportation and the emergence of nationally unified markets;
4 the rise of commerce, finance and the wealthy merchant class;

5 the rise of pre-modern manufacturing;
6 industrial promotion by local governments (sometimes successful but not always);
7 high level of education.

These are the features of the Edo period that are commonly cited by many researchers. It is interesting to note that these conditions are not met by some developing countries even today. We may even say that developing countries of the twenty-first century are rarely equipped with all of these conditions, and those that satisfy some of these conditions are also not many. In this sense, Japan in the Edo period was on the verge of industrialization waiting for external stimuli to start new growth. Though it did not yet have steam power or modern machinery, political, economic and social conditions were ripe. How this situation was created historically was explained, at least partially, in the previous chapter. This chapter will selectively examine these conditions in detail.

Features of the bakufu-han system

Features of the Edo society can be described as follows.

1 It was a class society. The ruling class was the samurai (military men who were permitted to carry a sword). The ruled included farmers (ranked no. 2), craftsmen (no. 3), and merchants (no. 4). These four classes were called *Shi-Nou-Kou-Shou* (from top to bottom).[1] There was a big gap between the samurai class and other classes. Farmers were officially placed no. 2 because they paid the rice tax, but they were not particularly respected. Below all of these classes, there were also outcasts, *eta* and *hinin*, who were institutionalized and used by the Edo government (see QAs at the end of the book).
2 Politically, it was a centralized system. The Bakufu had absolute political power over the fate of hans and could even remove or abolish them at will. The shogun gave daimyos the land to rule. In return, daimyos pledged loyalty to shogun.[2] Any sign of disobedience was met with the sternest punishment including *seppuku* (ritual suicide) and the termination of the family.
3 Economically, it was more decentralized. The Bakufu was not very capable of (or interested in) conducting consistent economic policies. Its policies were unstable and often myopic. On the other hand, each han could decide its internal policies including administration, taxation, education, industrial promotion, issuing paper money and other economic regulations as long as it was not explicitly prohibited by the Bakufu.
4 The Bakufu imposed the following expenses on hans:

(i) *Sankin kotai* (alternative attendance) which means bi-annual commuting of the han lord between home and Edo. Every daimyo was required to reside in Edo every other year and stay in his han the rest of the time. This cost a huge sum of money in travel and residence since a large number of retainers also had to move with the daimyo, and proper style in travel and residence must be prepared to match each daimyo's prestige.
(ii) Random and irregular assignment of public works such as building and repairing castles, moats, roads, reservoirs, canals, river banks, etc. Because of this system, the Bakufu could dispense with the public investment budget as any construction work was simply ordered to hans.
(iii) Other ad hoc and arbitrary taxes and charges, for example, for celebrating the birth of a son in the shogun family.

Imposition of these arbitrary expenses on hans had the effect of weakening the financial capability of hans so they were left with no resources to rebel. Many hans sank deeply into debt and eventually defaulted on their obligations—except those which succeeded in reforming their financial structure, promoting local trade and industry, and producing sufficient revenues. Tokugawa Ieyasu and his posterity were clever enough to devise these stifling methods. Absolute power over the fate and size of hans, along with huge and unpredictable expenses imposed on them, kept each daimyo at bay. This must have been considered necessary to end the warring period, which had lasted for a few centuries, once and for all.

Agriculture

The Edo society was agrarian, particularly at the beginning, with about 90 percent of the population being peasants although this ratio subsequently declined a little. The basic unit of production was the small family. Previously, one farming household often contained dozens of people including many families and their servants. But a series of official land surveys and peasant registration (kenchi) conducted before and after the beginning of the Edo period dismantled the big family system into small farming units, with each family guaranteed (and obliged to cultivate) its portion of the farmland.

According to the law, peasants had no right to move and were tied to the land as a labor force and a tax base. But in reality, some farmers moved to new land, sometimes to avoid a high tax burden or unreasonable policies and sometimes to simply improve their life. Later, as rural income rose, many well-to-do farmers enjoyed village festivals and theaters as well as trips to Ise Shrine, climbing Mount Fuji and travelling to other religious sites—officially for worship, but actually for fun. Traditionally, peasants in the Edo period were often described as hungry, repressed and vexed by high taxes, corrupt and greedy officials, and famines and other natural disasters. However, recent studies find them relatively wealthy by the standard of agriculture in latecomer countries. This was particularly true in Western Japan and toward the end of the Edo period.

Tanaka Keiichi (2000), an Edo historian, argues that farmers were very dynamic and independent, and they often rejected Bakufu or han officials who tried to introduce inconsistent or unreasonable policies. According to Tanaka, the Bakufu generally had no long-term policy vision; most of their laws and regulations were ad hoc responses to ongoing historical changes that could not be stopped. The Regulation of Keian, first promulgated in 1649 and reissued throughout the Edo period, is the case in point. The Regulation was a collection of prohibitions on farmers—don't smoke tobacco, don't buy sake or tea, divorce a wife who likes to travel for fun and so on. This document should not be viewed as evidence on how strictly the government constrained peasant life but as a hollow depiction of ideal farmers that no longer existed and the Bakufu had no power to restore.

The agricultural sector grew in two phases: quantitative expansion first, then qualitative intensification (Figure 2.1). From the mid-fifteenth century to the late seventeenth century, which includes the previous Sengoku period and the early Edo period, there was an enormous expansion of cultivated land (especially rice paddies). Earlier, rice was produced in narrow valleys where mountains ended and plains began, because this was the only place where constant water supply was available. But during this period, large-scale water management projects were carried out all over Japan by daimyos and influential farmers to control floods and use rivers for irrigation. As a result, land under cultivation expanded dramatically.

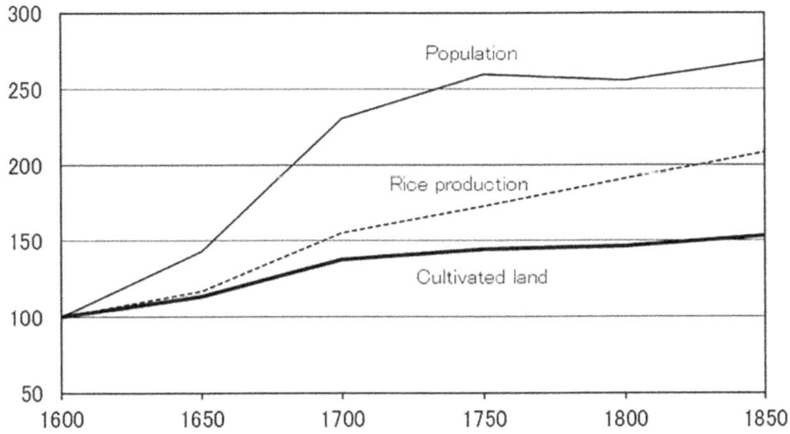

Figure 2.1 Population and rice production (1600 = 100)

Source: Hayami and Miyamoto, eds, 1988, p. 44.

The plains, which had hitherto been uninhabitable marshlands, were turned into productive paddy fields. The population increased rapidly in a way rarely seen in a pre-modern society. Oishi Shinzaburo (1977) calls this "The Great Age of Opening Fields."

By the late seventeenth century, land expansion came to a halt. The rapid growth of farmland in the previous period also brought some negative effects including labor shortage, deforestation, and frequent occurrence of floods. From this period onward up to today, Japanese agriculture has emphasized intensive cultivation with large inputs of labor, fertilizer and technology rather than the quantitative expansion of arable land.

From the eighteenth century onward, the area of cultivation and population remained relatively stable, but rice output continued to grow thanks to increased productivity. Contributing factors included double cropping, new species of rice, organic fertilizer (dried fish was especially popular), and the introduction of new farming tools. Many guidebooks were published to teach farmers how to produce crops more effectively. Miyazaki Yasusada's *Nogyo Zensho* (Encyclopedia of Agriculture) in eleven volumes, published in 1697 and reprinted many times subsequently, was one of them. Okura Nagatsune and Sato Nobuhiro are the other two agriculturalists who published 79 volumes and over 300 volumes, respectively, of farming guidebooks.

At the beginning of the Edo period, peasants cultivated mainly for family consumption. They ate what they produced and their living standards were at a subsistence level. From the middle Edo period, because land productivity rose and agricultural surplus was created, peasants began to sell their rice and other crops to the market which was often nationally integrated (see below). Cash crop production increased and commercial farming began. Some farmers, especially near Osaka, specialized in cash crops and purchased rice for consumption. In many developing countries today, transformation from subsistence to commercial farming is a common policy target. Japan in the late Edo period had already achieved it.

Villages were well organized and permitted autonomy as long as they paid rice taxes as stipulated by the central or local government.[3] The rice tax was levied on villages, not on individual farmers. Village leaders, who were often themselves farmers, allocated the rice tax burden among villagers. In this sense, village leaders played the role of the lowest-level tax administration. Thanks to them, the Bakufu and hans could raise tax revenues with little administrative cost.

However, everything was not rosy. Farmers' uprisings frequently occurred during the Edo period, especially at the time of famine and toward the end of the Edo period. Rebellious farmers were unhappy with taxes, inflation, famine, corrupt officials or government policies. Uprisings were not impulsive or random. Strategies were discussed within the village or among participating villages, objectives were set, leaders were appointed and proper procedure and discipline were followed. Physical assets were targeted for destruction but no harm was done to humans. Farmers' uprisings in the Edo period were not uncontrolled phenomena; they were highly organized.

Officially, all farmers belonged to (were tied to) assigned land as recorded in the kenchi registration book. By the nineteenth century, however, the income gap between rich and poor farmers emerged, the number of landless farmers increased, and large landowners began to hire tenant farmers to cultivate their land. Small-holder family farming, which was the production and tax base of the Edo economy, started to disintegrate.

Budget and money

The Bakufu's revenues included the following:

- rice tax from the land directly owned by the Bakufu (areas not distributed to other daimyos);
- monopoly on mining, foreign trade and minting money;
- direct control on major cities (Edo, Kyoto, Osaka, Nagasaki, Sakai, etc.);
- financial contributions from merchants in exchange for monopoly and cartel rights.

In addition, as noted above, the Bakufu freely ordered hans to various public works, eliminating the need to have their own public investment budget. On the other hand, the hans' revenue consisted of the rice tax from their territory and the revenues from promoting local industries (if this is successful).

The entire fiscal system was based on the rice tax. The fiscal unit of account was the "koku" (volume unit, about 180 liters of rice). The han's economic size (and its prestige) was measured in koku and samurai salaries were also paid in rice—but of course rice salary had to be cashed before buying things. Rice tax was collected by each village and physically transported to major rice markets, then redistributed to the rest of the country. The Bakufu and han rice revenues were also cashed in those markets. Osaka was by far the most important national rice market.

This rice-based economic system had the following consequences and developments:

1. Since rice had to be physically shipped across regions, this tax system required a nationally unified transportation and distribution mechanism. Private merchants provided the required services but the Bakufu and han governments often regulated and supported them. As land transportation (by horse) was very costly and inefficient, water transportation on the sea, river and lake was mainly used.

2 The center of economic activity gradually shifted from subsistence farming to commercial agriculture, then to handicraft industries. But the government's tax base basically remained on rice. There were occasional attempts to levy on commerce but this did not become a reliable tax base. Non-rice production expanded while rice became an increasingly small part of the national economy. As time went by, the Bakufu and han governments faced fiscal crises while farmers and merchants enjoyed increasing income and wealth.

3 Faced with chronic fiscal deficits, the Bakufu repeatedly resorted to the following measures: (i) monetary debasement (similar to printing money, which led to inflation), (ii) spending cuts, (iii) tax increases and ad hoc levies, (iv) price controls and administrative reforms. Some commercial policies were tried such as forcing designated merchants to form cartels with exclusive marketing rights in exchange for additional financial contribution. However, such monopoly creation was often reversed and the Bakufu soon reverted to free entry policy. These measures cannot be considered a set of consistent policies backed by a long-term vision.

Money consisted of both gold and silver (see Figure 2.2). Gold was popular in Edo (Eastern Japan) and silver was mainly used in Osaka (Western Japan). Copper coins were also used for small transactions. Hans were allowed to issue paper money which could be circulated in the han's domain. But when local paper money was issued excessively, or when the han's finance was broke, there was no taker for such paper money. Inflation rose at the time of famine and accelerated towards the end of the Edo period, especially after international trade was resumed in 1859.

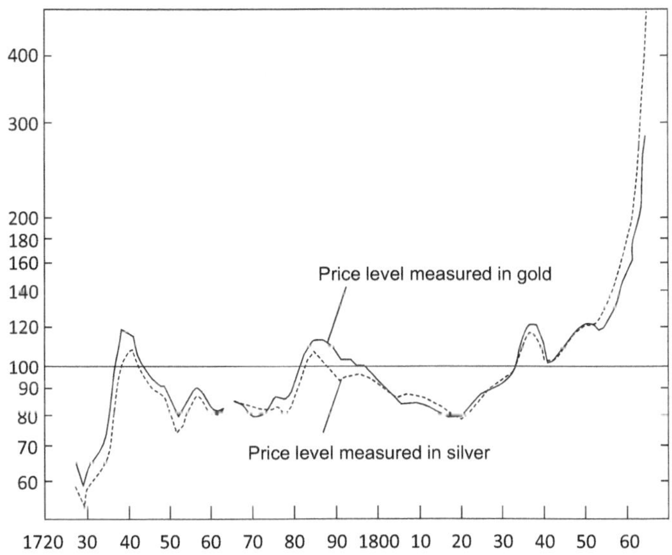

Figure 2.2 General price level (1840–1844 = 100)

Source: Shimbo and Saito, eds, 1989, p. 71.

Note: The general price index in Kyoto and Osaka, five-year moving average, semi-log scale.

Transportation and commerce

The Bakufu designated five official highways and opened major sea lanes. They covered the entire nation from North to South and East to West, but no international routes were permitted. The private sector provided necessary travel services such as inns, restaurants, tea houses, shippers, baggage carriers, etc. As part of non-tax obligation, farming villages near official highways were required to provide horses at the time of heavy travel needs. *Sankin kotai* (daimyos' alternative residence between Edo and their hans) increased travel spending and further stimulated the development of the road system. At the same time, out of military concern, the Bakufu did not permit the free movement of people and merchandise. At strategic points, *sekisho* (passport controls) were created. Some rivers were intentionally left without bridges, to block the march of a potential enemy to Edo. Hans were not allowed to build large military ships or maintain navies.

As noted above, from the very beginning, the Edo tax system presupposed a nationally unified rice market. The development of cash crops and handicrafts further accelerated nationwide commerce. Osaka was the commercial center with a large number of wealthy merchants and money changers and lenders, while Edo was the political center as well as a large consumption city. Naturally, the sea lane between the two cities was well developed. In Osaka, even the futures market in rice was established in 1730. This is said to be the first futures market in the world.

Active commerce produced *gosho*, or rich merchant families, such as Yodoya, Konoike, Onogumi, Tennojiya, Hiranoya, Shimadagumi and Kajimaya. Some even survived the political change from Edo to Meiji to become Japan's leading business groups. The two merchant families of the Edo period that survived and lead the Japanese economy even today are the Mitsui group, initially engaged in kimono trade and money changing, and the Sumitomo group, which specialized in copper mining and smeltering.

The fact that indigenous business groups emerged in the Edo period to later form *zaibatsu*, playing key roles in absorbing Western technology, import substitution and competition with foreign enterprises, was remarkable. In the history of latecomer industrialization, not so many countries could withstand the powerful presence of foreign competitors and build their national industries. Another important fact was that business entries and exits were very frequent in the late Edo to the early Meiji period under the impacts of international trade, shifting demand and relative prices, new technology and institutions, political change and issuance of many new policies. No business groups could overcome these difficulties without effective internal reform and creation of solid linkage with newly emerging commercial activities. Using a series of unofficial ranking of wealthy merchants, Miyamoto (1999) finds that the survival ratio of the top 231 merchants from 1849 to 1864 was 44 percent. The ratio falls further to 15 percent by 1888 and a mere 9 percent by 1902. From this perspective, Mitsui and Sumitomo are the exceptions rather than the rule. Most gosho declined or disappeared within decades. In a rapidly changing economy with fierce competition, it is hard to stay profitable for a long time.

As with agriculture, the Bakufu's policy towards commerce and industry was ineffective and incoherent. Its physiocratic ideology and insistence on the rice economy prevented it from turning to new tax bases in emerging agro-processing, commerce, finance and manufacturing. In response to fiscal crisis, the Bakufu resorted to austerity, squeezing farmers, imposing arbitrary contributions on daimyos and rich merchants, monetary debasement and price control. Occasionally the idea of vitalizing the private sector through deregulation or industrial promotion surfaced, but it was always crushed by so-called reforms that tightened economic austerity and regulation even more.

At times the Bakufu controlled and taxed private businesses, while at other times free market was encouraged. Cartels were sometimes imposed and other times prohibited. Economic historians still debate whether the Edo economy was more dynamic under the free market policy than under the pro-cartel policy. According to Miyamoto and others (1995), the sound development of the market economy depends on a number of institutions and customs to facilitate transactions such as the bill of exchange and provision of credit. From this perspective, the authors defend the cartels in the Edo period as a private mechanism to generate such services. From the viewpoint of historical institutional analysis, Okazaki Tetsuji (1999) also tries to show that estimated GDP grew faster during the time when cartels were permitted than when they were banned. He argues that trade cartels were a positive factor for the development of the Edo economy rather than an impediment. However, the available data and his regressions may be too crude to draw a strong conclusion.

Based on Miyamoto and Uemura (1988), Figure 2.3 illustrates national transaction patterns of the late Edo period. In the early Edo period, which is not shown, Osaka was the

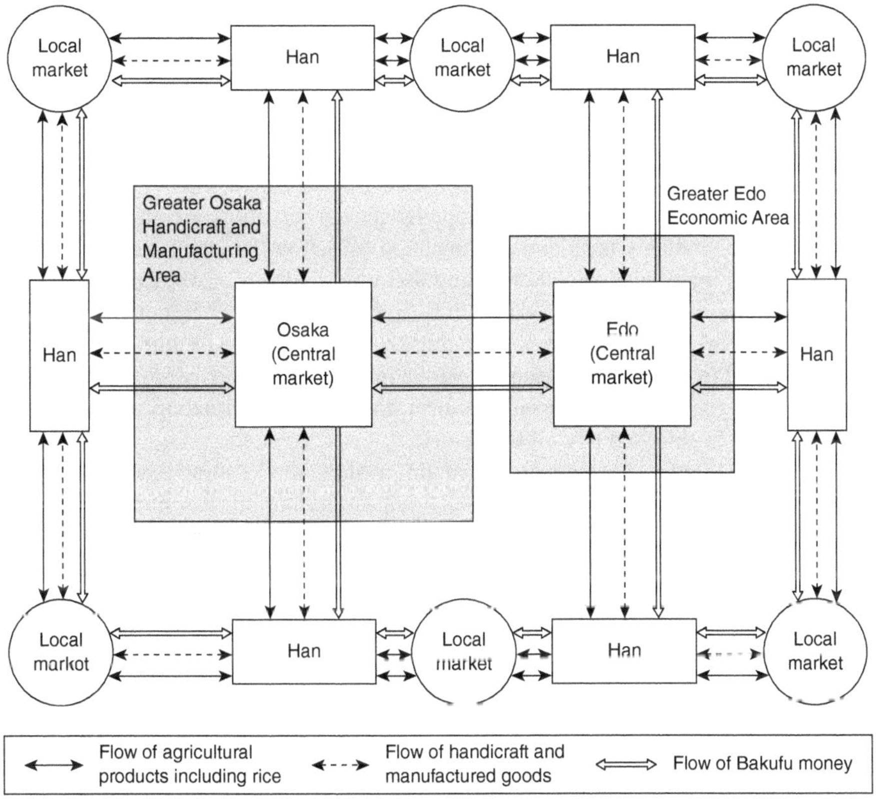

Figure 2.3 Inter-regional economic linkage in the late Edo period

Source: Miyamoto and Uemura, 1988, p. 285.

center of production and commercial activities. Edo, the large consumption market, and all hans traded bilaterally with Osaka while transactions among hans were limited. In the late Edo period, the production capacity of the area surrounding Edo, regional cities and han economies grew. As a result, local markets and direct trade among hans emerged without the intervention of Osaka merchants. In addition to rice, a large number of agricultural and manufactured products were traded in nationally and regionally integrated markets. The center of economic activity gradually shifted eastward, from Kansai (Osaka and Kyoto) to Edo and Eastern Japan. The relative weight of Osaka in the national economy decreased.

Industrial promotion

As agriculture and commerce grew, pre-modern manufacturing such as handicrafts and food processing also began to develop. Each region created specialized products that were marketed all over Japan. For example, tea, tobacco, wax, indigo, salt, knives, sword, pottery, lacquer ware, silk, cotton, soy sauce, sake, paper, cut stone, medicine and chemicals were traded widely. Emergence of these regional specialties was mainly the result of private effort, but in some cases the support of local governments also made a difference.

In order to enrich the local population and increase the tax revenue, many hans promoted local industries, and some even succeeded (Nishikawa and Amano, 1989). Here are some examples:

- *Yonezawa Han* (adding value to local inputs)—When Uesugi Yozan (1751–1822) became the daimyo of Yonezawa Han in Northeast Japan, the han finance was bankrupt and samurai and farmers were destitute. Retainers even considered closing the han and returning it to the Bakufu. Yozan introduced austerity measures, encouraged research and learning, and promoted industries. He repelled the conservative faction who opposed his reform. He opened new farmland and installed irrigation. His main strategy was to add value to local materials instead of selling them in raw form. *Aoso*, a plant material for high-quality textile, was transformed into finished kimono by importing weaving technology. Mulberry plantation was encouraged for producing silk kimono. Lacquer trees were planted to manufacture lacquer ware and wax. Safflowers were introduced to produce orange dye. Thanks to Yozan's reform, the economic situation improved and Yonezawa Han was able to repay all the debt.
- *Tokushima Han* (indigo)—Farmers produced indigo along the Yoshino River in Shikoku Island and their output gradually grew. But indigo distribution was monopolized by Osaka merchants who imposed high interests on loans. In order to protect local farmers and encourage local merchants, Tokushima Han created an indigo exchange and provided financial and distribution services. The Bakufu objected to this move, prohibiting official bodies to engage in such activity. In reality, the Bakufu wanted to protect Osaka merchants who contributed financially to its coffer. In response, the han privatized the indigo exchange and other services.
- *Takamatsu Han* (sugar)—This local government, also in Shikoku, issued local paper money to promote various industries but its attempts generally failed, and its money depreciated. After many failures, the han finally succeeded in pilot production of sugar from sugar beet and commercializing the technology. As sugar production greatly increased, the han encouraged inter-han trade to expand the market. But again, the Bakufu intervened to discourage such trade not brokered by Osaka merchants.

- *Satsuma Han* (trade gains for military buildup)—Satsuma Han in southern Kyushu was also broke with huge debts in the early nineteenth century. Zusho Hirosato (1776–1849), Satsuma's high official, adopted austerity and implemented administrative and agricultural reforms. He intimidated merchant lenders into rescheduling Satsuma's debt for 250 years with no interest, which was practically cancellation. He started han monopoly of sugar trade with southern islands as well as illegal trade with China via Okinawa, both of which were very profitable. After international trade was resumed in 1859, Satsuma Han vigorously traded with China and the West, and purchased new technology including blast furnaces, cannons, western ships and the latest guns. By building wealth and military capability, Satsuma Han later played the leading role in toppling the Bakufu and establishing the Meiji government.

Other hans were also successfully engaged in industrial promotion of one kind or another including Choshu Han (paper, wax), Akita Han (silk and silk dress), Hizen Han (pottery, coal) and Higo Han (lumber, silk). In the late Edo period there was dynamic competition among hans to supply nationally marketable products that was either privately driven or policy triggered. Industrial promotion combined with fiscal reform was the key to the survival of impoverished hans. But we should not forget that there were also many hans that were less innovative and fell deeply into economic difficulty and debt. These hans borrowed large sums of money from private merchants that they never repaid.

Thus, at the local level, some hans produced economic leaders who solved the domain's fiscal crisis, promoted local industries and actively engaged in domestic (and later international) trade. This is in sharp contrast to the central government which was throughout unable to propose any policy to support and tax the growing national economy. Japan at the end of the Edo period was ripe for a new set of economic visions and policies that were more proactive than those put down by the Bakufu leaders.

Education

The popularity of education in the Edo period is often cited as the cause of fast industrialization in the later periods. Education in the Edo period ranged from the recondite study of ancient Chinese philosophy and literature at government schools to children's basic education at private schools. Education fever was not just in such large cities as Edo, Osaka and Kyoto but also a nationwide phenomenon. Here, the four main types of learning institutions are introduced.

1. Bakufu schools—Bakufu schools mainly taught Confucianism, an ancient Chinese philosophy started by Confucius in the sixth to fifth century BC. It emphasized social order, proper rituals, the way of good political leadership and respect for the elderly and superiors. The Edo government vigorously promoted Confucianism as an ideology to legitimize and maintain the class society. Fujiwara Seika (1561 1619), Hayashi Razan (1583–1657) and Arai Hakuseki (1657–1725) were the leading Bakufu scholars. Students had to memorize and interpret ancient Chinese books. How to modify this foreign doctrine to fit the Japanese reality was one of the important theoretical questions. Toward the end of the Edo period, the Bakufu also established schools for Western language (Dutch) and Western technology in medicine, navigation and military technology.

2 Han schools—Hans also established schools to educate their young samurai. Some even accepted non-samurai students. The curriculums were basically the same as those of Bakufu schools with Confucianism at the center of learning. Later, as with Bakufu schools, progressive han schools adjusted curriculums to teach more practical skills such as military training and foreign language. At the end of the Edo period, there were approximately 300 hans and 230 han schools, which means about three quarters of hans were equipped with han schools. Many han schools were transformed into new educational institutions in the Meiji period.
3 Private professional schools—Eminent scholars often set up their own private schools and recruited students. Depending on the instructor, various subjects were taught: Confucianism, kokugaku (research on ancient Japanese literature that later influenced nationalism and anti-foreigner movement), Western languages (Dutch, later also English), medicine, science and technology, and so on. These schools normally accepted both samurai and non-samurai students. In the late Edo period, after the ports were open to the world, they attracted talented and passionate young people with the desire to contribute to the country. Their eyes were opened to the international situation and Japan's precarious position in it. A large number of national leaders in the late Edo period and the early Meiji period came from these schools. The most renowned among such incubator schools are listed in Table 2.2.
4 Terakoya (private elementary schools)—These schools were run by self-appointed teachers to teach the 3Rs (reading, writing, and arithmetic which meant abacus) to small children.

Table 2.2 Examples of private professional schools (late Edo period)

School and location	*Teacher and year of establishment*	*Main teaching*	*Prominent students*
Kangien (Hita, Bungo Han)	Hirose Tanso 1817	Confucianism and ancient Chinese literature	Takano Choei (Western studies) Omura Masujiro (military reformer)
Narutaki Juku (Nagasaki)	Philipp F. B. von Siebolt (German) 1824	Western medicine	Takano Choei (Western scholar) Ito Genboku (medical doctor) Ito Keisuke (medical doctor and botanist)
Teki Juku (Osaka)	Ogata Koan 1838	Dutch language and Western medicine	Fukuzawa Yukichi (founder of Keio Univ.) Omura Masujiro (military reformer) Hashimoto Sanai (Western studies) Otori Keisuke (Bakufu & Meiji statesman)
Zoyama Shoin (Edo)	Sakuma Shozan 1835	Western studies and military technology	Yoshida Shoin (Shokason Juku teacher) Katsu Kaishu (Bakufu official) Yamamoto Kakuma (politician)
Shokason Juku (Hagi, Choshu Han)	Yoshida Shoin 1855 (until 1857)	Social and political philosophy	Takasugi Shinsaku (anti-Bakufu fighter) Kusaka Genzui (anti-Bakufu fighter) Ito Hirobumi (prime minister) Yamagata Aritomo (prime minister)
Keio Gijuku (Edo/Tokyo) Later, university	Fukuzawa Yukichi (1858, renamed 1868)	First Dutch, later English and Western political economy	Obata Tokujiro (politician and thinker) Yano Fumio (official and scholar) Nakamigawa Hikojiro (official and business leader) and many others

Initially, terakoya was a charity organization but later evolved into a profit-seeking entity charging tuition fees. Normally one teacher taught a few dozen children who received individual assignments. There was no rigid regulation or guideline on schooling age, but most children entered terakoya at the age of seven or eight and stayed until the age of twelve or thirteen. Standard daily curriculum included brush letter writing in the morning and arithmetic and moral studies in the afternoon. There were monthly and year-end exams as well as letter writing exhibitions. Children's education was not compulsory and the Bakufu and han governments neither intervened nor promoted it. As the general public realized the importance of studying letters and arithmetic, a large number of terakoya were established from urban to rural areas contributing to the high literacy among the population.

After the Bakufu fell, the Meiji government took education into the public realm and introduced the national school system. In the eighth year of Meiji (1875), there were about 24,000 elementary schools in Japan, the vast majority of which had been converted from terakoya. This suggests the rough number of terakoya that existed in the late Edo period. In the same year (1875), primary education enrollment was 50.5 percent for boys and 18.6 percent for girls.

Box 2.1 Proto-industrialization and population dynamics

Economic historians have noted that certain areas of Europe, such as Flanders in Belgium and Lancashire in England, were "industrialized" in the seventeenth and eighteenth centuries even before the Industrial Revolution took off in the United Kingdom. This industrialization was characterized by rural, family-based production of textiles and garments without modern machinery and was often brokered by urban merchants.

The concept of proto-industrialization was proposed to explain why this happened, and why it was observed in certain areas only (proto means primitive or early). The proponents have advanced a hypothesis to explain rural industrialization from the unique interaction among agriculture, population and commerce. Population growth is often regarded as given in economic modeling. But in the hypothesis of proto-industrialization, population dynamics is a crucial endogenous element. F.F. Mendels and P. Deyon, who proposed this idea, define proto-industrialization as a phenomenon satisfying the following three conditions:

- it is a manufacturing activity for market sales, not for home consumption;
- it is undertaken by peasants in a rural area where soil quality is poor and plots are small;
- it is located near an area of commercial agriculture with large farm size and high productivity.

Proto-industrialization begins as a side job in villages where agricultural productivity is low. They can sell cloth and garments to nearby rich villages where agricultural productivity is high. It is a sort of specialization (division of labor) within a relatively small geographical area: villages with fertile soil produce farm products and villages with poor soil produce manufactured goods, and they exchange output with each other. They sometimes also sell their products to larger markets.

Furthermore, the hypothesis of proto-industrialization assumes certain demographic dynamics in the following sequence:

(1) For some reason, villages with poor soil face a population increase, leading to food shortages.
(2) Poor peasants engage in the production of garments for sale to relieve the population pressure.
(3) This increases their income, which prompts them to get married sooner and have more children.
(4) Population growth continues to keep the peasants just as poor as before, even though they are more "industrialized."
(5) The supply of cheap labor is thus increased, and rich farming villages and urban merchants continue to accumulate wealth. (This widening income gap may possibly generate capitalists and landless farmers leading to industrialization under full-fledged capitalism in the Marxian sense. However, this historical linkage is not convincingly proven empirically.)

According to Saito Osamu (1985), the Japanese data in the Edo period does not support the hypothesis of proto-industrialization. There is no evidence of systematic population increase in the areas where peasants engaged in pre-modern manufacturing. On the contrary, it is observed that Edo period farmers practiced birth control, sometimes even killing new-born babies, to manage the population pressure.

Proto-industrialization assumes a rather peculiar population dynamics that may be applicable to certain European regions in certain periods, but not in the rest of the world or at other times. Also, there is no evidence that it was linked with or stimulated the Industrial Revolution that occurred later. However, the idea of population growth responding to the process of pre-modern early industrialization is an interesting one. In our age, people's life style including urban migration, the timing of marriage and the number of children to be had is clearly influenced by the income level of each person and the economic situation of the nation.

Notes

1 Historically, Vietnam also had the distinction of Si-Nong-Cong-Thuong (the Chinese characters are the same, only the pronunciation is different). The idea originally came from Confucius in ancient China, but the top ranking "Si" in Vietnam meant scholars, not fighting men. Moreover, in China and Vietnam, the four-way classification merely indicated what type of people were respectable in society and had no political implications. The Edo government turned this idea into an ideology that legitimized a class society with samurai on top.

2 This land-based leader–follower relationship is called feudalism as explained in the text. But feudalism had another, more colloquial and negative connotation for people, especially those in the Meiji period, who looked back to the Edo period with critical eyes. For them, feudal is an adjective that goes with anything rigid, inhumane and suppressive.

3 Each han separately decided the rice tax rate and the way to collect it. Similarly, the Bakufu levied rice taxes from the areas directly ruled by it. Rice tax revenue thus belonged to each collecting government.

3

TRANSITION FROM EDO TO MEIJI

The opening of ports and the fall of the Bakufu

After the establishment of the Edo government in the early seventeenth century, foreign travel and trade were restricted in steps. From 1639, the Bakufu banned any foreign contact except highly regulated trade at Nagasaki's Dejima (tiny artificial island) under strict official control. In other words, the Bakufu monopolized limited foreign trade. Only Chinese and Dutch merchants were allowed to trade with Japan, while Korea and Ryukyu (Okinawa) had diplomatic relations with Japan. Contact or transaction with all other nations was strictly prohibited. No Japanese were allowed to go abroad or come home from abroad. Under this isolation policy, the only channel for absorbing Western knowledge, mainly medical and scientific information, was through Dutch books and products. This situation lasted for about one-and-half centuries.

However, from the end of the eighteenth century, Western ships began to approach Japan with an intention to use Japanese ports and even to resume trade. The Russians and the British were particularly eager but the Bakufu refused to even talk to them. Meanwhile, the news of the Opium War (1840–1942), in which Britain defeated China, took possession of Hong Kong and forced China to open its ports, arrived. This was a big shock to the Bakufu.

Ultimately, in 1853, four American military ships ("Black Ships") led by Commodore Matthew C. Perry entered Edo Bay. The Bakufu was forewarned about their coming but could do little to counter it. This was a well-planned US mission for which a negotiating strategy with Japan had been carefully designed. Perry was convinced that the show of force, not peaceful diplomacy, was most effective in producing results with the Japanese. Firing powerful cannons, Perry demanded a "friendship" treaty that allowed American ships to use Japanese ports for refueling and restocking water and food. The Americans left, saying that they would return in the following year to hear the answer.[1] The entirety of Japan was thrown into chaos and a fierce debate began as to whether Japan should yield to the American demand and open its ports or repel foreigners. When Perry and his troops returned to Edo Bay in the next year, the Bakufu agreed to sign the friendship treaty with the United States and opened Shimoda Port and Hakodate Port for foreign ships. Similar treaties were immediately concluded with the Europeans.

The next demand from the US was the conclusion of a full bilateral commercial treaty. In 1858, the Bakufu asked for imperial permission to sign commercial treaties with the major powers. This was supposed to be a mere formality but Emperor Komei refused to grant permission. The Bakufu signed the treaties anyway without imperial approval. Politically, it would have been more advisable to hear out the views of various domestic groups,

DOI: 10.4324/9781315444048-4

especially influential daimyos, before making such an important national decision—and actually, free opinions were collected at first—but new *Tairo* (highest Bakufu official) Ii Naosuke turned to a more despotic method. In 1859, as ports were opened for international trade, he suppressed all dissenting voices, jailed his opponents and even executed many of them. Naturally, this policy was severely criticized and increased anger and violence. Ii was assassinated in the following year, in 1860, by samurai infuriated by his disregard of the emperor and submission to foreign pressure.

With the conclusion of the friendship and commercial treaties, foreign diplomats and merchants began to settle in Japan. However, they were permitted to stay only in designated foreign settlements and travel only in the vicinities. Free contact or trade with the Japanese public was prohibited. The largest foreign settlement was Yokohama, a small fishing village turned into a modern port city for the purpose of fulfilling the treaty obligations.

The opening of Japanese ports led to significant social and economic changes.

1. Foreigners brought new ideas, technology and systems which the Japanese began to absorb very rapidly. At the same time, the Japanese were also afraid of the superior military power of the West.
2. Silk and tea suddenly found huge overseas markets. Many villages turned to their production. The rising output and soaring prices of these commodities enriched rural farmers who produced them.[2]
3. Enriched farmers began to buy imported clothes from England instead of wearing homemade or secondhand clothes. This profligacy even worried high officials of the government.
4. A new merchant class, called *Yokohama merchants*, emerged to link Japanese producers and markets with foreign merchants. As noted above, foreigners were not permitted to travel outside the foreign settlement and thus needed the help of Japanese merchants to penetrate the market.
5. As inflation surged, samurai and the urban population were impoverished. The relative price structure was transformed after the opening of ports. Old industries and merchants declined and new ones emerged.

The commercial treaties that the Bakufu signed with the West were unequal in the sense that (i) Japan had no right to decide its own import duties; and (ii) the Japanese court was not allowed to judge foreign criminals in Japan. In 1866, Japanese import duties were set uniformly at 5 percent, and this situation lasted until 1899 when the tariff rights were partially regained (the full restoration of tariff rights took nearly half a century, until 1911). Inability to indict foreign criminals was considered to be a great national humiliation. The opposition blamed the Bakufu for signing defective treaties. They also criticized the Bakufu for economic change and inflation, in addition to yielding to foreign pressure without national consensus or imperial approval. However, it should be noted that no "undeveloped" non-Western countries in the late nineteenth century, including China, were allowed to have equal relations with the West. The Bakufu did not stand a chance of getting equality with the West, given the military and economic backwardness of Japan at that time. In this humiliation and frustration, creation of a first-class society on a par with the West became a national obsession, not only for regaining pride but also for revising the unequal treaties.

The flexible structure of transition politics

After the opening of ports, severe political fights ensued for about fifteen years. To summarize the highly complicated developments, events unfolded over the two key issues of (i) promotion of open door policy versus anti-foreigner nationalism, and (ii) upholding the emperor versus supporting the Bakufu. Anti-foreigner radicalism was very strong and prevalent at first, but wise daimyos and samurai gradually realized the impossibility of repelling the foreigners as the West was too modern and powerful. Satsuma and Choshu, the two most powerful hans, learned this lesson in a hard way by actually exchanging fire with Western gunships. The political fight gradually shifted to the question of who would end the power monopoly of the Bakufu and establish a new government to cope with the external crisis.

Japanese political process in the late Edo period to the early Meiji period exhibited a flexible structure that was very unique in latecomer countries that faced the pressure of global integration (Banno and Ohno 2010ab). The years from 1858 (signing of the commercial treaties) to the early 1880s was a period in which Japan had to reorganize politics, redefine national goals and decide on concrete plans to achieve these goals. Despite the exiting of the Bakufu as a political loser in 1867–68, the dynamism of transition politics did not change very much. The Meiji Revolution was achieved through flexible politics, in which flexibility was seen in (i) the pursuit of multiple and evolving goals; (ii) constant regrouping of leaders and (iii) flexibility of leading groups themselves. Politics was a complex process with many leaders, many phase shifts and changing priorities, far from the image of a solid authoritarian state under one charismatic leader that single-mindedly pursued industrialization while suppressing democracy. In reality, Meiji Japan was quite different from the typical developmental states of East Asia in the post-WW2 era such as Korea, Taiwan and Singapore.

National goals continued to evolve. Initially, the political goal of *kogi yoron* (government by public deliberation) was intended to replace the Bakufu's despotic rule. It evolved from a simple proposal of alliance among four or five influential hans into the idea of a conference of all 300 hans and even the creation of a bicameral system. As it turned out, this plan which intended peaceful political reform was interrupted by the Boshin War of 1868–69. The military showdown was ignited by the refusal of the Bakufu to be downgraded to a minor power in the proposed political scheme. In early Meiji, Kido, Fukuzawa as well as former samurai of Tosa Han upgraded the feudal assembly model to the idea of creating a Western style constitution and parliament. They were then split into those promoting a British style parliamentary system and those advocating a German style constitutional monarchy. Regardless of particular form or style proposed, the installation of a government by public deliberation of one sort or another was a political requirement for legitimizing the Meiji Revolution and the new government established by it.

On the other hand, *fukoku kyohei* (enriching economy, strengthening military) in the late Edo period was the idea that each han should set up a trading house, collect products from all over Japan for export, purchase guns and military ships from the West with the proceeds and bolster the han's military capability to ultimately emerge as a winner in the political transition. In reality, the hans that could do this effectively—Satsuma and Choshu, and to some extent Tosa also—became the main powers to topple the Bakufu and occupy central places in the new government. Under the new government, *fukoku* was transformed from the mercantilist idea of trading local products for profit to the notion of industrialization, i.e., building factories equipped with modern machinery to raise domestic production. As to *kyohei*, the armies of the strong hans that had achieved the revolution, but had nothing more to do in the Meiji period, began to demand foreign campaigns. Because of this, *fukoku* and *kyohei*, which were initially integrated, became two separate goals—industrialization versus military expansion—that competed for the same budgetary resource.

Another aspect of flexible politics was the constant regrouping of leaders. Each national goal stated above had its champions. Industrialization was guided by Okubo Toshimichi (1830–78), foreign expedition was backed by Saigo Takamori (1827–77), a parliamentary system was strongly proposed by Itagaki Taisuke (1837–1919) and the drafting of a (German style) constitution was planned by Kido Takayoshi (1833–77)—and supporters gathered around these leaders. However, no one group could yield sufficient power to carry out desired policies, and could pursue them only by forming a coalition with one or two other groups. Dominance of one group invited intervention from other groups, and the defeat of another group was compensated by the assistance from others. This continuous political rebalancing hardly resulted in permanent grudges or vengeance against each other. Even before the Bakufu fell, hans were practicing such flexible diplomacy. This process, which from outside looked like endless political fights, was surprisingly successful in avoiding chaos and achieving multiple national goals in the long run.

Moreover, leaders themselves were variable and multifaceted. Initially, virtually every han was split between open trade and anti-foreigner movement, and between allegiance to the emperor and to the Bakufu. But in hans that ultimately emerged as winners, all retainers followed the han's official line once it was set. The policies of Satsuma and Choshu oscillated between anti-foreigner and pro-foreigner stance, but both chose the open trade, pro-emperor stance at the end. Even though the two hans fought previously and hated each other, they decided to join military forces to end the Bakufu's rule. The amazing thing was that these policy swings were made by the same leaders changing their minds rather than one faction driving out another within the han. Such flexibility in leadership is hardly observed in internal wars anywhere else, then or now. Two sides are usually ensconced in uncompromising positions and do not stop fighting unless one side annihilates the other.

The Meiji government and its goals

As a result of relatively minor battles between the emperor side and the Bakufu supporters in 1868–69 (one of the fiercest battles was fought in Edo where Ueno Park now stands), the Bakufu was defeated and the new Meiji government was established in 1868. The emperor moved from Kyoto to Edo, which was renamed Tokyo (meaning eastern capital).

The Meiji government was run by former young samurai from strong hans in Western Japan (especially Satsuma, Choshu, Tosa and Hizen[3]) and a few influential noblemen. The young emperor, fifteen years old at the time of the Meiji Revolution, was elevated to the head of state for legitimacy and as a unifying symbol of the new regime. The Meiji government had a very clear policy objective of promoting rapid Westernization and modernization of Japan. At first, the most serious external challenge was to avoid colonization by the West. But this fear subsided in the early Meiji period as Japan began to aggressively absorb Western systems and technology under solid national unity and identity. Thereafter, the top national priority was to catch up with the West in every aspect of civilization, i.e., to become a "first-class nation," as quickly as possible.

After a "long, peaceful sleep" (international isolation) imposed by the Bakufu, Japan suddenly discovered that Europeans and Americans were far more advanced in technology and industry while Japan was a backward agricultural country. This was a big shock to the Japanese. The painful recognition of backwardness and shattered pride was the psychological driving force behind Japan's industrialization during the Meiji period. In order to modernize Japan, the Meiji government had three clear goals: industrialization, political reform (introducing a modern constitution and parliament) and external expansion through military modernization. These were shared goals among all politicians, officials, academics, media and even the general public. As explained in the previous section, Meiji leaders fought over prioritization and the concrete content of these three goals while accepting the importance of all goals.

The biggest headache for the Meiji government in its early years was the resistance from conservative groups who disliked radical reforms. The previous samurai class, now deprived of their rice salary and the privilege of carrying swords, were particularly unhappy with the new government which was established, ironically, by former young samurai. But step by step, the new government succeeded in reducing their influence and consolidating power. It abolished the samurai class and their rice salary, and offered them government bonds as a compensation whose value rapidly depreciated under inflation. Local autonomy under the han system with inherited daimyo rule was replaced by a centralized government and prefectures whose governors were appointed by Tokyo. A new land tax at the initial rate of 3 percent of the assessed land value replaced the old rice tax that was levied on the annual yield of rice.

In 1871–73, the Iwakura Mission, a large high-level official delegation headed by Iwakura Tomomi (1825–83; equivalent to the Prime Minister), was dispatched to the US and Europe for nearly two years. As they departed from Yokohama, the mission counted 107 members including the Prime Minister, Minsters, officials, secretaries and the students sent abroad. The main objectives of the Iwakura Mission were to (i) conduct preliminary negotiations for revising the unequal treaties; and (ii) study Western technology and systems. They failed miserably in the first objective because the West would not treat Japan equally as long as its institutions remained "backward." But the mission succeeded in gaining insights in their second objective, which helped the new Japanese leaders to map out the future course. The Mission was very warmly welcomed and widely reported wherever they went.

Industrialization

Among the members of the Iwakura Mission, Okubo Toshimichi was deeply impressed with Western technology embodied in a large number of British factories he visited. Returning to Japan, Okubo vigorously promoted industrialization as the Minister of Finance (later, as the Minister of the Interior). His policies included hiring foreign advisors, hosting of domestic industrial fairs, and the construction of roads, railroads and agricultural research centers. Many state-owned model factories were established in military production, silk spinning, shipbuilding and mining (most of them were rehabilitated mines from the Edo period). New systems, such as metric weights and measures, the Western calendar, a new monetary system, banking, and joint stock companies, were introduced. Okubo was assassinated in 1878 but his supporters, especially Kuroda Kiyotaka (1840–1900) and Okuma Shigenobu (1838–1922), continued his policies.

The Meiji government sometimes confused businesses with inconsistent policies. But more often, it strongly supported the emerging private sector in establishing domestic industries and driving out foreign rivals. This policy was called *yunyu boatsu* (import substitution). With official assistance, big businesses started to develop. Politically well-connected businessmen were called *seisho* and their business groups were called *zaibatsu*. Some of them, for example Sumitomo and Mitsui, dated back to the Edo period, but many others such as Mitsubishi, Furukawa, Yasuda and Asano emerged in the Meiji period. Some big names included the following:

> Iwasaki Yataro (1835–85)—he was a businessman from Tosa Han who started a maritime transport company. Okubo's government gave him support and monopoly so that he could drive out foreign shipping firms. Iwasaki made a huge profit with an exclusive contract with the government to provide military transport to Taiwan in 1874. Iwasaki was the founder of the Mitsubishi Zaibatsu whose business empire expanded to include banking, international trade, shipbuilding, coal mining and, later, virtually everything. He was often criticized for his government connection.
>
> Shibusawa Eiichi (1840–1931)—born in Saitama, he was first a Bakufu retainer serving the last shogun, then an energetic official at the Ministry of Finance of the new government, and finally a super coordinator of Japanese industries. Shibusawa helped to establish hundreds of joint stock companies such as Imperial Hotel, Nippon Usen, Nippon Steel, Bank of Tokyo, Osaka Spinning and Sapporo Beer as well as business and social organizations such as the Tokyo Chamber of Commerce, Imperial Theater, Japan Women's University and Central Charity Association. Unlike Iwasaki, he did not form his own zaibatsu.
>
> Godai Tomoatsu (1836–1885)—he was a business coordinator from Satsuma Han. Like Shibusawa, he contributed to the creation of many companies and business organizations in Kansai area (Western Japan).
>
> Mitsui Zaibatsu—Mitsui was a big merchant family in the Edo period. Its original business was trade in *kimono* (Japanese dress) and money-changing. In Meiji, the Mitsui family gained the status of a treasury depositary of the new government, which was very profitable, and succeeded in internal organizational reform. Banking, coal mining and international trade ("Mitsui Bussan") became the main business areas.
>
> Sumitomo Zaibatsu—the Sumitomo group operated Besshi Copper Mine in Shikoku during the Edo period. The old copper mine was modernized in Meiji. The business expanded to include coal mines, banking, electrical cables, fertilizer, etc.

Most of the state-owned enterprises (SOEs) were commercially unsuccessful, but they had strong demonstration effects on emerging Japanese entrepreneurs. These factories also trained a large number of Japanese engineers under Western supervisors using the latest machines, who later migrated to other factories or established their own. These SOEs were later privatized except military establishments. They were sold "cheaply" to business groups such as Mitsubishi, Mitsui and Furukawa, triggering a political scandal in 1881. However, it must be reminded that many of the previously loss-making SOEs were restored to profitability through restructuring and additional investment by new private owners. It may be a bit unfair to criticize them for stealing state assets.

The Meiji period saw the births of many business groups and enterprises that survived and prospered into the current period. At the same time, and somewhat contradictorily, the ups and downs of enterprises were extremely volatile from the late Edo to the Meiji period. Economic shocks such as the beginning of international trade, demand shifts, foreign institutions and technology, and changing relative prices led to the decline of old enterprises and the rise of new ones. Even influential merchants and established producers in the past failed to survive these shocks unless they undertook bold internal reforms or built linkage with the emerging merchant class.

Figure 3.1 depicts the attrition of millionaires calculated from the nationwide data in Miyamoto (1999), indicating how many of the biggest businesses managed to stay in the millionaires' list in the following periods. The new rich of the late Edo to early Meiji period exited very quickly. The speed of disappearance seems even faster for the millionaires that emerged in the later periods. Among the 231 millionaires in the Edo period, only twenty survived into the late Meiji period.

This proves, at least in terms of the number of richest business families, that the main driving force of Meiji industrialization was not the merchants from the Edo period. Meiji industrialization was attained not by the same business groups expanding over time but by frequent entries and exits of newcomers. In this sense, Mitsui and Sumitomo from the Edo period, and Mitsubishi from the Meiji period, which continued to grow and prosper to this date are the exceptions rather than the rule.

The constitution and parliamentary government

In the political sphere, establishment of a Western style parliament and constitution was a nationally shared goal whose achievement was absolutely necessary to legitimize the Meiji Revolution and for Japan to be treated equally by the West. Under this agreed goal, different views on the timing and content of the proposed constitution generated much political turmoil as explained in Section 2.

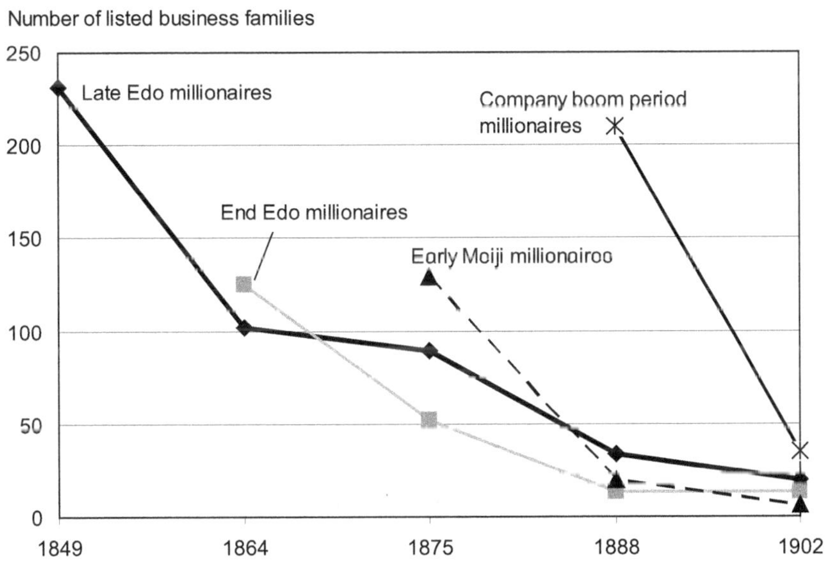

Figure 3.1 Survival of millionaires in the late Edo and Meiji period

Source: computed from Miyamoto (1999), p. 53. Each line indicates how many of the largest business families of each period continued to stay on the lists in later periods.

With respect to timing, from 1873 onward, many political groups outside the government, including high officials expelled from the government, demanded a constitution as soon as possible. Political oppositions, intellectuals and rich farmers joined this Freedom and People's Rights Movement, which spread to the entire nation. The government cracked down on this movement and the advocates of an early constitution also at times turned violent. Meanwhile, the majority of the top government officials wanted to go slow. They argued that, because Japanese people were only "semi-developed," careful preparations were necessary and gradualism rather than radical change was suited for Japan.

As to the contents of the constitution, an acute debate arose on the choice between a more advanced British-style democracy and parliamentary system and a less democratic German-style constitutional monarchy. Many intellectuals and progressive politicians favored the British system, but conservative politicians in the government preferred the German model. The latter feared that if too much freedom was allowed when people's political views remain primitive, violence and instability would result. They pointed to the violence that occurred in the aftermath of the French Revolution as a thing to be avoided at all cost.

In this regard, the contrasting opinions of Okubo Toshimichi and Fukuzawa Yukichi are worth attention. After coming home from the official mission to America and Europe, Finance Minister Okubo submitted the Proposal on Constitutional Politics to the government in 1873 whose key arguments can be summarized as follows. Democracy and monarchy each has merits and demerits. Ideally, there is no doubt that democracy is far superior. But the actual working of democracy is often marred by party politics, and by the tyranny of majority over minority in the worst case. On the other hand, monarchy functions well if people are unenlightened and the monarch is excellent, but citizens will suffer enormously if corrupt officials pursue their personal interests under a cruel ruler. In comparison with Britain, Japan remains semi-developed and cannot rid itself of feudal customs easily. Monarchy is a thing of the past, but we are not yet ready for democracy. Moreover, the central government must have strong authority for the time being to carry out bold reforms. Thus, the most practical system Japan can now adopt is a constitutional government based on gradualism that matches the speed of social change. This means constitutional monarchy.

Meanwhile, Fukuzawa, Meiji's most prominent educator and thinker, argued as follows in his *Outline of the Theory of Civilization* in 1875. Countries can be classified into civilized, semi-developed and barbaric, and Japan belongs to the second group. Democracy and monarchy each has merits and demerits. The highest priority for Japan at present is to avoid being colonized by Western powers and remain independent (up to here, his views are the same as Okubo's and hardly unique). To achieve this great objective, Japan must throw away past traditions and customs and vigorously introduce Western civilization. There are two aspects, technical and spiritual, to civilization. Technical is easy to copy while spiritual is difficult to internalize. In adopting these, we must "pursue the difficult first and the easy later; by first reforming people's mind, then change politics and laws, and finally introduce tangible objects" (Fukuzawa, 1962[1875], vol. 1, ch. 2).

In other words, Okubo's strategy is to design new policies and institutions by taking people's backward spirituality as given, while Fukuzawa wants to transform the spiritual structure of the nation as a matter of priority. The contrast between the pragmatism of Okubo, the high official, and the idealism of Fukuzawa, the enlightenment thinker, is remarkable. Their debate is far from outdated today since it contains a fundamental question about the sequencing of economic development versus political modernization (democratization) in latecomer countries.

Under the mounting popular pressure, Emperor Meiji declared in 1881 that a parliamentary government would be established within ten years. To study and prepare the content of the proposed constitution, Ito Hirobumi, another high official, and his assistants stayed in Europe for more than a year to consult German and British legal experts. After returning to Japan, his team drafted a constitution based on the German model while partially incorporating opinions of foreign legal advisors such as Albert Mosse and Hermann Roesler. The final draft was submitted to the Privy Council, an organ newly created to assess the draft constitution, and discussed chapter by chapter in closed sessions. The Meiji Constitution was promulgated in 1889 and, after an election, the first imperial parliament was convened in 1890. Japan became the first non-Western country with a functioning constitution (among the non-Western countries, Turkey also had a constitution but it was shortly suspended).

Foreign policy

The most important diplomatic goal in the Meiji period was to revise the unequal commercial treaties with the West that lacked tariff rights and the right to judge foreign criminals. This was needed to regain national pride and join the ranks of the "first-class countries." But to succeed, Westernization of Japanese society was considered necessary. To show that Japan was Westernized, the government even built *Rokumeikan*, a state-run ballroom, and invited foreign diplomats and business leaders for evening balls with Western music and food.[4] Such superficial Westernization was severely criticized by nationalists and opposition groups. Nevertheless, over time as Japanese modernization and industrialization proceeded successfully, treaty renegotiation became possible and the revision was accomplished. Tariff rights were partially regained in 1899 and completely restored in 1911. The court rights were reinstated in steps during 1894–99. Japan's legal humiliation lasting nearly half a century was finally over.

Another feature of Meiji diplomacy was expansionism. To guard Japan's independence and national interests against Western, Chinese and Russian intervention, it was considered necessary to construct a "Line of Interest," a sort of buffer zone, beyond Japanese borders. This practically meant putting Korea under Japanese control. The government was eager to "open up" Korea, which was maintaining its closed door policy, and force an unequal commercial treaty in Japan's favor, just like the West did to Japan earlier. Naturally, Korea resisted. In 1873, military invasion of Korea was proposed but rejected within the Japanese cabinet. In the following year, the government sent troops to Taiwan over an incident in which Okinawa fishermen were killed by the Taiwanese. These external expeditions were often planned to deflect the anger of former samurai who were deprived of rice salary and the privilege of carrying a sword. Crafting an external crisis to deflect domestic anger is a common tactic everywhere.

In the 1880s Japan became more aggressive in its attempt to place Korea under its influence. Japan's main rival was China (Qing Dynasty) which considered Korea as its protectorate. Japan started to aggressively intervene in Korea's internal politics and stage military provocation, which led to the Japan–China War of 1894–95. Although the Chinese naval fleet was larger and more modern than the Japanese, the disciplined and organized Japanese army and navy had the upper hand. Defeated, China had to pay a reparation of 365 million yen, equivalent to four times the annual budget of Japan, and cede Liaodong Peninsula, Taiwan and Penghu Islands to Japan. However, Japan had to immediately return Liaodong Peninsula to China under the joint pressure of Russia, Germany and France.

Japan was too weak to ignore this demand from these Western powers. The return of Liaodong Peninsula was another great humiliation in Japanese diplomacy.

After the Chinese were expelled from Korea, Russia came to occupy a large part of Northeast China (Manchuria) including Liaodong Peninsula. Russia gained territorial and economic concessions, kept large troops there and built military bases, batteries and ports. Japan was greatly alarmed. The Japan–UK alliance was formed to deter Russia, and Japan began to prepare for a final showdown. When the Japan–Russia War (1904–5) broke out, few people predicted Japanese victory against the huge Russian Empire. To cover the war cost, Japan issued government bonds in London and New York. At first there were no takers, but finally the deal was done. Battles were fought on land and at sea. The fall of Russia's Lushun Fortress on the Liaodong Peninsula, at great human cost to the Japanese army, and the defeat of Russia's Baltic Fleet in the Japan Sea were decisive. Many were surprised that a non-Western latecomer could beat a powerful White nation.

Box 3.1 The lecture of Natsume Soseki

Natsume Soseki (1867–1916) perhaps was and is the most popular novelist in Japan. His life largely coincided with the Meiji period. He was an expert in both English and ancient Chinese literature. His early novels were comical (*I Am a Cat*, *Bocchan*) and sometimes romantic (*Sanshiro*) or pedantic (*Kusamakura*). But his later novels exposed a dark side of modernized Japan, especially individuals who struggle under human limitations in modernized life without success (*Sorekara*, *Mon*). Desperate love triangles were his favorite theme.

In his famous lecture in Wakayama, "Development of Modern Japan" (1911), Soseki warned his fellow Japanese against newly emerging complacency. In late Meiji when this lecture was delivered, Japan already had a functioning parliamentary government and had recently won a victory over Russia. Industrialization was proceeding rapidly. Japanese people were elated. But Soseki said that Japan's modernization was superficial.

Since Japan opened its ports to foreigners in the mid-nineteenth century, Western impact transformed Japan completely. But all these influences originated in the West, and Japan only copied them passively without really digesting and internalizing them. The arrival of Western waves was too fast for the Japanese to make them their own. Forced absorption of foreign ideas and systems would make the Japanese nervous and unhappy, but there was no good solution to this problem. This was the essence of Soseki's message whose excerpts are cited below. Soseki touched on the fundamental dilemma of Japanese identity which remains unsolved even today. In the twenty-first century, Japan is sometimes ill at ease in the company of the advanced Western nations, while unable to build true trust and friendship with its Asian neighbors.

> Development in the West is *endogenous*, while Japan's development is *exogenous*. Here, *endogenous* means emerging naturally from within, like a bud blooms into a flower in an outward motion, and *exogenous* means being forced to take a certain form because of external influences...

Western societies are evolving naturally but Japan after the Meiji Restoration and foreign contact is quite different. Of course, every country is influenced by its neighbors, and Japan was no exception. In certain periods, Korea and China were models for us. But overall, throughout history, Japan was developing more or less endogenously. Then suddenly, after two centuries of isolation, we opened up and encountered Western civilization. It was a big shock we never experienced before. Since then, the Japanese society began to evolve in a different direction. The shock was so severe that we were forced to change directions...

Western tides dominate our development. Since we are not Westerners, every time a new wave arrives from the West we feel uneasy like a person living in someone else's house. Even before we can grasp the nature of the previous wave, a new wave arrives. It is as if too many dishes are brought in and soon removed before we can start to eat. In such circumstances, people will inevitably become empty, frustrated, and worried.

(Source: Yukio Miyoshi, ed., *Soseki's Writings on Civilization*, Iwanami Bunko, 1986)

Notes

1 When the American Black Ships left, the Bakufu ordered the Administrator of Izu to quickly build several new *odaiba*, or fortified islets, off the coast of Shinagawa. Apparently, these tiny forts were not enough to stop the Americans and they were never used. Today, the two remaining odaiba can be seen at the foot of Rainbow Bridge from Yurikamome train.

2 Some economists regard global integration and free trade as the engines of growth. In reality, a sudden and unprepared opening of developing economies often leads to bankruptcies of local firms, deindustrialization, rural impoverishment and widening income gaps. For example, *The Least Developed Countries Report* of the UNCTAD (2004) states that a consistent development strategy is the prerequisite for poverty reduction without which export promotion under international integration alone will not produce desired developmental effects. In this context, the Japanese experience in which the export of silk and tea enormously enriched the farmers in the late Edo to the early Meiji "port-opening" period is unique and very different from the cases of most other latecomer economies.

3 It must be noted that former samurai from Hizen (also called Saga), such as Okuma Shigenobu (1838–1922), Eto Shimpei (1834–74), Oki Takatou (1832–99) and Soejima Taneomi (1828–1905), joined the new government by the merit and connection of each person rather than as a former han team. Hizen Han pursued *fukoku kyohei* independently from and cooperated little with other strong hans, thus being unable to become a party to shape the new government.

4 Rokumeikan was located in Hibiya, near where Imperial Hotel now stands. Since most foreign diplomats and business leaders lived in Yokohama, the government even prepared a special late-night train from Shimbashi to Yokohama to bring them home after the ball.

4

IMPORTING AND ABSORBING TECHNOLOGY

Meiji industrialization

The three salient features of Meiji industrialization are very strong private sector initiative supported by appropriate official assistance, successful import substitution in the cotton industry, and parallel development of the modern sector and the indigenous sector. These will be discussed more fully in this and the following chapters.

As noted in the previous chapter, one of the agreed policy objectives of the Meiji government was industrialization. The official policies of introducing Western institutions, building infrastructure, hiring foreign advisors, renovating education and training, establishing state-owned factories and research centers, organizing trade fairs, assisting zaibatsu and so on, were all important and played crucial roles. At the same time, it should be stressed that private sector dynamism was even more essential. Such powerful business leaders and coordinators as Shibusawa, Iwasaki and Godai provided leadership, and large zaibatsu groups began to form. At the grass-roots level, traditional and newly emerging merchants, skilled engineers, proud craftsmen, rich farmers and village leaders all over the country became the driving force of broad-based technical absorption. Without this private sector capability, even good policies would have failed to produce significant results.

It should also be recalled that many contributing factors to Meiji industrialization were inherited from the previous Edo period. They included agricultural development, nationally unified markets, transportation and distribution networks, a strong merchant tradition, the development of financial services, a well-educated population and experiences of industrial promotion by local governments yielding various results.

The cotton industry was one of the leading industries of the world in the nineteenth century. At first, British products dominated the global market. In Asia, India was the main producer. But Japan absorbed textile technology very rapidly in the late nineteenth century. After the opening of ports, Japan first imported British cotton clothes as rural demand for such clothes surged. Later, it imported cotton yarns and wove clothes for the domestic market. By around 1900, Japan began to export cotton yarns while importing raw cotton from India initially, and also from the US later. In the early twentieth century, Japan became a major exporter of cotton clothes (finished products). Today, international development institutions such as the World Bank often discredit import substitution policy or at least remain suspicious about its effect. In this light, Meiji Japan's brilliant success in turning its major imports (textile products) into major exports in less than half a century is all the more striking.

DOI: 10.4324/9781315444048-5

However, the introduction of modern Western technology did not drive out all traditional technology inherited from the Edo period. In the textile industry as well as in other industries such as metal-working, printing and food processing, indigenous production methods existed side-by-side with modern machines and factories. Sometimes the two sectors produced differentiated products for different market segments. At other times they were vertically related with one sector producing inputs for the other. New technology influenced traditional methods, but local conditions and requirements also modified imported technology. This pattern observed in Meiji Japan, in which foreign technology and indigenous technology influenced each other in the early days of industrialization rather than the former wiping out the latter, is termed the *dual structure* or *hybrid technology* by economic historian Odaka Konosuke (1990, 1999).

By the end of Meiji (1912), shortly before the outbreak of WW1, Japan can be said to have been successfully industrialized in light manufacturing, especially textiles. But heavy and machinery industries were still embryonic. Vigorous development of these industries started later, during and after WW1.

The macroeconomy and industrial development

The Japanese economy underwent several stages after the opening of ports in the late Edo period. Major developments are explained chronologically below.

1 *Initial impact of foreign trade* (1850s–60s): foreign ideas, technology, institutions and products flowed in to radically transform the Japanese society. The resulting shifts in relative prices and industrial structure forced many of the production regions of various traditional goods to decline and be replaced by newly emerging regions and products. Inflation shot up toward the end of the Edo period.
2 *Monetary confusion and continued inflation* (late 1870s): the Meiji government initially adopted the US monetary model in which there was no central bank and certified private banks issued money against their gold reserves. But this system did not work well and produced confusion in the nascent banking sector. Inflation accelerated as paper money was printed to finance the military operations to suppress Saigo Takamori's rebellion in Kyushu in 1877. As the prices of rice and other agricultural products rose, farmers and landlords got rich while former samurai were generally impoverished.
3 *Matsukata Deflation* (early 1880s): Chancellor of Finance Matsukata Masayoshi adopted a deflationary policy to end inflation and introduce a modern monetary system. This resulted in establishment of the Bank of Japan as a central bank in 1882, replacing the failed US monetary model. As the prices of agricultural commodities plummeted, rural income fell and the number of landless farmers increased.[1]
4 *The first "company boom"* (late 1880s): after inflation subsided and modern banking was installed, there was a rush to establish joint stock companies in the private sector. Exchange rate depreciation, easy money and low interest rates also encouraged their emergence. Rich landlords and merchants as well as former daimyos invested in newly issued stocks, but they were mainly interested in quick dividends rather than long-term business growth.
5 *Continued waves of company booms* (1890s–1910s): a large number of joint stock companies were established in the late 1890s, late 1900s and during WW1, interrupted by recessions. Booms and busts became a permanent feature of Japan, a young capitalist nation. Initially, textile mills and railroad construction and operation were the two most popular sectors for investors. Later, company creation spread to all sectors.

6 *Two wars* (Japan–China 1894–95; Japan–Russia 1904–5): these wars were fought as Japan asserted its political and economic influence in the Korean Peninsula and then the Northeastern part of China. The Qing Dynasty of China and the Russian Empire stood in front of Japan's expansive intention. In both wars, Japan emerged as a winner although the war with Russia was particularly costly in terms of human lives and budgetary finance. After each war, fiscal activism, instead of a return to fiscal prudence, was adopted. Large public investment was undertaken to build more railroads and the national telephone network. In addition, military spending was kept up even during peacetime. Economic management of Taiwan, Japan's first colony acquired in 1895, also began with institution-building and public investment. Local governments issued foreign-currency denominated bonds to invest in infrastructure for water works, roads, tramcar networks and so on. As a result, the general budget size (combining central and local governments) ballooned and the balance-of-payments deficit widened. Gold reserves (i.e. international reserves) were gradually lost, and the public debt stock rose to about 40 percent of estimated GDP. Roughly half of the public debt was denominated in foreign currency.

Choice between fiscal activism and a small government was the main arguing point of Japan's first parliament convened in 1890, and the fight between two camps continued into the twentieth century. From the late Meiji period onward, fiscal activism was promoted by Seiyukai, with the full name of Rikken Seiyukai, a political party established in 1900 by Ito Hirobumi, the drafter of the Meiji Constitution and the first Prime Minister. Ito's idea was to create a party to strongly support the government's policies rather than insisting on *chozen-shugi*, or ignoring the demands of opposition parties in the parliament, an obviously untenable tactic adopted initially by the Meiji government. Seiyukai's main support base was rich farmers and landlords who welcomed aggressive public investment in rural areas.

But fiscal overspending produced by Seiyukai governments naturally led to mounting balance-of-payments pressure as noted above. Macroeconomic belt-tightening was clearly necessary in the first years of the twentieth century. In reality, this economic crisis was unexpectedly overcome by the outbreak of WW1 (1914–1918) rather than by orthodox fiscal and monetary austerity. As the European powers started military confrontation, they stopped exporting machinery and industrial inputs to the rest of the world including Japan. World demand for manufactured goods shifted to Japanese products despite their inferior quality, allowing the Japanese economy to enjoy an enormous export-led boom. But these are events of the following Taisho period which will be dealt with more fully in Chapter 7.

No reliable GDP statistics exist for this period, but we have some estimates. According to them, Japanese output was very bumpy with the average real growth rate of 2 to 3 percent per year. By today's standards, this is not particularly impressive for a developing country although there may be a problem of data quality. Nevertheless, low growth may have been a fact rather than a statistical concoction. Such relatively low growth seems to have been sufficient for a latecomer economy to emerge as a new economic power in the nineteenth to the early twentieth century. As for the employment structure, the share of agricultural employment was dominant, at about 70 percent in the early Meiji period, but it gradually declined.

International trade

Regarding trade structure, raw silk—silk yarn rather than finished silk products—dominated Japan's exports, followed by tea, cereals, seafood, minerals and coal. Clearly, Meiji Japan was a primary commodity exporter. Raw silk remained the top Japanese export, not just during the Meiji period but in the entire pre-WW2 period up to the 1930s. The largest importer of Japanese silk and tea was the United States. Stockings made from Japanese silk were very popular among American ladies until artificial fibers such as rayon and nylon were invented.

The United States, a young developing country at that time, maintained high import protection throughout the nineteenth century (see Box 4.1). It protected its silk weaving industry with tariff rates of 45 to 50 percent, but the industry needed silk yarn as an input. An attempt to increase domestic silk yarn production failed, so the US industry was compelled to continue to rely on Japanese yarn.

On the import side, dramatic shifts occurred in Japan's trade structure as the cotton industry succeeded in import substitution as discussed earlier. Initially, finished products (clothes) were imported. Later, imports shifted to intermediate input (cotton yarn) and then to raw material (raw cotton). In Figure 4.1, we can see a clear product cycle of this industry moving from import to domestic production, and finally to export. Domestic production shifted downstream from spinning to weaving as well as from low to high quality products. At first, Britain was the main exporter of finished textile products and machinery to Japan. But over time, Japan increased competitiveness against British textile products and drove them out of the Asian market.

In early Meiji, Japan's trade pattern was a "vertical" one typical of a developing country. It exported raw silk, tea leaves and other primary commodities to Europe and America while importing manufactured products from them. By late Meiji, Japan developed a more complex trade pattern. Against Europe and the US, trade remained basically vertical. But with the rest of Asia, which included China, Korea, India and Southeast

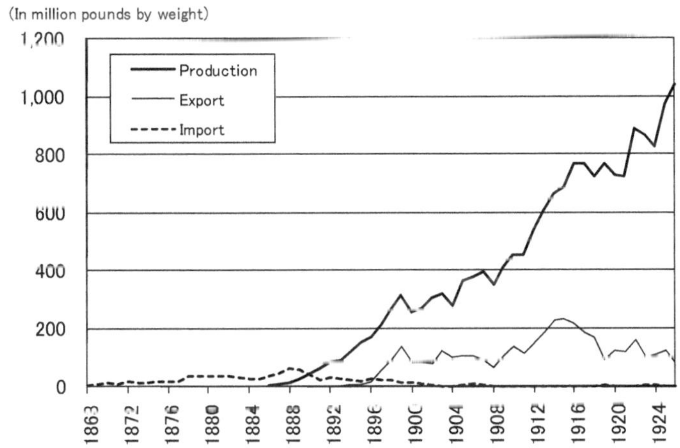

Figure 4.1 Production, export and import of cotton yarn

Sources: Iijima Manji, *History of Japanese Textile Spinning Industry*, Sogensha, 1949, pp. 502–504.

Asia, Japan began to export light manufactured goods such as cotton yarn, cotton clothes, knitwear, matches, umbrellas, clocks, lamps, glass products and so on. Japan also began to import materials needed to produce them, especially Indian raw cotton which was short-fiber. Japan also imported US cotton which was long-fiber. Due to the emergence of Japan's cotton industry, India was driven out of the position of an exporter of cotton products into an exporter of raw cotton (Figure 4.2).

As the export of cotton yarn and the import of raw cotton both rose, the government abolished the cotton yarn export tax in 1894 and the cotton import tariff in 1896. This benefited modern cotton factories that used Indian cotton as inputs, but hurt traditional producers who spun domestically produced cotton (Figure 4.3). In order to establish a monopolistic position in importing Indian cotton vis-à-vis foreign marine cargo carriers, Japanese textile companies formed a cartel and used only Nippon Yusen (a Mitsubishi-group shipping company) and Menka Shosha (Cotton Trading House) as the sole carrier and distributor of Indian cotton to Japan. This secured a stable supply of Indian cotton at low prices for Japanese textile companies.

How Western technology was transferred

Western technology was imported and internalized in phased but overlapping steps (Uchida 1990). Different technological transfer schemes were adopted depending on project type and time periods, from simple turnkey contracts and management contracts to engineering education, selective technical advice, copy production based on reverse engineering and original invention after studying foreign models. The method progressed sequentially from easy to more complex as Japanese technological capability steadily rose. In addition, we should not forget the role of policy support that allowed Japanese firms to climb the technological ladder.

The earliest method of technology transfer was hiring of foreign advisors. In early Meiji, especially in the 1870s, new factories and infrastructure were constructed and operated with significant assistance from foreign engineers and managers. In the late nineteenth century, there were many unemployed British railroad engineers since the British railroad system had

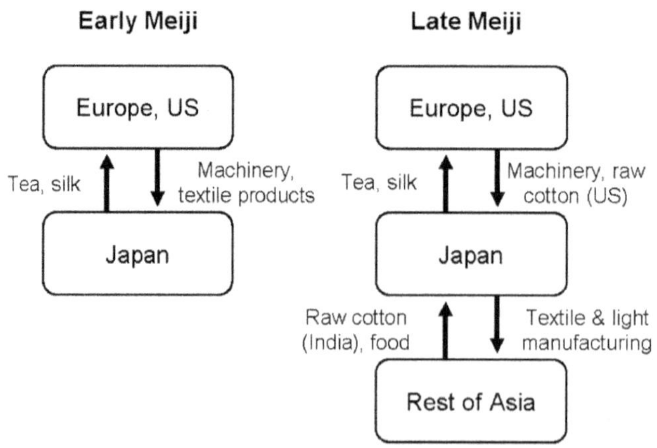

Figure 4.2 Trade structure

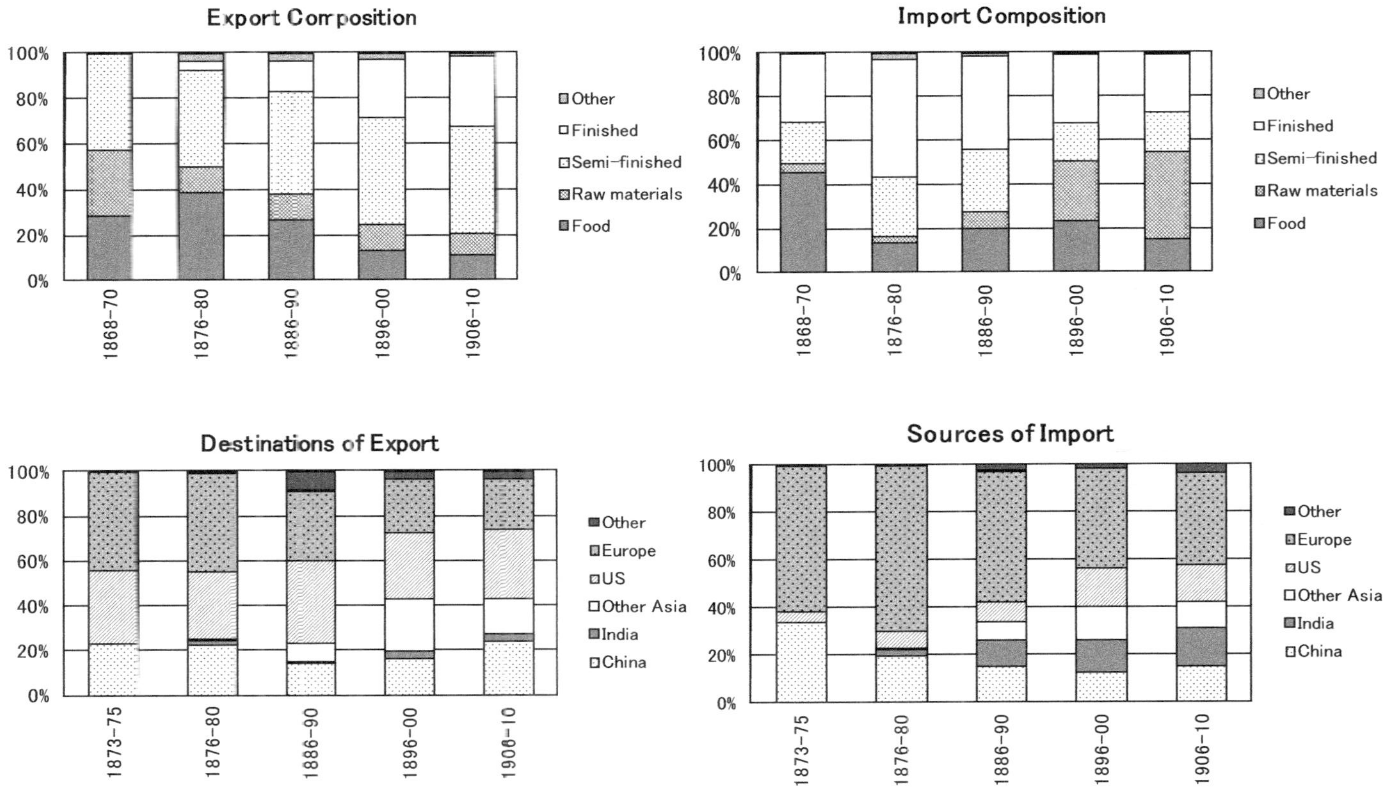

Figure 4.3 Structure of expcrt and import

been more or less completed. They often traveled abroad in search of jobs. The salaries of such foreign advisors were very high and sometimes even higher than that of the Japanese Prime Minister[2] which became a great financial burden on the government. In 1874, the salaries of hired foreign engineers accounted for 34 percent of the current budget of the Ministry of Industry.

Figure 4.4 indicates the number of foreigners employed by the central and local governments. The number—especially the number of engineers—declined significantly toward the end of Meiji as Japanese engineers steadily replaced foreigners. Since contracts that the government signed were turnkey projects with fixed terms, foreigners returned home or went elsewhere when the contract expired. The government took utmost care to prevent important national projects, such as mines, railroads and shipyards, from falling into foreign hands. From the mid Meiji onward, foreign teachers, including language teachers, hired by private universities and other academic institutions (not shown in Figure 4.4) became the dominant form of foreigners' employment in Japan.

The second form of technology transfer was training of Japanese engineers. Since foreign advisors were too expensive to keep, the government vigorously promoted "import substitution" by Japanese engineers. Excellent students were nominated by the government to go abroad to absorb the latest ideas and technology at universities and colleges in Europe and America with financial support from the Japanese government. Students were sent to the most appropriate institutions for the subject and they studied very hard, easily replacing foreigners after returning to Japan. However, the amount of Japanese government scholarship was not very large.

Domestically, Kobu Daigakko (Institute of Technology) was established in 1877 as the highest academic institution for absorbing Western technology, where foreign professors taught mostly in English. It was located in Kasumigaseki at the heart of Tokyo where the Ministry of Finance now stands. It developed from a training school for Japanese operators at industrial projects under the Ministry of Industry. Later, the Institute was merged into the Faculty of Engineering of Tokyo University under the Ministry of Education. Henry Dyer, a British engineer, was contracted as the first president of Kobu Daigakko, where he pursued a judicious combination of theory and practice, an ideal that had not been realized in his home country. The institute offered courses in civil engineering, mechanical engineering, shipbuilding, telecommunication, chemistry, architecture, metallurgy and mining. The six-year

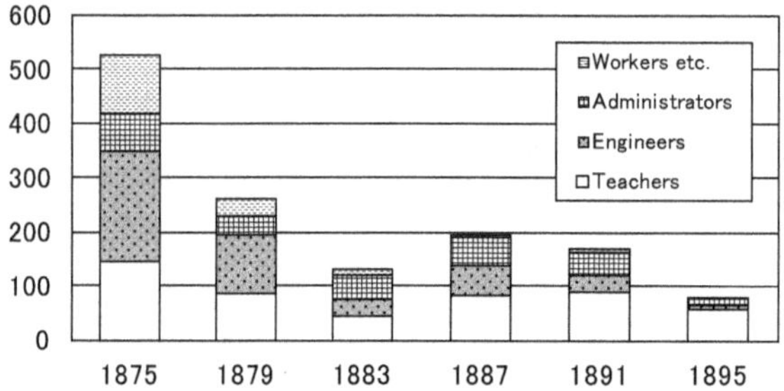

Figure 4.4 Foreign advisors employed by the Meiji government

Source: Umetani Noboru, *Hired Foreign Advisors*, vol.1, Kajima Research Institute Publishing House, 1968. Private sector employment is excluded.

program consisted of a preparatory period (mainly language learning), specialized studies and internship at government projects, each lasting two years. Top students were sent abroad to study. Kobu Daigakko produced many industrial designers and engineers who built the Biwako–Kyoto Canal and a power station, Tokyo Station, the Bank of Japan Headquarters, Nara Hotel, and so on.

In addition, Koto Kogyo Gakko (industrial high schools) played a critical role in equipping Japanese factories with competent mid-level engineers. Tokyo Craftsmen School was established in 1881 and upgraded, together with Osaka Industrial School, to Koto Kogyo Gakko in 1897. Four more Koto Kogyo Gakko were created by the end of Meiji, with many more added during the following Taisho period. Good students who lacked financial means to go to Kobu Daigakko were attracted to Koto Kogyo Gakko, which taught practical technology and supplied a large number of engineers and technicians to private enterprises. This no doubt greatly increased the technical absorptive capacity of the country. However, proud and ungovernable craftsmen were more influential on the factory floor than newly trained engineers during much of Meiji. Furthermore, workers were hired by a labor broker who supplied them to factories on a contract basis. Transition from craftsmen to trained engineers as main factory labor, and from indirect employment to direct management of workers by the enterprise, progressed slowly but steadily (Odaka 2000).

In the latter half of Meiji with an increasingly broad base of Japanese engineers, copying, licensing, joint venture and technical cooperation became the dominant forms of technology transfer. Graduates from Kobu Daigakko often played an instrumental role in selecting and importing new technology. In economic ministries and large private firms, they took initiative in collecting information, purchasing machines, and adjusting them to Japanese requirements. Besides this, trading houses such as Mitsui Corporation and Takada Shokai provided customers with product information and technical assistance in ordering and installing equipment. Many US and European machines were copy-produced by reverse engineering, but this became illegal by the revisions of the commercial treaties in 1894 and 1899. Thereafter, Japanese firms had to learn technology by more formal and costly ways.

Unlike today's developing countries which covet foreign direct investment (FDI), there was relatively little FDI in Meiji Japan (Table 4.1). FDI into Japan was prohibited until the revision of the commercial treaties in 1899, and Japanese government and businesses continued to remain hostile to foreign investment even under the revised treaties. This was in sharp contrast to the industrial experiences of China and India which received large amounts of FDI in this period. The Japanese government was also afraid of borrowing from foreigners, especially in early Meiji (Chapter 6). Bytheway (2005) estimates that, during Meiji, FDI was

Table 4.1 Selected foreign investment projects during Meiji and Taisho

Year	*Japanese name*	*Foreign partner*	*Foreign ownshp*	*Remark*
1893	Standard Oil	Standard Oil (US)	100%	Later sold to Nippon Oil
1899	Nippon Electric (NEC)	Western Electric (US)	54%	Later under Sumitomo
1900	Murai Brothers	American Tobacco (US)	50%	State-owned in 1904
1900	Rising Sun	S. Samuel & Co. (UK)	100%	Oil business
1901	Singer Mishin	Singer Sewing Machine (US)	100%	

(continued)

Table 4.1 (continued)

Year	*Japanese name*	*Foreign partner*	*Foreign ownshp*	*Remark*
1902	Osaka Gas	Mr A.N. Brady US)	50%	Brady capital exits in 1925
1903	Tokyo Electrical Train	Mr Malcolm (UK)	–	
1905	Tokyo Electric	General Electric (US)	38%	Later Toshiba, 1939
1906	Osaka Glass Manufacturing	Private syndicate (UK, Bel, Fr)	56%	
1907	Nippon Steel	Armstrong & Vickers (U K)	50%	Weapon manufacturing
1907	Imperial Spinning	J&P Coats (UK)	60%	
1909	Dunlop Rubber	Far East Dunlop (UK)	100%	Later, 100% Japanese
1910	Shibaura Manufacturing	General Electric (US)	24%	Later Toshiba, 1939
1910	Nippon Okijenu & Asechiresu	L'air Liquide (FR)	100%	
1910	Lever Brothers Amagasaki	Lever & Brothers (UK)	100%	
1910	Nippon Chikuonki Trading	Mr. F.W. Hohn (US)	–	Phonograph
1917	Yokohama Rubber Manuf.	F.B. Goodrich (US)	50%	Presence since 1912
1918	Japan-US Sheet Glass	Libby Owens Sheet Glass (US)	35%	From 1922, under Sumitomo
1920	Sumitomo Electric Cable	Western Electric (US)	25%	
1922	Asahi Silk Weaving	Vereinigete Glanzstoff Fabriken (Germany)	20%	From 1929, under Nicchitsu
1923	Fuji Electric Manufacturing	Siemens (Germany)	30%	Japanese partner: Furukawa
1923	Mitsubishi Electric	Westinghouse Electric (US)	10%	
1925	Japan Ford	Ford Motor (US)	100%	Previously, sales through agents
1927	Japan General Motors	General Motors (US)	100%	
1927	Japan Victor	Victor Talking Machine (US)	100%	From 1937, under Nissan
1927	Daido Match	Sweden Match (Swe)	50%	From 1932, under Nissan
1928	Japan Columbia Phonograph	Columbia (UK)	59%	From 1935, under Nissan
1928	Toyo Babcock	Babcock & Wilcox (UK)	71%	Boilers, steam turbines
1929	Japan Benberg Silk Fiber	J.P. Benberg (Germany)	20%	In 1933, merged with Asahi Silk weaving
1931	Mitsubishi Oil	Associated Tidewater Oil (US)	50%	Japanese partner: Mitsubishi
1931	Sumitomo Alminum Smelting	Aluminum Co. of Canada (Can)	50%	
1932	Toyo Otis Elevators	Otis Elevators (US)	60%	Japanese partner: Mitsui
1932	Japan Submarine Cable	Int'l Standard Electric (US)	12%	Under Sumitomo
1933	National Cash Register	National Cash Register (US)	100%	
1937	Japan Watson	Watson Computing Tabulating Recording Machine (US)	100%	
1939	Shibaura Kyodo Industries	United Engineering (US)	–	Japanese partner: Shibaura

Source: Bytheway (2005), pp.166–169.

a very small part of foreign saving mobilization with the share of only 0.7 percent, while issuance of government bonds (82.5 percent), municipal bonds (7.8 percent) and corporate bonds (9.0 percent) was the dominant form of borrowing from abroad. Though quantitatively small, Bytheway argues that FDI played crucial roles in technology transfer in certain sectors such as electric machinery, telephone equipment and light bulb production.

In the early twentieth century, a number of automobile and electrical machinery companies signed licensing agreements and technical cooperation contracts with Western firms. However, in such cooperation the Japanese partners quickly absorbed needed technology and often dissolved the relationship with the Western partner.

Japan is said to be a country of *monozukuri* (manufacturing things). In many European countries including nineteenth-century Britain, engineers who worked in oily factories did not have a high status compared with managers, lawyers and accountants who remained in clean offices. But in Japan, university graduates loved to build, adjust and repair machines and manage factories. They had no problem working side-by-side with machine operators on a noisy factory floor. This was true in the Meiji period as well as until the recent past. The best students chose engineering, rather than law or economics, as their field of specialization.

Labor market

The Japanese labor market in the Meiji period and up to the middle of the twentieth century hardly resembled the post-WW2 Japanese model where lifetime employment and loyalty to the company were the norm. In the early days of Japanese industrialization, the labor market exhibited many of the neoclassical traits in which workers were wage-sensitive and footloose, felt little allegiance to the company, and did not follow managers' instructions closely. The Survey of Industrial Workers by the Ministry of Agriculture and Commerce in 1901 found that Japanese workers were frequent job hoppers who did not stay with one company for long. Moreover, they lacked work discipline and hardly saved from their income. The Ministry concluded that these lamentable labor characteristics constituted a serious barrier to industrialization.

According to another survey conducted in 1902 by the Tokyo Metropolitan Police, 29.9 percent of male workers at mechanical factories in Tokyo quit jobs in less than a year; 17.6 percent lasted between one and two years, and 15.2 percent stayed between two and three years while only 4.2 percent worked at the same place for a decade or more. Subsequent annual surveys confirmed that rapid labor turnover, despite fluctuations due to economic cycles and other conditions, remained virtually the same from 1902 to 1913.

However, from the perspective of technology learning, such disloyal behavior was a positive factor in Japan's early industrialization. Among talented and ambitious craftsmen in the Meiji period, it was customary to absorb as much knowledge as possible at factories supervised by foreigners and equipped with the latest machines. Frequent migration across state-owned factories and military mills was a natural means to achieve this. After learning sufficient technology and operational skills, many craftsmen set up their own companies, often to supply components and production services to mother factories. By the early twentieth century, industrial clusters in textile, steelworks, shipbuilding and fertilizers formed in low areas in Tokyo such as Honjo, Fukagawa, Asakusa, Kanda, Shiba and Kyobashi.[3] Similar developments were also observed in Osaka. Many of these industrial areas saw large-scale anchor firms surrounded by a great number of manufacturing small and medium-sized enterprises (SMEs). It is noteworthy that these early industrial clusters formed autonomously without designated industrial zones, factory relocation policy or other interventions by the state. Market forces prompted skilled engineers and manufacturing SMEs to emerge strongly, a feat that many of today's developing countries try to achieve by technical training and SME support measures with mixed results.

Company management viewed job hopping by most competent engineers as a great challenge to long-term business development. As the weight of Japanese industrial activity shifted gradually from light manufacturing such as cotton textiles using young female labor to heavy and chemical industries, demand for more faithful and experienced workers grew because the success of the latter depended critically on accumulated skills and company-specific experience. Thus, around the 1910s, large private firms began to offer internal incentives such as promotion and/or salary increase to retain workers longer, although the footloose situation of workers at SMEs and the service sector was hardly affected. Much later, during the Japan–China War (1937–1945) which led to the Pacific War (1941–1945), Japanese workers were forced to remain at establishments assigned by the government as part of total war effort.

Another salient feature of Meiji industrialization was the prevalence of female domestic workers called *jochu* (Odaka, 1989). In any rapidly industrializing society, labor migration from rural villages to cities is activated and Meiji Japan was no exception. Expanding urban industry and lingering rural poverty and labor surplus were the pull and the push factors of such migration. The end of Meiji to early Showa was the peak period of *jochu* which included young unmarried girls who lived with the family as well as older married helpers who commuted. In 1930, toward the end of this period, jochu accounted for 17.5 percent of Japanese non-farm female employment, second only to textile workers, and 5.7 percent of Japanese households hired jochu. Housemaids were also popular in other rapidly industrializing countries. The percentage of domestic workers in total non-farm female employment was 11.4 percent in the UK in 1851, 11.8 percent in the US in 1910, 10.6 percent in Thailand in 1960 and 34.3 percent in the Philippines in 1975. As income and wages rose and the labor market tightened, the age of jochu came to an end (the Japanese labor market turned from general surplus to shortage around 1960). The gender gap in wage also persisted over time and across sectors, with female workers receiving only about 55–65 percent in comparison with male workers in farm employment, textile work and domestic service, as exemplified by the wage data collected by the Ministry of Agriculture and Commerce from 1885 to 1920.

Hybrid technology

Odaka (1990) argues that Meiji industrialization was achieved by combining existing traditional technology and new Western technology in an appropriate manner. He calls this "hybrid technology." Although Western technology was far superior to Edo-period technology, the former did not completely replace the latter. This can be considered as one example of the "translative adaptation" introduced in Chapter 1.

According to Odaka, different types of industrial evolution can be identified. In Figure 4.5, intermediate points such as I* and M* can be called hybrid technology[4] (M stands for "modern," I stands for "indigenous" and the asterisk means modified).

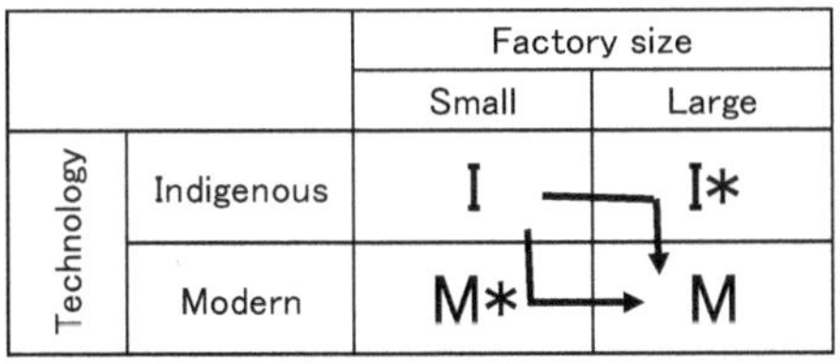

Figure 4.5 Technology and factory size

M→M For a completely new technology, the Western model must be imported as a whole; there was no corresponding traditional technology (e.g. railroads, telephone system, electrification).

I→I*→M Indigenous technology was first adjusted and expanded. Later, there was a switch to a new Western method (e.g. shipbuilding, sake making).

I→M*→M Indigenous technology was first replaced by Western technology but at a small scale that fitted Japanese reality. Later, the size was expanded (e.g. printing, machine production).

Indigenous and modern technology often coexisted because they played complementary roles in vertical industrial linkage in which one industry produced an input to the other, or because their markets were differentiated with, for instance, modern plants producing for export and traditional ones serving the domestic market. As Figures 4.6 and 4.7 illustrate, despite the steady growth of modern industries from Meiji to early Showa measured by output, it was not the largest part of the Japanese economy when measured by employment. The largest absorber of labor force was still the primary industry whose share, however, was gradually declining. The share of employment of indigenous manufacturing and service sectors remained relatively stable at slightly over 30 percent.

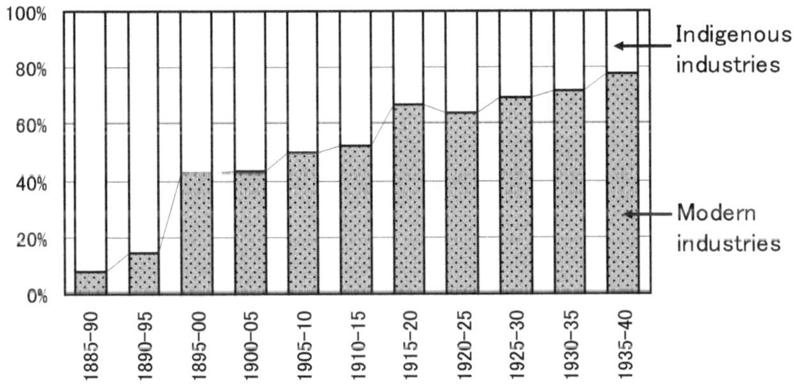

Figure 4.6 Manufacturing output in prewar Japan

Source: Matsumoto and Okuda (1997).

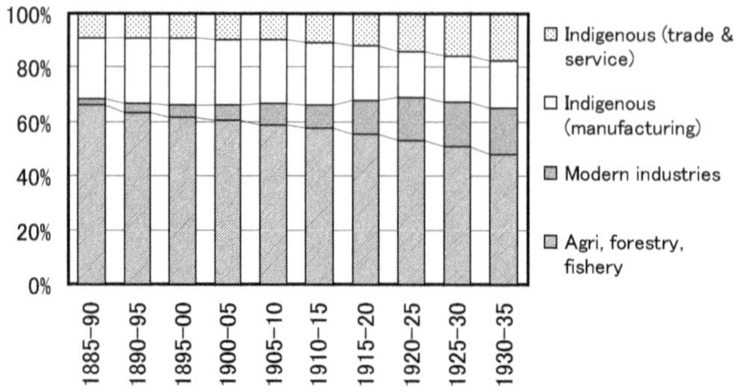

Figure 4.7 Employment structure in prewar Japan

Source: Matsumoto and Okuda (1997).

Box 4.1 Meiroku Zasshi

Mei is the first syllable of Meiji. *Roku* means six. *Zasshi* means journal. Meiroku Zasshi (*Journal of the Sixth Year of Meiji*) was a series of publications by Meirokusha (Society of the Sixth Year of Meiji) in 1874 and 1875. Meirokusha, in turn, was a free discussion forum founded in 1873 (the sixth year of Meiji) by Mori Arinori, who later served as the first education minister. *Meiroku Zasshi* was a collection of relatively short essays covering a wide variety of issues such as lessons from Western history, proposals for reforming the Japanese language, religious questions, social policy and economics. At the outset of each issue, the following message was printed in archaic Japanese:

> Recently, we friends gathered to discuss social issues and foreign situations in order to deepen our knowledge and enjoy high spirits. As meeting records have accumulated, we have decided to publish and share them with our colleagues at large. While it is only a small booklet, we would be happy if it helps to improve the knowledge of the Japanese people.

As an example, here is the summary translation of "The Argument against Tariff Protection" by Tsuda Mamichi (1829–1903), a scholar in Western studies. This article was published in the fifth volume of Meiroku Zasshi on April 15, 1874.

> Our trade deficits were 8 and 7 million yen in 1872 and 1873, respectively. In addition, we pay 2 million yen annually as salaries for foreign advisors and teachers. This means that gold and silver flow out of Japan at the rate of roughly 100 million yen every decade. Our international reserves may be exhausted in one or two decades.
>
> Pessimists say, "If we lose precious metals like this, how can Japan survive? We must stop this outflow. Europe used tariff protection in the past. The US is still practicing it. We must also adopt this policy."

I disagree with this idea. European economists state clearly that protection is the worst policy which harms the nation's welfare. The US is still resorting to tariff protection because American industries are less developed than European, with higher cost. Therefore, Americans levy high tariffs on imported goods to promote domestic industries.

But the development level of Japanese industries is far below even that of the American. Needless to say, comparison with Europeans is out of the question. It is like a small baby trying to compete with a giant. That is why we have to pay 2 million yen for foreign teachers. Evidently, copying American policy is not suitable for Japan. More specifically, there are several reasons why tariff protection is undesirable.

First, commercial treaties with the West prohibit raising our tariffs.

Second, there is a huge gap in technology between Japan and Europe. For example, the price of domestic steel is higher than imported steel even after paying the transportation cost. Protection is not enough to narrow this gap.

Third, Japanese people now like to consume a wide variety of imported products such as food, clothes and household goods for which domestic supply is nonexistent. For many goods, no Japanese factories can produce them.

Fourth, under the policy of rapid Westernization, a large amount of imports is hardly avoidable.

Fifth, Japan is a student learning Western knowledge and technology. To study more and faster, we need to pay high tuition.

Some say, "If we do nothing, we will lose all international reserves soon." But don't worry. The trade balance may be in surplus or in deficit in the short run, but there will be no great imbalance on average. The movement is natural and cyclical. When we first opened our ports, we had trade surpluses for a few years. Then, imports exceeded exports for the next three to four years. It is certain that we will have surpluses again in the near future. The natural balance is always maintained, and this is the condition under which technology and civilization should progress.

Meiroku Zasshi was Japan's first modern scholarly journal which greatly stimulated policy debate among intellectuals. However, the journal was terminated by a government order under the tightened speech control in November 1875. Its publication lasted only one and half years.

Notes

1 Using an old-fashioned Marxian language, we may say that Matsukata Deflation founded the basis of Japan's coming capitalism and industrial revolution by producing the proletariat class detached from productive assets (including land) and establishing the modern banking system that supported the expansion of capitalists.

2 In the early 1870s, among the top earning foreigners in Japan, with their position, nationality and monthly salary, were William Walter Cargill (advisor to the Railroad Department, Ministry of Industry, British, 2,000 yen), Thomas William Kinder (advisor to the National Mint, British, 1,045 yen), Edmund Morel (advisor to the Railroad Department, Ministry of Industry, British, 850 yen),

and Horace Capron (advisor on the development of Hokkaido, American, 833 yen). Udaijin (equivalent to Prime Minister) Iwakura Tomomi received only 600 yen per month.

3 These industrial areas were severely affected by the Great Kanto Earthquake of 1923. Honjo recovered strongly but Fukagawa, badly damaged by fire, did not. After the quake, key industrial areas of Tokyo generally shifted toward the south. Omori and Kamata emerged as new industrial clusters. Additionally, coastal industrial areas were created by landfill in the Keihin Area (between Tokyo and Yokohama). Asahi Glass, Asano Shipbuilding, Asano Cement, Ajinomoto, Nippon Cable, Fuji Electric, Tokyo Electric Power, Nisshin Flour, Mitsubishi Oil and Meiji Confectionery gathered in this area by the Taisho period.

4 Nakamura Takafusa (1997) proposes the concept of new indigenous industry, which is an indigenous industry modified by Western technology. This corresponds to I→I* in Odaka's terminology.

5

DEVELOPMENT OF KEY INDUSTRIES

In this chapter, we will examine several important industries of the Meiji period. As noted earlier, silk reeling was the top export sector of Japan throughout the Meiji and up until the early Showa period, exporting silk yarns to the United States was the principal market. At the same time, the cotton textile industry was a dynamically emerging sector shifting from traditional, largely family-based technology to modern factory production, thereby achieving import substitution, overtaking the British industry and leading Japan's Industrial Revolution. Meanwhile, the machinery industry was gradually taking root but was still relatively weak. Late Meiji was a period of learning for the producers of railroad locomotives, modern ships, electrical equipment, steel and automobiles. In the early years of the twentieth century, most Japanese machinery was cheap but low in quality, and could hardly compete with American or European products.

Silk industry

Silk production had been a traditional industry in Japan dating back to ancient times, perhaps to the fourth or fifth century AD. During the Edo period, many hans promoted and produced cloth and kimono made of high quality silk. When Japan opened its ports and resumed foreign trade in the mid-nineteenth century, Japanese silk suddenly found a voracious overseas demand, especially in the United States, mainly as a material for ladies' stockings. The export-led silk boom had several important consequences.

First, silk production—mulberry cultivation, silkworm raising and silk spinning—was greatly stimulated and spread all over Japan, especially in eastern regions. Virtually all farmers and villages fit for silk production tried to produce silk. This raised rural income significantly, together with the production of dried tea leaves, another highly demanded export product. This greatly changed the rural landscape and livelihood of Japan in the Meiji and subsequent periods even though one can hardly find any mulberry tree plantation or silk production anywhere in Japan today.

In many developing countries in the past and present, rapid industrialization and global integration often impoverishes farmers and widens the income gap between urban rich and rural poor (UNCTAD, 2004). In late nineteenth-century Japan, however, economic integration with the mighty West did not generate such an income gap, thanks largely to the silk boom. The tea export boom and rice inflation also contributed to rural income enhancement. However, rural prosperity now critically depended on the market gyrations of these primary commodities. When the prices of silk and/or rice were high, enriched farmers and rural landowners enjoyed low tax rates (since the land tax was fixed nominally)

 DOI: 10.4324/9781315444048-6

and greater consumption, vigorously absorbed foreign ideas and technology, and staged a political movement demanding Japan's first constitution and criticizing the Meiji government for delaying it.[1] When commodity prices plummeted, their reform movement lost momentum and indebted farmers became landless. This was the risk of global integration for a developing country facing domestic and international market fluctuations, which is also present in today's integrated world economy.

Second, a new class of merchants emerged. Under the unequal commercial treaties, Japan had no tariff rights but, in turn, foreigners in Japan were without travel rights. Foreigners were confined to the designated foreign settlements and their surrounding areas,[2] with Yokohama as the largest foreign settlement, and could not build their own commercial network in Japan. Thus they were compelled to rely on Japanese merchants to procure silk and tea for export, and supply British clothes and other Western goods to local markets. Japanese merchants who played this role were new traders unrelated to rich merchant families of the Edo period. They communicated price information, provided short-term trade credit to rural producers, established new marketing channels, and even assisted in purchasing and installing new machines and acquiring foreign technology. The so-called Yokohama merchants, and other new merchants, mediated business between foreign traders and rural producers. Securing ties with honest and helpful merchants was a life-or-death matter for regions engaged in the production of export commodities. Renowned silk-producing localities emerged or expanded in Nagano, Yamanashi, Gunma and Tohoku Region (all Eastern Japan) where such merchants played critical roles in informing and restructuring producers. When successful, producers and merchants shared huge profits. Quick and spontaneous emergence of producer-supporting (rather than cheating) merchants at a time of great economic change was a unique Japanese feature not always visible in other countries.

To be objective and fair, however, it must be reminded that not all Meiji-period merchants were truthful. Foreign traders often bitterly complained about the dishonesty and corruption of some Japanese merchants. Water was sometimes added to silk yarn before weighing because silk was sold by weight. Foreign buyers had to check whether the merchandise was dry inside. At one time, the quality of Japanese silk became so low that its demand and price fell significantly in the global market. In response, the government was forced to impose quality standards and worried producer associations had to devise ways to ensure quality.

Third, the continuation of silk export was accompanied by the transformation of production method and organization. Manual labor was gradually replaced by mechanized spinning (I ➔ M*: see Chapter 4 for notation). At first, silk production was undertaken by farming families, which was later joined by mechanized factories (M* ➔ M). To be more precise, silkworm raising still remained family-based and spread across the country, but silk reeling became increasingly automated in modern factories. Silk yarn remained the top export item for nearly eight decades from the opening of the ports in 1859 up to the 1930s providing a stable source of foreign exchange for Japanese industrialization.

Traditional cotton industry

The production of cotton textile products undergoes the following steps: (i) cotton harvest; (ii) ginning and cleaning; (iii) spinning (producing yarn); (iv) weaving (producing fabric); and (v) sewing and cutting (producing garment). Other processes such as knitting, dyeing and printing may be added. As Odaka Konosuke emphasized (Chapter 4), indigenous and modern sectors often coexisted in Meiji industrialization, and the cotton industry was no exception. For this reason, let us examine the traditional and the modern cotton industries in turn. This section looks at the traditional production.

Like silk, the cotton industry has a long history in Japan. However, the indigenous method of using wooden looms and household labor was far less productive than Western technology. The traditional production was often organized as a putting-out system, where a merchant concluded contracts with individual farm households to produce specified goods. The merchant provided all materials and sometimes even tools, received finished products and paid commission per piece. Production took place in farmers' households using (usually female) family labor. The question is how this antiquated mode of production survived the onslaught of British imports and installation of modern factories. Why were they not wiped out?

There were several reasons. First, domestic demand for cotton products rose so fast that, while imports increased, domestic production also had room to expand. Domestic demand was rising because (i) farmers were enriched by the silk and tea booms noted earlier, and they switched from homemade or second-hand clothes to external purchase; (ii) new merchants, including Yokohama merchants mentioned above, succeeded in establishing a nationwide sales network and (iii) the price of clothes relative to the general price level declined, which further stimulated demand.

Another important reason was that Japanese and British cotton products were different in use and not easily substitutable (Kawakatsu, 1991). Japanese cotton products used low-count fibers and were thicker, which made them suitable for daily or workplace wearing, while British cotton products used high-count fibers which were thinner, and were more fashionable and formal.

While the traditional cotton industry thus survived and coexisted with the inflow of Western merchandise, the impact of global integration significantly altered its production organization. Vertically integrated producers that combined the production of raw cotton, yarn and fabric declined, while specialized weavers using imported yarn prospered. Among traditional cotton products, demand for plain white cloth fell while high-value, more differentiated products such as creased, patterned and colored fabrics found a larger customer demand. Some cotton-producing villages disappeared while new ones popped up. The survival and prosperity of traditional cotton regions under the integration shock depended very much on the existence of helpful merchants who introduced appropriate imported materials and developed new domestic markets for the producers (Saito and Tanimoto, 1989). Again, the merchant's productive role was essential in adjusting to a new environment.

Toward the end of the Meiji period, machines began to be introduced even in the traditional cotton sector. This was prompted by the need to improve efficiency in the face of rising wages, cyclical recessions, and the worsening of the terms-of-trade, which means the falling price of output (fabric) relative to input (yarn). Even though machines were introduced, they were not exactly the same as the Western original. Production scale was smaller and modifications were often made, including the use of as many wooden parts as possible in place of steel. These can be considered modifications of the indigenous method (I ➔ I*).

Modern cotton industry

We now turn to the modern cotton industry. This large factory-based production had to be introduced as an entirely new technology from the beginning (M ➔ M).

In early Meiji, Japan imported a large amount of cotton yarn as an input to domestic cotton fabric production. The government considered *yunyu boatsu* (import substitution) of cotton yarn to be an important national goal. Model factories in cotton spinning were established in the 1870s, but these state-owned enterprises did not succeed commercially. The reasons for this included the lack of capital, the production scale (2,000 spindles) which was too small for efficiency, the use of water power which was constrained by location and operation time, and the lack of technical expertise.

The turning point came when Osaka Spinning (Osaka Boseki Kaisha), a private company, was established in 1883 by the strong initiative of Shibusawa Eiichi, the super business promoter who assisted establishment of hundreds of business firms and economic organizations (Chapter 3). Worried about rising cotton yarn imports, Shibusawa decided to create a new company that could overcome the known defects of state-owned cotton spinning mills. In particular, Osaka Spinning introduced the following innovations (Abe, 1990):

- It was a joint stock company subscribed by big merchants and former daimyos who were personally persuaded by Shibusawa to invest. As for working capital, loans from the First "National" Bank,[3] of which Shibusawa was the president, were made available.
- It had a sufficiently large capacity of 10,500 spindles attaining economies of scale.
- It had the use of a steam engine that permitted 24-hour operation.
- It was located in an urban area which facilitated worker recruitment.
- Yamanobe Takeo, who studied theory and practice of the textile industry in the United Kingdom, was appointed as Chief Engineer (see Box 5.1).
- It used low-cost Chinese cotton instead of domestic cotton.
- It used advanced machinery, including the adoption of the latest Ring Spinning Machine instead of the Mule Spinning Machine.

Osaka Spinning was an instant success. Although 1883, the year of its establishment, was a year of business recession (Matsukata deflation, Chapter 4), the company was profitable from

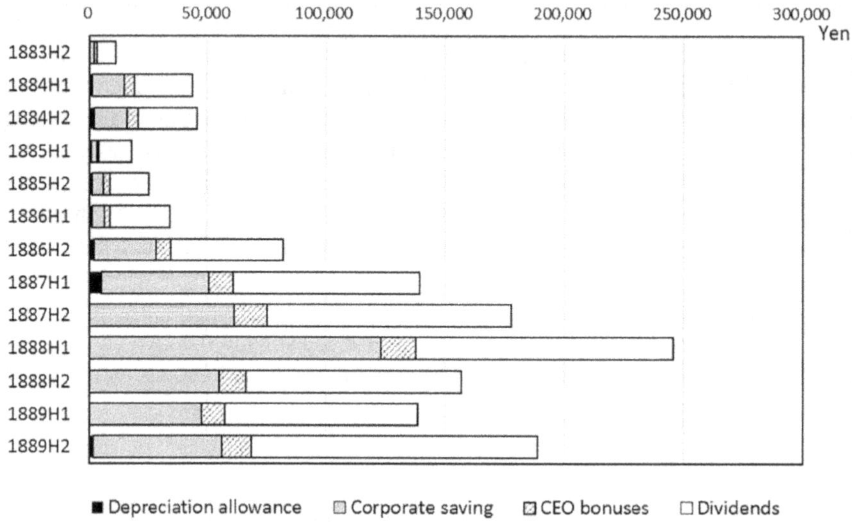

Figure 5.1 Profits of Osaka Spinning in the early years

Source: compiled from Hanai (2000), pp. 120–121.

the outset (Figure 5.1). The lesson we can draw from the experience of Osaka Spinning is that competitiveness depends critically on the choice of appropriate technology which includes the size, location and mode of operation. In addition, the combination of strong managerial leadership (Shibusawa) and deep practical knowledge (Yamanobe) was instrumental. Without these, purchasing expensive machines alone would not have achieved efficiency.

The success of Osaka Spinning had a powerful demonstration effect. Soon, several spinning factories modeled after Osaka Spinning were established. Largest among them were Hirano, Amagasaki, Settsu and Kanegafuchi (later renamed to Kanebo), which were concentrated in the Kansai area in Western Japan. Initially, their products were sold to domestic traditional weavers and contributed to import substitution of cotton yarn as Shibusawa intended. Later, their products were also exported as well as used internally to produce fabric within these factories. Young female workers were recruited to work in these factories often under hard and inferior working conditions. Factories competed fiercely to hire and retain such female workers. Recruiting missions were often dispatched to rural areas. Competent male textile engineers were in even greater shortage.

As the modern cotton industry emerged to become the mainstay of Japanese manufacturing, it faced two problems. The first was the recession that peaked around 1900, forcing even large factories to restructure, merge or even close. The number of modern spinning factories declined from 78 in 1899 to 49 in 1904. After the shakeout, the three largest spinners, Osaka, Toyobo and Dainihon, began to dominate the industry.

Another problem was the conflict of interest between company owners and management. The shareholders of spinning companies were rich merchants or former daimyos not interested in the textile business per se and wanting quick and high returns on their investment. By contrast, top managers and skilled engineers were well informed about technology and market trends. Their priority was to invest in technology and capacity to ensure long-term growth of the enterprise. The former pressed for large dividends while the latter preferred retention of profits for reinvestment. This tension sometimes escalated to the level where shareholders demanded the resignation of the management. In the early years of Osaka Spinning, the profit was divided roughly equally between dividend payments and retention for further investment (Figure 5.1).

The machinery industry

Meiji industrialization was light manufacturing industrialization led by textiles while the machinery industry was still feeble and internationally uncompetitive. Japanese machines were imitations of Western models. The machinery industry still heavily depended on foreign technology and imports. "Made in Japan" meant low price and low quality. During Meiji, machinery was only imported and not exported. Nevertheless, technology was being absorbed, and preparation for the giant leap in the Taisho and Showa periods (1910s–1930s) was being made (Sawai, 1990).

Initially, state-owned military mills dominated the machinery industry. Backed by the central government and its budget, they were large in size and equipped with the newest machines imported from Europe and America, and directed by hired foreign managers. By contrast, private companies were smaller and less modern, and used second-hand or Japanese machines.

But private-sector manufacturing was also growing, albeit gradually. Largest among private companies were shipyards and railroad carriage factories (Table 5.1). Medium-sized ones included electrical companies such as Shibaura (later Toshiba), NEC, Oki and Hitachi. Meanwhile, small companies produced miscellaneous components and devices. The input–output linkage between large and small firms was still weak. Large factories imported most machines and produced the remaining machines and inputs internally. Domestic procurement from Japanese subsidiaries and suppliers was insignificant at first. In other words, "supporting industries" (a term used for component suppliers and material processing firms serving large assembler firms) did not exist during Meiji.

In Tokyo and Osaka, manufacturing SMEs began to emerge in certain areas and spontaneously formed industrial districts. They tended to gather around large anchor factories. In Shiba area in Tokyo, near Tokyo Tower and Hamamatsu-cho Station today, large anchor

Table 5.1 Largest enterprises by employment size (1907)

No.	*Enterprise*	*Employees*	*Ownership*
1	Ministry of Communications	152,869	State-run
2	Railroad Agency	88,266	State-run
3	Furukawa Mining	30,125	Private
4	Mitsubishi Mining	24,245	Private
5	Kure Naval Factory	21,056	State-run
6	Monopoly Bureau, Ministry of Finance	20,563	State-run
7	Tokyo Army Weapons Factory	19,668	State-run
8	Mitsui Mining	17,472	Private
9	Mie Spinning	13,393	Private
10	Kanegafuchi Spinning	12,204	Private
11	Kaijima Tasuke (coal mining)	12,144	Private
12	Yokosuka Naval Factory	11,937	State-run
13	Osaka Army Weapons Factory	11,545	State-run
14	Mitsubishi Shipbuilding	10,921	Private
15	Hokkaido Coal Mine Steamers	10,201	Private
16	Kyoeki Trading	10,000	Private
17	Fuji Gas Spinning	9,573	Private
18	Osaka Spinning	9,474	Private
19	Fujita Gumi (zaibatsu)	8,837	Private
20	Yawata Steel Works	8,584	State-run
21	Kawasaki Shipbuilding	8,483	Private
22	Yasukawa Keiichiro (coal mining)	7,241	Private
23	Sesebo Naval Factory	6,858	State-run
24	Settsu Spinning	6,450	Private
25	Tokyo Railway	6,373	Private
26	Sumitomo Kichizaemon (mining)	6,114	Private
27	Osaka Shosen (shipping)	5,271	Private
28	Osaka Godo Spinning	4,615	Private
29	Kenshi Spinning	4,114	Private
30	Imperial Hemp Spinning	3,914	Private
. . .			
101	Shibaura Manufacturing (Toshiba)	989	Private
126	Seikosha	700	Private

Source: Ministry of Commerce and Industry, *Factory Database*, 1907.

Note: Numbers include workers and miners only. Office staff are not counted.

firms such as Shibaura Engineering Works (private), Naval Weapons Factory (state-owned) and Mita Manufacturing (state-owned) were located. Surrounding them, small private firms were established to produce mechanical devices and parts.[4] Another industrial district in Tokyo was Honjo-Fukagawa area on the left bank of the Sumida River. This district specialized in metal products such as nuts, bolts, springs and the like. In these industrial districts, SMEs not only competed for orders but also cooperated in production with each other. If one factory did not have the right equipment to do a certain work, it would ask a neighboring firm to do it, and vice versa. Some of the SMEs became subcontractors of larger firms. The accounting system of SMEs long remained informal and pre-modern.

Capable engineers liked to move from factory to factory for experience and skill building. Inter-firm migration such as this facilitated technology transfer and emergence of manufacturing SMEs. Graduates from the Institute of Technology and technical high schools (Chapter 4) first worked at state-owned factories or at relatively large private companies. After acquiring sufficient skills and knowledge, many of them moved to smaller private companies or established their own. In this way, Western technology was diffused widely and naturally within the machinery industry.

Japanese managers and engineers were generalists rather than specialists, and job hopping was very common. Japanese workers were also characterized by their lack of discipline and low savings. Japanese labor force in the late nineteenth and early twentieth century was more "neoclassical," quite different from the faithful labor force in the post-WW2 era. To further promote industrialization, Japan had to transform these light-footed engineers and workers to stay in one place in order to let them absorb and develop firm-specific skills and knowledge. Japan later succeeded in doing this partly during the 1910s and more during the war time (1937–45, see Chapter 9).

The following sections will look at some of the prominent subsectors within manufacturing.

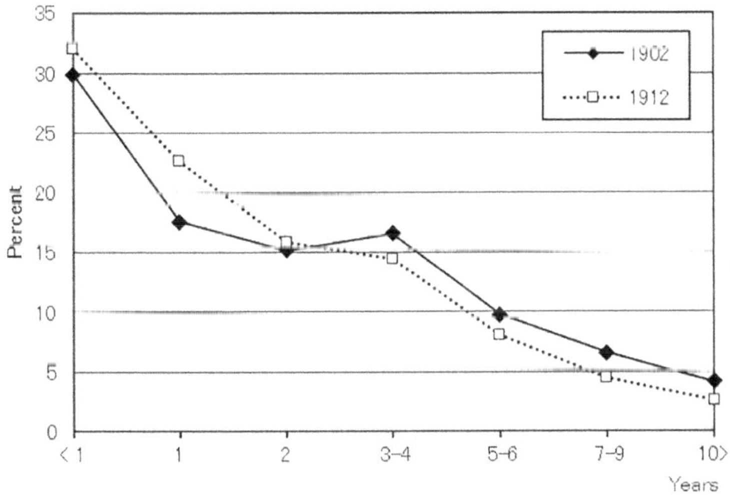

Figure 5.2 Average duration of male employment in manufacturing

Source: compiled from Sawai (1990), p. 218.

Steel

In mid to late Meiji, Japanese steel production was able to cover only about 20 percent of domestic demand, with the rest supplied by imports. This figure was much lower than those of other late industrializing countries in the nineteenth century such as France, Germany and the United States whose domestic supply ratios ranged from 70 to 90 percent (Suzuki, 2000). This partly reflected the backwardness of Japanese steel technology, but the lack of tariff protection, imposed by the unequal commercial treaties with the West, also contributed significantly to the penetration of imported steel. Japanese tariff rates were uniform 5 percent over all goods while the countries mentioned above carried steel tariffs between 20 and 100 percent. The higher transport cost to the Far East, which provided natural protection for Japanese producers, was not enough to offset the higher cost of domestically produced steel. It was estimated that Kamaishi, the first Japanese steel mill using blast furnace technology, established by the government in 1880 but soon privatized, needed at least 30 percent tariff protection to compete with imported steel.

In 1895, the government decided to build a state-of-the-art steel mill by using part of the reparation received from Qing Dynasty, China as a result of a victorious war in 1894–95.[5] After research, German technology of Gutehoffnungshütte (GHH) was selected and Yawata in Northern Kyushu was identified as the appropriate location. A large number of German managers and engineers were mobilized with high salaries for construction and operation.

The first blast furnace of Yawata Steel Works went into operation in 1901, but production was often interrupted, output was far below capacity and a loss was incurred. German technology, without local adjustments, did not ensure smooth operation. The causes were found to be the lack of coke oven and the unsuitable content of iron ore. The government additionally built a coke oven and began to select materials carefully. Japanese engineers from Kamaishi were called to actively adjust the blast furnace and modify the operation method. By 1905, steel production at Yawata became efficient and smooth. From then on, Yawata's capacity was expanded in many aggressive steps to serve as the largest steel mill in Japan for half a century up to the WW2 period. Yawata is often cited as the proof of Japanese capability to quickly learn, adjust and internalize imported technology so it works best in the local context.

As Japan gradually regained tariff rights, steel tariffs were raised to 5–10 percent in 1899 and 10–20 percent in 1911. This stimulated Mitsui and Mitsubishi Groups to invest in steel production, but Yawata's dominance and technological edge were not affected by additional entry.

Railroad carriages and locomotives

Railroad locomotives and carriages are quite different in technological requirement. The former are far more difficult to manufacture than the latter. Throughout Meiji, about 25 percent of railroad carriages were imported and the rest were domestically produced. Among domestic producers, Shimbashi Factory and Kobe Factory, both state-owned, were the largest, which together accounted for 64 percent of domestically produced railroad carriages.

As for locomotives, all had to be imported at first but the government wanted to promote domestic production. In 1900, the first railroad locomotive was test-produced through cooperation of the state and private sector. State-owned Shimbashi Factory provided the blueprint to Japan Railroad and Kansai Railroad, two targeted private companies, and engineers were exchanged between the state and the private sector. In 1912, the Railroad Agency nominated four private companies to copy-produce locomotives. But since these companies were still technically incompetent, the government offered handholding support, making available technology, materials, production management, training (which included opportunities to study abroad) and the guarantee of official procurement of finished products. In this way, the government pampered the burgeoning railroad industry which, thanks to such assistance, eventually came to possess world-class locomotive technology during the inter-war period.

During the Meiji period, railway construction was booming. There were both state-run and private railroad operators. However, in 1906, the government nationalized virtually all private railroad companies. This was carried out partly for military reasons and partly because many of the private railroad operators were unprofitable due to excessive construction relative to transport demand. Railroads tended to be overbuilt because politicians liked to promise more and more railroads in their constituencies in preparation for the next election. Vote-buying such as this is prevalent in any age and country.

Shipbuilding and ocean transport

Among domestic shipyards, two private firms, Mitsubishi Shipbuilding in Nagasaki and Kawasaki Shipbuilding in Kobe, dominated. Both were former state-owned factories sold to influential business groups. In the early days, ship repairing was more profitable than building new ships.

About half of the orders for new ships came from domestic private ship operators, and the rest were produced for the navy or exported to China, Thailand and other countries. Under the Shipbuilding Promotion Law of 1896, the government supported the shipbuilding industry by offering subsidies for companies that built large-sized ships above 700 tons (later, above 1,000 tons). The construction of naval ships was not very profitable but the government supplied all materials. Due to the lack of supporting industries, shipbuilders produced most parts internally.

Approved in the same year, the Navigation Promotion Law subsidized ocean transport operators if they operated international routes or possessed large ships over 1,000 tons or fast domestic ships. These thresholds were also raised in steps and the amount of subsidies was increased over time.

As a result of these conditional (performance-based) but generous subsidies, the shipbuilding industry expanded significantly. Japanese ship production, which hardly reached 10,000 tons per year before 1896, rose to 80,000 tons per year by the time of the outbreak of WW1 (1914). As noted above, Mitsubishi and Kawasaki were the two largest shipbuilders as well as the largest receivers of state subsidies related to tonnage, ship type, engine type and horsepower. Osaka Shipbuilding was the third largest but the amount of subsidies received was much less than the top two firms. Even smaller shipbuilders such as Ishikawajima, Ono and Uraga built fewer ships and received far less in subsidies. As for ocean transport, Nippon Yusen, established by the Mitsubishi Group and later merged with a rival firm, dominated. It also received ample subsidies from the state, with amounts in some years so large as to turn the operational loss into profitability (Ando, 1979).

Electrical machinery

Shibaura Engineering Works (later Toshiba) was founded by inventor Tanaka Hisashige. Initially, it was a relatively small operation with 502 workers producing military goods. When naval factories stopped procuring from Shibaura and started internal production of components, Tanaka shifted to the production of electrical machines for private use such as generators and transformers. When Shibaura faced a financial crisis, Mitsui Zaibatsu came to the rescue. Shibaura also established business cooperation with General Electric (United States). Similarly, Mitsubishi Electric Company cooperated with Westin House (United States) and Furukawa Electric Company worked with Siemens (Germany).

Even with hard efforts for domestic production, imports still dominated the Japanese market of generators and transformers in Meiji. Foreign products, mainly from the United States, accounted for about 75 percent of the total supply in 1911. Toshiba had a market share of 16 percent and produced low capacity generators compared with American products.

There was a debate within the Japanese government regarding whether the national telephone network should be laid privately or by the state. The government finally decided to build it by itself. The business of supplying telephone equipment to this national project was considered highly lucrative. To win this contract, Western Electric approached Oki Electric to produce telephone equipment but Oki refused. Western Electric then set up Nippon Electric Company (NEC), a joint venture with Japanese partners, in 1898 with the American capital share being 54 percent. Oki and NEC subsequently competed for the official procurement of telephone equipment.

NEC was initially only a sales agent for Western Electric products, but soon began to produce its own products and became more independent from Western Electric. NEC's success was due to the availability of foreign technology and capital, secured markets of telephone equipment through government procurement and the Japanese company's high technical absorptive capacity.

Box 5.1 Shibusawa, Yamanobe and others

In 1877, Yamanobe Takeo was a twenty-six-year-old student majoring in economics and insurance theory in London. One day he received a letter from an unknown gentleman in Japan. The sender's name was Shibusawa Eiichi. The letter said something like this: "Dear Yamanobe, your name was mentioned by a friend of mine. Japan imports too much cotton yarn today. We need to establish a domestic spinning industry. We need people who know both management and technology. Will you please study the cotton industry? I will create a company."

Perhaps Yamanobe was annoyed. Who is this man to tell me to change my subject? But after thinking a while, he decided to follow Shibusawa's advice. He went to King's College where he studied textile industry theory. But theory alone was not enough. He moved to Manchester, the then world capital of the textile industry. He posted ads in newspapers: HIRE ME AS COTTON INDUSTRY TRAINEE, WILL PAY, but no company responded. Finally, he met Mr. W. E. Braggs who allowed Yamanobe to work and absorb practical knowledge in his factory for eight months. Learning included technology, marketing and shipping. Yamanobe worked very hard. Shibusawa sent him 1,500 yen to support the study. Shibusawa later recollected that this was a huge sum even for him and sending it to Yanamobe was like jumping off the stage of Kiyomizu Temple (a phrase implying a bold and very risky decision).

When his study ended, Yamanobe placed orders to buy textile machines and steam engines from renowned manufacturers such as Platt and Hargreaves, and returned to Japan. In 1882, Shibusawa and Yamanobe selected an appropriate factory site in Osaka. To establish the company, 250,000 yen was collected from rich merchants and friends of Shibusawa. Shibusawa's bank, First National, would lend working capital. Osaka Spinning was successfully launched in 1883. Yamanobe became the Chief Engineer of the factory.

Around 1900, there was a severe textile recession. Shareholders demanded higher and quicker returns. But Yamanobe insisted on long-term development of the company. Even the General Director criticized him. Being desperate and wanting to quit, Yamanobe visited Shibusawa's residence. Shibusawa assured Yamanobe that he would support him 100 percent and requested him to continue to work for the company. Convinced, Yamanobe stayed. When the recession ended, Yamanobe was promoted to the President of Osaka Spinning Company.

Let us meet one more person in the textile industry, Fuji Masazumi, a super factory renovator of Kanegafuchi Spinning (Kanebo). He graduated from Keio University and worked in the sales department of Suminodo Factory of Kanebo. This factory suffered from obsolete machines, a lack of work discipline and low capacity utilization. He worked 18 hours a day to replace or repair old machines and recruited 500 new workers. He restored the factory to full operation in three months. He was then promoted to the Managing Director of Kanebo's Tokyo Factory. This factory was another disaster. He repaired, invested and improved. He reduced the workforce from 4,000 to 1,620. After three years, the factory became very profitable. If Mr. Fuji were still alive, he could be dispatched to any failing factory in any country.

What do we learn from these stories? Meiji industrialization was achieved by these powerful and risk-taking individuals brimming with energy, vision and leadership. Meiji Japan, whether urban or rural, was full of such people, not just Shibusawa, Yamanobe and Fuji, and Japan relied on them for realizing a latecomer industrial revolution. New laws, deregulation and level playing fields are perhaps not enough. If Shibusawa did not write the letter to Yamanobe in London, Japan's textile industry may not have taken off. If so, the real question is, how can we generate such wonderful people continuously in a society? Japan also has ups and downs and it currently seems unable to produce great business heroes or statesmen in sufficient abundance to overcome economic stagnation.

Notes

1 Under the Movement for Freedom and People's Rights, it was decided in 1880 that local chapters of the Movement should draft their own constitution proposals. At least 90 constitutional manuscripts were prepared by opposition politicians and intellectual groups all over Japan. Spontaneous study groups in rural areas also participated actively in this drafting, whose proposals were usually more advanced and democratic than the Meiji Constitution which was actually adopted by the government in 1889.

2 The commercial treaties permitted foreigners to travel freely within ten Japanese miles (about 40 kilometers) of foreign settlements. For foreign residents in Yokohama, this meant free access to a large part of today's Kanagawa Prefecture and a small western part of the Tokyo Metropolitan area.

However, Edo (Tokyo) and Hakone were excluded. To travel outside, an internal passport had to be obtained, with the purpose of academic research or medical treatment only (not for trading). The Western diplomatic corps demanded relaxation of this regulation, and a simplified procedure was later adopted for visiting hot springs in Hakone and Atami.

3 The Meiji government initially tried to create a banking system modeled after the American system which had no central bank. Private banks were nationally certified to operate as banks and issue money provided that they held specified amounts of reserves (Chapter 6). The First National Bank established by Shibusawa, who at that time was a Ministry of Finance official, was the first private bank to be certified by the government. Subsequent private banks were numbered sequentially up to the One Hundred and Fifty-third National Bank. Eventually the American model was abandoned and the Bank of Japan, a central bank, was established in 1882.

4 Later, in 1939, Toshiba was created by merging Shibaura Engineering Works and Tokyo Electric Company. Today, one can see Toshiba Head Office from *Yurikamome* train—that is where Shiba Industrial District was located. However, the area was twice destroyed, by the Great Kanto Earthquake in 1923 and US aerial bombing in 1945, so no sign of Meiji industrialization remains.

5 However, the closing balance of the Special Account for Japan–China War Reparation in 1902 reveals that only 580,000 yen (0.2 percent) of total reparation amounting to 365 million yen was allocated to the construction of Yawata Steel Works while 84 percent went to military buildup.

6

BUDGET, FINANCE AND THE MACROECONOMY OF MEIJI

The two wars

One of the key national goals of Meiji was external expansion. Japanese political leaders, spearheaded by Yamagata Aritomo who served as prime minister in 1889–91 and 1898–1900, felt that it was necessary to create a sphere of influence around the nation to protect its interests from interventions of the West or neighboring countries. In late Meiji, the greatest potential threat to Japan was the eastward expansion of Russia's Romanov Empire. To guard its national interests, Japan wanted to construct a "line of interest" beyond its national border. That specifically meant placing Korea under Japanese influence.

In his speech at the just-established Imperial Parliament in 1890, Prime Minister Yamagata argued as follows:

> There are two ways to secure national independence and integrity. The first is to protect the line of sovereignty. The second is to protect the line of interest. The former means the nation's border and the latter includes areas closely related to national security. Every country defends both. Under the present circumstance, to maintain our independence and stand against the Western powers, defending the line of sovereignty is not enough. We need to protect our line of interest as well.

But China's Qing Dynasty considered Korea as its protectorate. Japan's ambition over Korea naturally clashed with Chinese interests. In Korea, the political situation became unstable as the Japanese army staged military provocations and the assassination of a Korean queen. Finally, Japan and China opened fire over Korea in the Japan–China War (1894–95). Japanese battleships, strategy and discipline won over China's older method of fighting. Although Chinese equipment was also modern, its strategy was poorly designed and the morale of soldiers was low. After this victory, Japan obtained from China reparations amounting to 310 million yen in gold (paid in sterling-denominated checks which Japan held as gold reserves in London), the territory of Taiwan as Japan's first major colony and the Liaodong Peninsula facing the Yellow Sea. However, Japan was immediately forced to return the Liaodong Peninsula to China under joint pressure from Russia, Germany and France (led by Russia). Japan felt deeply humiliated at this incident which proved that it was still a much weaker power than the West.

Even after Japan's victory over the Qing Dynasty, Korea and the northeastern region of China, called Manchuria, remained under Russian influence. Russia gained territorial and

 DOI: 10.4324/9781315444048-7

economic concessions and kept large troops in Manchuria. This inevitably collided with Japan's expansionist policy. To deter Russia, Japan went into military alliance with the United Kingdom in 1902. Within ten years of the Japan–China War, another major war, the Japan–Russia War (1904–5), broke out over the sphere of influence. Most foreign observers predicted an easy Russian victory. But surprisingly, despite a heavy human toll, the Japanese army conquered Russia's mighty Lushun Fortress located on the Liaodong Peninsula and the Japanese navy decisively defeated Russia's Baltic Fleet in the Battle of the Japan Sea. Following this naval triumph, the Japanese government asked the United States to mediate a peace treaty between Japan and Russia because continuation of the war would surely lead to a serious fiscal crisis for Japan (the approach to the American government had been made in advance).

The victory over Russia was regarded as a proof that Japan, a non-Western latecomer, had finally become a first-class nation on a par with the West. National pride ballooned and the rest of the developing world took notice. At the same time, Japanese people and media were infuriated at Russia which paid no war reparation—even though Japan obtained from Russia the southern half of Sakhalin Island as well as the Liaodong Peninsula which included the military port of Lushun and the commercial city of Dalian. An angry mob gathered in Hibiya Park began to attack police stations, a newspaper firm and American facilities. Meanwhile, the Japanese government was happy just because the war ended before it went bankrupt.

Japan annexed (colonized) Korea in 1910. Meanwhile, in 1917, the Russian Revolution terminated the Romanov Empire as a communist regime took over.

Fiscal activism and postwar management

What impact did the two wars have on Japan's industrialization and macroeconomic policy stance? To consider this, we need to look back a little.

When the first session of the Imperial Parliament was convened in 1890, the hottest issue was whether Japan should adopt fiscal activism or fiscal austerity. The government wanted more spending for industrialization and military buildup while the opposition parties, which held the majority, demanded tax and spending cuts. The latter reflected the voice of voters, most of whom were rich farmers and landlords obliged to pay the land tax. The government responded with the principle of *chozenshugi*, or ignoring demands of political parties in policy formulation, a clearly untenable proposition if parliamentary politics was to be guarded. The first parliamentary session managed to avoid a complete showdown but the subsequent sessions were not so easy. Gradually, some opposition parties changed tactics and began to cooperate with the government. Instead of demanding a small government, they asked for active public spending in their constituencies. On the government side, Ito Hirobumi, the first Japanese prime minister who formed governments three more times, proposed that a pro-government party should be established rather than permanently insisting on *chozenshugi*. *Rikken Seiyukai*, headed by Ito, was established in 1900 as a conservative pro-spending party.

During the two wars, military spending sharply increased. Prior to the Japan–Russia War, even foreign bonds were floated in America and Europe to cover roughly half the war expense. This practically ended the debate over the fiscal policy stance as the national budget had to be increased to execute wars. Moreover, even after each war, public spending was expanded rather than contracted to a previous level. Because of this fiscal ratchet effect, the size of government continued to rise. The term Postwar Management referred to the aggressive public investment and spending programs of both central and local governments after the Japan–China War and the Japan–Russia War, which included:

- continued military buildup, with the largest bill for battleship construction;
- railroad construction;
- integrated steel works in Yawata (Chapter 5);
- laying of a national telephone network;
- management of Taiwan which included colonial administration and business investment;
- infrastructure such as roads, water supply, urban trams, etc. which was mainly built by municipal governments;
- education spending undertaken mainly by local governments.

As a result of continued fiscal expansion, balance-of-payments pressure mounted and the Bank of Japan was quickly losing gold reserves. Japan prior to WW1 was facing an increasingly serious macroeconomic crisis (Figure 6.1).

Exchange rate policy

Britain adopted the gold standard in 1821 and all other major Western countries, including the United States, also shifted to the gold standard by the end of the 1870s. While the West was thus on the international gold standard, Japan, at least externally, remained on the silver standard. Gold, silver and copper coins circulated internally but silver was the

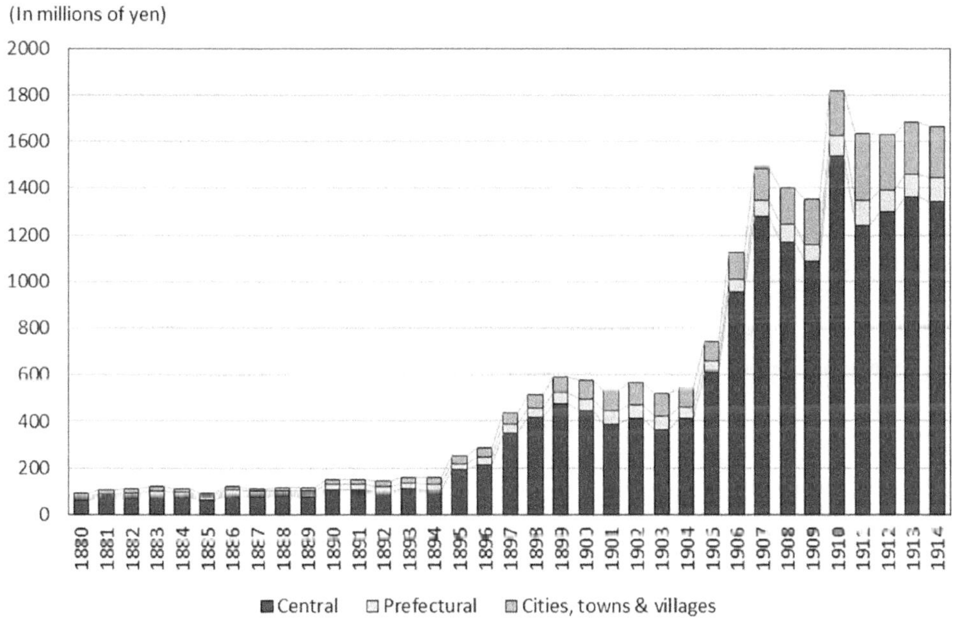

Figure 6.1 Central and local government expenditure

Source: Statistics Bureau of Management and Coordination Agency, *Historical Statistics of Japan Vol. 3*, pp. 240–241 and p. 289, 1988.

means of international settlement. This was mainly because the silver standard was dominant in East Asia where Shanghai was the center of foreign exchange markets.

The price of silver gradually declined against gold in the late nineteenth century. This meant that the Japanese yen, tied to silver, automatically depreciated against the world's major currencies, lowering Japanese costs and providing a favorable condition for export promotion (Figure 6.2). However, Finance Minister Matsukata Masayoshi, who earlier imposed what was called Matsukata Deflation to stop inflation and monetary confusion in the early 1880s, now insisted that Japan should adopt the gold standard as soon as possible to join the rank of first-class nations. Ignoring opposition, Matsukata introduced the gold standard in 1897. The initial gold reserves were secured by the reparation gold paid by China as mentioned above. From this time onward and up to WW1, the Japanese yen was fixed against major currencies at the parity of two yen to the US dollar.

As a result, automatic depreciation of the yen ended. Japanese inflation converged to world inflation, which was close to zero. Due to the disappearance of exchange risk and the confidence that came with the membership of the international gold standard, it became easier for the central and local governments of Japan to issue foreign currency-denominated bonds. They did frequently issue such bonds to cover war costs as well as the cost of building local infrastructure as explained above.

Banking and capital markets

In early Meiji, the Japanese banking system was chaotic, to say the least, and development of a modern and stable banking system took a long time. The initial policy in 1872 of creating "national" banks (actually, state certified private banks), copied from the United States, was not very successful. This decentralized system had no central bank, and each "national" bank could issue bank notes with the backing of gold reserves. But holding gold reserves was costly and initially only four banks were set up. Later, the gold reserve requirement was

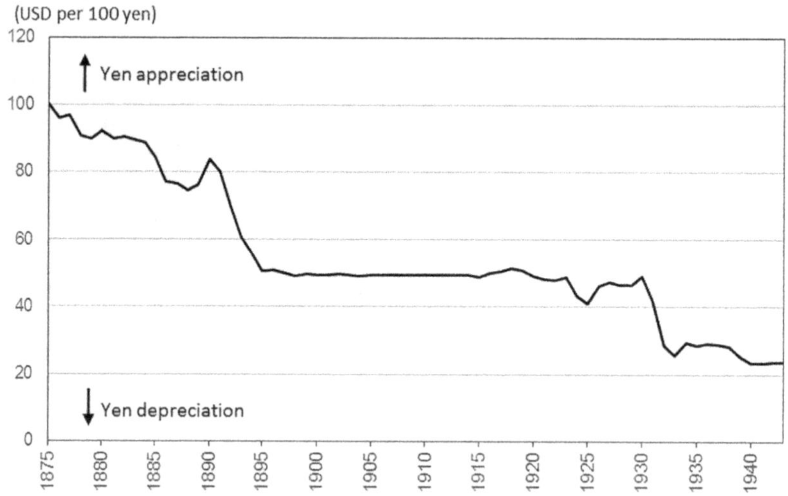

Figure 6.2 Yen–dollar exchange rate

Source: Management and Coordination Agency, *Historical Statistics of Japan*, vol. 3, pp. 104–107, 1988.

relaxed and a total of 153 banks were created. But eventually, this system was regarded as ineffective and abolished.

The modern banking system began to take root with the creation of a central bank (Bank of Japan) in 1882, which from then on was the only entity to issue the national currency. In addition to private commercial banks, the following specialized banks were created to fund national or important investment projects:

- Japan Kangyo Bank (later, through merger, Daiichi Kangyo Bank and now part of the Mizuho Financial Group created in 2000; Kangyo means industrial promotion);
- Hokkaid Takushoku Bank (bankrupted in 1997; takushoku means development by opening new land);
- Industrial Bank of Japan (now part of the Mizuho Financial Group);
- Bank of Agriculture and Industry (set up in each prefecture; merged into Japan Kangyo Bank by 1944).

In addition, postal savings, accepted at post offices, began to collect people's savings. Insurance companies, agricultural credit unions and urban credit unions also began to function as financial intermediaries.

Until late Meiji, despite such institutional developments, Japanese banks were not true financial intermediaries in the sense of taking deposits and making loans. At first, paid-in capital, reserves and government deposits—not people's small but numerous deposits—dominated the liabilities side of the banks' balance sheet. For early banks, designation as the government's fiscal depository was a very profitable business, because banks did not have to pay interest on official deposits between the time taxes were collected and the time they were withdrawn against government spending. Only towards the end of Meiji, banks began to rely more on private sector deposits as a funding source. But even then, many banks remained unsound on the assets side, with the general lack of information disclosure, risk management, portfolio diversification or project evaluation. Local banks were often lending to only one or a few business enterprises, with the bank and the enterprise usually both owned by the same owner. Such banks were called *kikan ginko*, which literally translates as "institution banks" but really means banks subordinated to and financing only a very small number of businesses. This situation subsequently exploded in an enormous bad debt problem in 1927 (Chapter 8).

The total number of banks, including all types, rose from the first establishment of two banks in 1872 to 320 in 1882, then stabilized around 350 for about a decade. But it began to shoot up in 1893 and reached the peak of 2,358 in 1901 and continued to stay above 2,000 until 1921 (Bank of Japan data). It is highly questionable whether a developing country with the economic size of Meiji and Taisho Japan needed more than 2,000 banks, most of which were very small and of dubious quality. The number began to fall thereafter and decline accelerated due to the banking crisis in 1927 and the wars in the 1930s and 1940s. From 1955 to 1985, during the post-WW2 high growth and subsequent slowdown, the number of Japanese banks was unchanged and much smaller at 86.

Limited data suggest that agricultural and industrial businesses relied heavily on informal finance throughout Meiji and even up to early Showa (Teranishi, 1990). In 1888, 92.8 percent of farmers borrowed from traditional sources that included money lenders, merchants, relatives, and mutual financing schemes. The percentage of informal finance gradually declined, but even as late as in 1932 it occupied 52.7 percent of farmers' borrowing. In the same year, manufacturers in Tokyo and Kobe sourced 39.2 percent of their external finance through informal channels. The prevalence of informal finance is a feature of virtually all developing countries, not just in pre-WW2 Japan.

All this points to the fact that creating a sound banking system in a developing country is a very difficult and long-term endeavor. The introduction of banking laws and financial deregulation will not be enough to achieve this. Transformation of commercial banks into genuine intermediaries between small savers and business investors requires proper institutions and ample experience in contract enforcement, project evaluation, risk management, prudential regulation, macroeconomic monitoring, financial innovation and much more.

As for the capital market, the first stock exchanges were created in Tokyo and Osaka in 1878. At first, few stocks were traded and these exchanges functioned mainly as a secondary market for government bonds. Former samurai who received government bonds in exchange for the previous rice salary often wished to sell them as they faced financial distress. In the 1880s, as many railroad companies were established, railroad bonds gradually became the most important instruments for stock trading. In the 1890s, the shares of maritime transport companies became popular. After 1906, when private railroads were nationalized, the shares of textile and food processing companies replaced railroad stocks.

Savings mobilization

If the banking system was still embryonic, where did the funds for Meiji industrialization come from? Data are incomplete, and economic historians are still debating. Here, let us look at the estimates provided by Teranishi Juro (1990).

Teranishi estimates the savings–investment balance of Japan from 1899 to 1937 (Table 6.1). He does not have data for early Meiji, before 1899, but his analysis covers up to early Showa.

Table 6.1 Estimated savings–investment balance by sector

(In millions of yen)

	1899–1902	*1903–1907*	*1908–1912*	*1913–1917*	*1918–1922*	*1923–1927*	*1928–1932*	*1933–1937*
Private farms	1	13	4	43	207	23	−12	222
Savings	121	159	175	240	657	523	402	580
Investment	120	146	171	197	450	500	414	358
Non-farm private sector	62	123	−87	175	81	−290	631	931
Savings	180	310	212	752	1724	858	1498	2637
Investment	118	187	299	577	1643	1148	867	1706
Government	−59	−233	15	120	−146	−112	−626	−1162
Savings	24	−142	205	317	441	801	251	−298
Investment	83	91	190	197	587	913	877	864
External sector (net)	5	−97	−68	338	143	−380	−6	−10
(Memorandum item)								
Land tax	104	115	154	166	290	291	188	145
(In percent of non-farm gross investment)	42.0%	38.4%	28.0%	24.2%	19.4%	13.8%	9.0%	11.3%

Source: Teranishi (1990), p. 68, p. 70.

Note: the S-I balance of private farms is transfer of surpluses to the non-farm sector through the financial system while land tax is transfer of surpluses through government budget.

He classifies the economy into four sectors: private farms, non-farm private enterprises, government and the external sector. He additionally estimates the size of the (agricultural) land tax. The following interpretation by Teranishi is consistent with his estimates though other interpretations may be possible.

First, in pre-WW2 Japan, the largest amount of funds for industrialization came from within the non-farm private sector itself. Retained profits, personal and family savings, and resources of rich merchants and businessmen seem to have been mobilized for private investments through self-finance, collected funds, the creation of joint stock companies and so on.

Second, fiscal transfer from agriculture to industry must also have played an important role to the extent that the land tax paid by rural communities was used to finance public investment and industrial subsidies. However, Teranishi somewhat downplays the role of landlords as a major contributor to saving mobilization since the ratio of agricultural tax to total investment declined over time. Nevertheless, such fiscal transfer may well have been substantial in early Meiji, a period that Teranishi's data does not cover.

Third, foreign savings played some role toward the end of Meiji as foreign-currency denominated bonds were issued by the central and local governments, as discussed above and explained in the next section.

The role of external funds

Quantitatively speaking, the contribution of foreign savings to industrialization was relatively small during the Meiji period. Almost all necessary funds were raised domestically. Meiji Japan did not welcome FDI or foreign loans for industrialization, except for the public-sector borrowing in late Meiji for the purpose of war execution and Postwar Management as mentioned above. Initially, as a matter of principle, the government rejected the incurring of external liabilities for fear of foreign control. This was in sharp contrast to other latecomers, such as Russia and Italy, during the same period. Russia borrowed heavily from financial markets in London to build railroads in the 1860s and 1870s. Italy also accepted large amounts of foreign investment in all sectors in the late nineteenth century.

In Japan, reliance on foreign saving did increase as Meiji progressed even though it did not become a major financial source for industrialization. Let us follow the events step by step.

In early Meiji, in 1870 and 1873, the government issued foreign bonds for railroad construction and the redemption of samurai salaries, respectively. After this, there was a debate within the government on the desirability of further borrowing for the purpose of creating a modern monetary system. But the idea was eventually turned down. Foreign borrowing was not resumed until the late 1890s.

After the victory of the Japan China War (1894–95) and the receipt of reparation gold from China, a fixed exchange rate and the gold standard were adopted. This made it easier for Japan to issue foreign bonds. On the other hand, a pursuit of fiscal activism, accelerated by the formation of Rikken Seiyukai in 1900 which strongly supported public spending, required additional financial resources. In order to ameliorate financial crises and credit shortage, the business community also began to call for external borrowing.

After the end of the Japan–China War, during 1897–1902, the Japanese government issued foreign bonds in three installments in London, totaling 190 million yen ($95 million) to fund war cost and public investment. During the Japan–Russia War (1904–5), the government again issued foreign bonds worth 800 million yen ($400 million) in four quick installments to execute the war. These bonds were denominated mainly in British pound or US dollar (the exchange rates were 2 yen per dollar and 4.87 dollars per pound). Between this war and the outbreak of WW1, the bond issue was repeated seven more times, mainly to redeem domestic government bonds and release more funds for domestic industries.

After the Japan–Russia War, Japanese municipalities (Kobe, Yokohama, Osaka, Tokyo, Nagoya and Kyoto) also began to actively borrow abroad. Municipal bonds and corporate bonds issued by local government-owned corporations were the two major forms of such borrowing. Funds raised through these instruments were used for building local infrastructure such as water works, port facilities, road, urban power and gas supply, and street trams.

Both Teranishi (1990) and Kamiyama (2000) interpret the increase of external public borrowing of this period by central government and municipalities as a way to finance balance-of-payments deficits while maintaining fiscal activism. Without external finance, fiscal and monetary policy stance had to be tightened to avoid macroeconomic calamity, as many developing countries are urged to do by the IMF today, but the Meiji government did not want to end vigorous spending for military buildup and infrastructure construction. At the end of Meiji, central government bonds outstanding, both domestic and foreign, were less than 40 percent of estimated gross domestic product (GDP), which implied that public borrowing was still within a manageable range.

As for FDI, inflow remained negligible in terms of both establishment of new enterprises as well as purchases of existing stocks by foreigners (Chapter 4). At first, FDI was prohibited except in the designated, tiny foreign settlements. As the unequal commercial treaties with the West were revised in 1899, restriction on FDI was lifted. But this did not prompt any sudden rush in foreign investment as policy makers and popular sentiment remained hostile to FDI. During Meiji, virtually all mobilization of foreign savings took the form of issuance of government, municipal and corporate bonds in the European and American capital markets as explained above, while FDI accounted for merely 0.7 percent of total inflow (Bytheway, 2005). It can safely be concluded that Japanese industrialization in Meiji as well as in the later, post-WW2 period was driven mainly by domestic investment and not FDI, although FDI provided limited but important functions in technology transfer in some industries.

Box 6.1 Japan becomes a new threat to East Asia and the world

By the 1910s, the three national goals set in early Meiji—industrialization, political reform and external expansion—were more or less achieved, and Japan began to consider itself to be part of the first-class world. Achievements of the Meiji period can be summarized as follows.

- An industrial revolution was attained in light manufacturing, especially the cotton textile industry, even though machinery and heavy industries were still weak.
- Japan now had a Western style legal system equipped with a constitution and accompanying laws, and a functioning parliament.
- As the unequal treaties were revised in steps, Japan regained tariff rights and the right to judge foreign criminals.
- Japan's sphere of influence was established as Taiwan and Korea had been colonized and interventions by China and Russia were repelled.

In the 1920s, as WW1 ended and the world entered the interwar period, Japan began to be invited to important international conferences as a member of the "Big Five," together with the United States, Britain, France and Italy. But Japan's accomplishments and emerging assertiveness raised new doubts among both the Western powers and its Asian neighbors. For the West, Japan was now a dangerous military competitor that might imperil their interests. For the rest of East Asia, Japan was acting as a new imperial invader threatening their independence. Suspicion and fear over Japan's intended action emerged after Japan's victory over Russia and intensified over time.

In 1915, while Europeans were busy fighting, the Japanese government delivered the "Twenty-One Demands" to China. These included demands for transferring German-occupied Chinese territory (Shandong Peninsula) to Japan, expansion of Japanese interests in Southern Manchuria and Eastern Inner Mongolia, a new industrial joint venture, prohibition of yielding Chinese territories to other countries, acceptance of Japanese advisors and others ("Manchuria" is a term then used to refer to the northeastern region of China). The Chinese government first resisted the Twenty-One Demands, but with an ultimatum from Japan, it finally yielded to the pressure. When China's protestation against the Japanese demands was ignored at the Paris Peace Conference in 1919, a large-scale anti-Japanese movement erupted in 1919, starting with student demonstrations, violence and a general strike in Beijing that spread all over China (May 4 Movement).

After the Russian Revolution in 1917, major powers sent troops to topple the new communist government, but the attempt was eventually unsuccessful. Japan sent the largest number of troops to Siberia and kept them there the longest after all other countries ended intervention.

These actions raised global suspicion against Japan. Even the United States, a traditional ally and the largest trading partner of Japan, began to express displeasure.

In fact, a thorny issue arose with the United States regarding the mistreatment of and discrimination against Japanese immigrants. Japanese migration to the West Coast of America began in the 1890s, which caused social and economic friction due to different work and life habits. The Japanese worked too hard, even on Sundays when most Americans were at church, which was blamed for stealing American jobs. Anti-Japanese movements intensified. The Japanese government was forced in 1907 to curb Japanese migrants in a Gentlemen's Agreement. Anti-Japanese legislation was passed in California in 1913 that restricted various civil rights of Japanese Americans. A ban on Japanese immigration was enacted in 1924. These events naturally hurt the feeling of Japanese people at home and in America, and worsened the bilateral relationship.

Thus, Japanese diplomacy in the 1910s and 1920s faced a grave choice. Japan had to choose between a path toward restoring friendship with the West and East Asia or continuing to assert its way against regional and global criticism.

7

WORLD WAR I AND THE 1920s

At the beginning of Meiji, the new government declared that, from then on, the Japanese calendar was to be renewed when and only when the ruling emperor departed. When Emperor Meiji passed away in 1912, his reign of 45 years, witnessing a great transformation of the nation from a samurai society to an industrialized and partly Westernized one, came to a close and a new era was ushered in. The Taisho period (1912–26), or the reign of Emperor Taisho, who suffered illness, was a relatively short one covering a large part of the 1910s and 1920s. It coincided with another transformation of Japan from a light manufacturing economy to one with emerging mechanical, chemical and heavy industries. A great export boom, followed by a prolonged period of lackluster growth, was the major economic landscape of the Taisho period.

Japanese life was also changing. Though most people continued to eat traditional food and wore traditional kimono, urban and Western cultures were becoming increasingly popular. A class of office workers, commuting daily from suburban home by rail and receiving a monthly salary, emerged. The female workforce found new job opportunities in department stores, cafés, the film industry and the transport sector, for example as bus conductors. In the political arena, Taisho Democracy movements demanded universal male suffrage, exits of unrepresentative cabinets and more rights for workers, women and the underprivileged.

Impact of World War I

When World War I erupted in July 1914, its consequences for the Japanese economy were at first uncertain. As the European powers began to engage in fighting, their international trade was suspended. Europe could no longer supply machinery, chemicals and other industrial goods to the rest of the world. It was feared that Japanese investment would be adversely affected. In reality, Japan did experience severe shortages of high-quality machines and industrial materials.

But it soon became evident that WW1 would bring a huge bonanza to the Japanese economy, at least for the moment, because of the sudden increase in global demand for Japanese products. An enormous export-led boom was generated as global demand shifted from European to Japanese goods, and also because the US economy was expanding strongly. Compared with manufactured products from Europe, Made-in-Japan goods were inferior but good enough as substitutes for now-unavailable European products.

The Japanese macroeconomy, which had faced mounting trade deficits and gold reserve losses prior to WW1, was greatly stimulated by a sudden and enormous rise in foreign demand. During WW1, the domestic price level more than doubled and real output surged, with an estimated annual real growth close to 10 percent. On the expenditure side,

DOI: 10.4324/9781315444048-8

export shot up, import declined slightly, investment increased, but only moderately, and with a lag (due to the shortage of machinery), and private consumption fell considerably (Figure 7.1). This situation can be explained as a sharp demand-driven output expansion without a corresponding capital stock increase. Existing machines were used fully which raised the "efficiency" of capital. People's consumption was compressed to make way for the rising foreign demand, and this was brought about mainly by forced saving under high inflation. Meanwhile, business profits surged and gold reserves accumulated. Japan was salvaged from the balance-of-payments crisis by the outbreak of a large foreign war, without having to resort to fiscal and monetary austerity.[1]

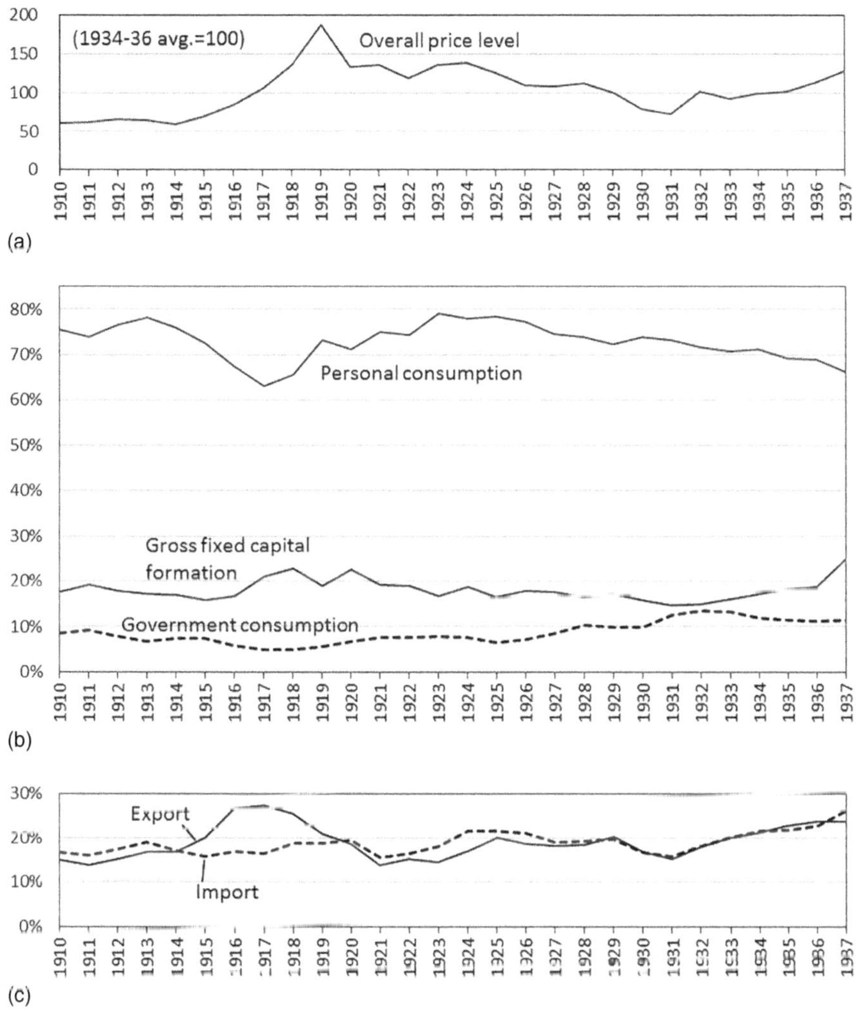

Figure 7.1 Price movement and the composition of gross national expenditure

Sources: Bank of Japan, *Price Indexes Annual*, 1985; GNP estimates by Ohkawa, Takmatsu and Yamamoto, in K. Ohkawa and M. Shinohara with L. Meissner, *Patterns of Japanese Economic Development: A Quantitative Appraisal*, New Haven, CT and London, Yale University Press, 1979.

The export-led boom was a broad-based one benefiting all industries. Among them, maritime shipping and shipbuilding sectors were extremely profitable and expanded most vigorously. Between 1913 and 1919, overall manufacturing output expanded 1.65 times, among which machinery industry jumped 3.1 times, steel 1.8 times and chemicals and textiles 1.6 times each.

Clearly, this export-led boom was artificial and temporary. It lasted only as long as WW1 continued, which meant about four years. Despite inferior quality, Japanese products captured overseas markets and import substitution accelerated domestically under this special condition. In retrospect, most of the business expansion was inefficient, excessive and unsustainable. Mediocre merchants and incompetent producers became suddenly rich and successful, and rapidly expanded their businesses. A class of nouveau riche called *narikin* emerged. In Japanese chess, *narikin* means a pawn turning into a gold general. They were often without culture or taste and fond of showing off their material wealth.

Japan participated in WW1 on the pretext of military alliance with Britain (1902–1923, with Russia as the potential enemy), but without engaging in any serious combat. It just captured German-occupied territories in Jiaozhou Wan (including Qingdao) in China and a number of islands in the Southern Pacific, and brought some German POWs to Japan. They were in general treated well and courteously.

Collapse of the bubble

When WW1 ended in 1918, a small business setback occurred. But the Japanese economy continued to do well in 1919. Then came the big crash of 1920. The war bubble finally ended and the postwar recession began. The prices of many commodities fell dramatically. In 1920 alone, the price of cotton yarn fell 60 percent, that of silk yarn 70 percent and the stock market index plunged 55 percent. Unlike the post-WW2 world where prices show downward rigidity, prices in those days were flexible in both directions. Macroeconomic adjustment was brought about mostly through large price changes rather than output fluctuation. One of the reasons for this was the behavior of most producers who tried to increase sales to offset falling prices, which collectively worsened the price decline. The lack of competitiveness and overcapacity of the Japanese economy, previously hidden under irrational exuberance, was exposed. Most narikin went bankrupt. Their happy days were short.

Throughout the 1920s, Japan experienced a series of recessions and banking crises. The most serious bank runs occurred in 1927 (Chapter 8). The economy slowed down significantly compared with the war boom period, but no severe contraction of output was recorded. Domestic demand was not buoyant but steady and sustaining. Recessions were frequent but short-lived. Prices remained flexible. Trade deficits returned and persisted, which was financed by the drawing down of the previously accumulated gold reserves. In the 1920s, the sky above the Japanese economy was neither sunny nor pouring. It was as if thick clouds gathered and stayed above the economy, depressing the economic mood of the country—somewhat like the recent period since the 1990s.

Faced with the onset of a recessionary period, it is worth noting how the Japanese government reacted. It had two policy options: generously rescue weakened industries and financial institutions saddled with bad debt, or have the courage to get rid of inefficient businesses and banks to restore industrial strength despite transitional pain. The Japanese government opted for the first. The Bank of Japan provided emergency loans to ailing banks and firms to avoid bankruptcies and unemployment. This policy eased the short-term pain but implanted a time bomb in the Japanese economy that was to explode several years later, as we will see in Chapter 8.

Development of heavy and chemical industries

Even under the cloudy sky of the 1920s, new sectors were growing. Heavy and chemical industries (HCIs) expanded strongly despite relatively weak aggregate demand. HCI growth was broad-based and included steel, chemicals, electrical machinery, general machinery and manmade fiber (rayon). Import substitution proceeded rapidly in these areas until, by the 1930s, Japan could produce most of these products domestically with sensible quality. Some engineered products, such as locomotives and ships, came to match global front-line technology. This was a big achievement in comparison with Meiji industrialization in which light manufacturing was the main pillar.

There were several reasons for strong HCI growth.

First, the WW1 boom ignited these industries under artificial protection from European products, as explained above.

Second, policy support was available. Fiscal activism, including military buildup, continued especially under Seiyukai Party governments (Chapter 9). Furthermore, high tariff policy for emerging HCIs was adopted. In 1899, freed from uniform 5 percent tariffs imposed by the unequal treaties, Japan began to raise tariffs on manufactured products. The government also promoted the formation of industrial cartels to avoid excess competition and overcapacity.

Third, electrification spread with the development of hydraulic power generation. Construction of hydraulic power plants occupied the largest share of private investment followed by railroad construction. As a result, electricity surplus was created in Kansai area in Western Japan. Power companies introduced discriminatory pricing by charging very low tariffs to large corporate customers. Once a dam, a power plant and transmission lines were completed, the marginal cost of producing electricity was almost nil. Discriminatory pricing helped to raise the operation ratio and the revenue of power companies. This in turn stimulated the growth of power-intensive industries such as chemicals, fertilizer, rayon and aluminum refinery.

Fourth, foreign technology was absorbed via FDI. Japanese companies including NEC, Shibaura, Mitsubishi Electric, Furukawa and Nissan tied up variously with American and European giants such as General Electric, Westinghouse, Siemens, Ford, GM, Dunlop and Goodrich in the fields of electrical machinery, automobiles, rubber tires and so on. Business cooperation took many forms including the creation of a Japanese subsidiary, joint venture, equity participation, technology licensing and other technical cooperation.

Fifth, vertical linkages were created between material producing and using sectors. Growth of the steel industry supported steel-using industries such as shipbuilding and mechanical engineering, and vice versa. Similar vertical interdependence emerged with chemicals, fertilizer, rayon and aluminum which stimulated both producers and users.

The use of tariff protection for heavy industrialization, mentioned above, deserves additional remarks. After examining a large number of historical cases, Chang (2002) finds that all industrializing nations in Europe, America and Asia in the past had adopted "infant industry promotion" by keeping high tariffs until domestic firms grew and became competitive. Japan was no exception. After the 5 percent uniform tariffs were repealed in 1899, the average tariff rate on non-zero tariff goods, calculated roughly as tariff revenue over total such imports, rose sharply (Figure 7.2). If we ignore the periods of WW1 and WW2, when trade in general and trade in manufactured goods in particular were severely limited, we can conclude that Japan maintained relatively high tariffs from the beginning of the twentieth century to the 1970s during which Japanese HCIs were catching up with the West. The fact that Japanese industries were protected for so long is not surprising, given similar practices in other latecomer economies of the nineteenth and twentieth century.

There is another important point here, namely: tariff protection becomes critical when and only when an economy progresses from the light manufacturing phase to heavy industrialization. When a country is mainly engaged in labor-intensive, low-skill production such as garments, footwear, food processing and electronics assembly, output and export can grow even without protection. But when it embarks on mechanical engineering and capital-intensive material production that require skills and experience, large upfront investment, long-term commitment and R&D, newcomers are usually unable to compete with global giants unless temporary support is provided. The lack of such support, or improper application of it, may lead to a middle income trap, among its many other causes. True, protection is a risky measure and many governments simply abuse it without producing any results. But historical experiences show that only those countries that master its proper use are likely to succeed in heavy industrialization and proceed to high income, not the ones that refuse to learn it (Ohno, 2013).

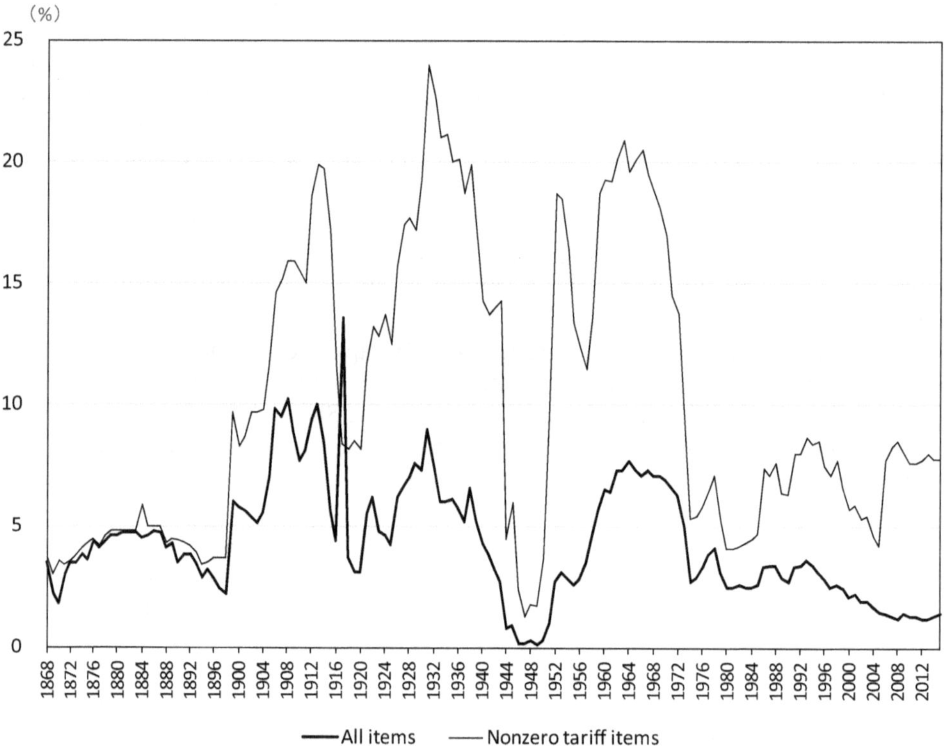

Figure 7.2 Estimated tariff protection

Source: Ministry of Economy, Trade and Industry. Tariff revenue is divided by import volume of respective goods.

From this perspective, Japan regained the tariff right from the West just when it was needed, that is, when Japan was ready to move from cotton textile industry to HCIs. It should also be added that, given the subsequent development of HCIs, Japan used this regained tool quite effectively.

Emerging new zaibatsu

With the development of HCIs, a new type of zaibatsu emerged in the 1920s and 1930s. Compared with old zaibatsu such as Mitsui, Sumitomo, Mitsubishi and Yasuda, new zaibatsu were HCI-based without much involvement in banking, commerce or light manufacturing such as cotton spinning. They invested aggressively in the Japanese colonies of Korea and Manchuria. New zaibatsu did not have a bank as core business, and instead raised funds by issuing stocks. Their business empire depended heavily on official support and political connection. The largest among them were Nissan, Nicchitsu and Mori.

Nissan was established in 1928 by Ayukawa Yoshisuke who specialized in management and company acquisition rather than engineering. Nissan was a short form of *Nihon Sangyo*, the company's full name which means Japan Industry. Raising capital from the stock market, business was diversified into mining, machinery, automobile, chemicals and fishery. Nissan invested heavily in Manchuria. Hitachi and Nissan Motors belong to this group.

Nicchitsu was established in 1908 by Noguchi Shitagau. The full name was *Nihon Chisso Hiryo* or Japan Nitrogen Fertilizer. The group's main business was electricity-intensive chemical

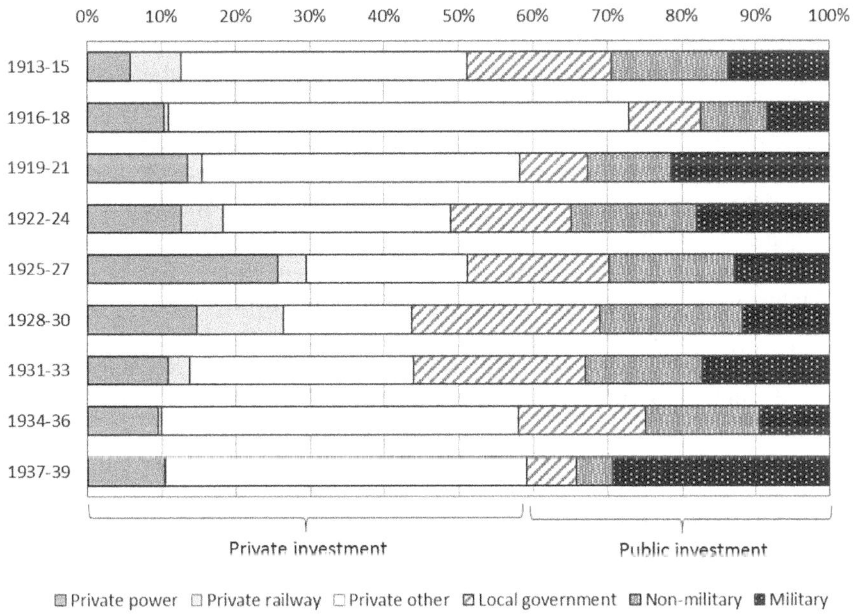

Figure 7.3 Gross capital formation

Source: Koichi Emi and Yuichi Shionoya, *Capital Formation*, Long-term Economic Statistics vol. 4, Toyokeizai Shimposha, 1971 (Part III, Tables 1 and 9).

Note: Percentage of total real investment in 1934–36 price.

industries such as fertilizer, rayon, medicine, explosives and metal refining. Micchitsu invested heavily in Korea.

Mori was established during the 1920s by Mori Nobuteru, who cooperated with Suzuki Saburosuke, the founder of Ajinomoto. Its main businesses included iodine, fertilizer, aluminum refining, electrical machinery and explosives.

Other new zaibatsu included Riken, which focused on chemical and medical research, and Nisso, which produced sodium hydroxide.

Because new zaibatsu did not have their own bank or trading house, financing and international trade functions were often provided by the subsidiaries of traditional zaibatsu such as Mitsui, Mitsubishi, Sumitomo and Yasuda. When Nissan purchased whole automobile plants from the United States, it asked Mitsubishi Trading Company to bring them to Japan (see below). The four zaibatsu banks—together with the Industrial Bank of Japan—were also active as underwriters or collateral trustees of corporate bonds issued by not only group companies but also companies belonging to other groups or independent companies. Corporate bond issue was a particularly important way of raising funds for power generation, railroad and paper where its share occupied 50–60 percent of total financial needs of each sector (Kikkawa, 2002, pp.173–176) (Figure 7.3).

Automobile production

The development pattern of the Japanese automobile industry was unique among latecomer countries. Instead of inviting foreign automotive giants to form an initial industrial cluster, the Japanese private sectors, from the outset, produced vehicles through copy production, trial-and-error, or technical cooperation with foreign partners. US car makers did invest in late Taisho Japan but they were in time forced to retreat due to the emergence of Japanese competitors and introduction of unfavorable policy. Moreover, instead of allowing only one or a few car makers to dominate in a relatively small domestic market and attain scale economy, as in the case of most other latecomer countries, Japan has had about ten domestic private producers since the pre WW2 period variously competing and aligning with each other. Even today, most of the original brands are present and globally competitive (Figure 7.4).

Cars began to be imported to Japan in 1899. There were initial attempts to build vehicles, but production was experimental and very small in scale. Imported models of Ford and General Motors were dominant in the nascent Japanese market. However, the Great Kanto Earthquake of 1923 suddenly increased the popularity of motorized cars in Japan as several thousand Model T Ford trucks were imported to augment transport capacity. Seeing this trend, Ford established a knock-down assembly plant in Yokohama in 1925 and General Motors followed two years later by building a similar plant in Osaka.

Nissan and Toyota were not the first companies to produce cars in Japan, but they emerged as the most serious car makers in the 1930s. They adopted very different approaches to acquire technology and boost production. Nissan opted for the fast way of purchasing existing plants and learning directly from foreign partners while Toyota chose the hard way of going it alone from scratch (Francks, 2015, pp. 97–102, pp. 220–223).

Ayukawa, the founder of new zaibatsu Nissan, was an aggressive business manager interested in expanding his empire through purchases, mergers and acquisitions (M&A), direct transfer of foreign technology, and extensive business and official connections. His initial casting firm manufactured motors for boats and agricultural machines as well as components for Ford and General Motor cars. In 1933, Ayukawa acquired the Datsun factory of

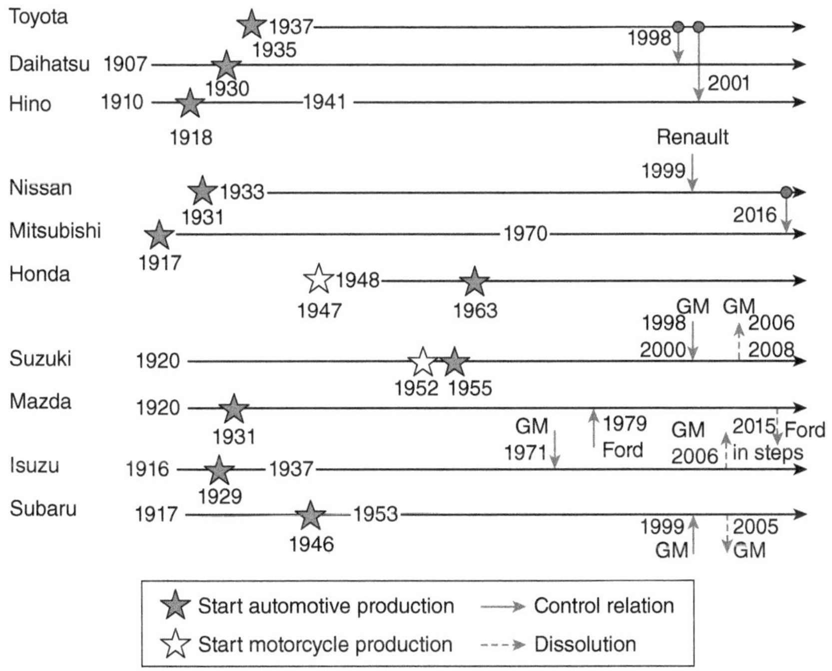

Figure 7.4 Timelines of Japanese automobile producers

Sources: websites of automobile companies. Years of automotive and motorcycle production are indicated. Unmarked years show other landmark events.

DAT Motors and combined it with his casting firm to create the Nissan Motor Company. Mitsubishi Trading supported Nissan to import a whole set of the latest machinery and equipment from the United States to replicate mass-production assembly lines. American engineers were hired to teach the most advanced design, construction and operation methods for the plant. In 1935, Ayukawa decided to move into the production of military trucks. Through its connection with General Motors, Nissan found an American company willing to sell a complete truck plant together with blueprints. Mitsubishi Trading again helped Nissan to bring the entire equipment to Japan and also to purchase additional equipment. It should be noted that automobile production was not the exclusive business area of Nissan as it also covered mining, metallurgy and mechanical engineering, with Hitachi as its core company.

Toyoda Kiichiro was the eldest son of Toyoda Sakichi, the founder of Toyoda Loom. He visited the massive production lines of Ford Motors in Detroit and was greatly impressed. He wanted to create a Japanese car maker independent of foreign giants. Though the weaving machine company was against this crazy idea, he began visiting Japanese factories, universities and government offices, purchased German and American equipment, and reverse engineered the latest GM Chevrolet. Recognizing Kiichiro's early results, the Toyoda Board finally approved establishment of the Automotive Department in 1933. Kiichiro declared that the first Toyota car would roll out within one year. His engineer friends helped, American models were further analyzed, a large factory was built in what was to become Toyota City, and additional equipment was imported. The engine was modeled after General Motors, the chassis was Ford-based, and the design was copied from Chrysler. After many failures, the team succeeded in casting the cylinder block and cylinder head of the engine. The first Toyota car was ready in May 1935—five months behind schedule. After WW2, automobile production was firmly established as the firm's core competency.[2]

In the 1930s the military and the Ministry of Commerce and Industry became increasingly eager to promote home production of military trucks. The Automobile Manufacturing Industry Law of 1936 offered generous incentives such as tax holidays, import duty exemption and financial access to license holders. A license was required to produce more than 3,000 vehicles and applicants must have majority Japanese ownership. Toyota and Nissan were the only companies that were granted licenses, and they switched to production of military trucks following the official instruction and demand. Meanwhile, increased tariffs on completely built units and knockdown components, as well as restricted access of foreign subsidiaries to foreign exchange, made it difficult for Ford and General Motors to stay in the Japanese market. They stopped operation in 1940 and 1941 respectively.

Among other Japanese automobile manufacturers, Daihatsu, founded by university researchers and producing tricycles, was the oldest. Hino and Isuzu were created by government-instructed mergers and specialized in commercial vehicles. Mitsubishi, as part of a large zaibatsu, had interaction with the group's shipbuilding and aircraft production. Meanwhile, Subaru, Suzuki, Mazda and Honda had engineer-type founders and moved into automobile production by expanding the original lines of business which were the production of aircraft, weaving machines, pumps and motorcycles, respectively. Among these, Honda starting automobile production in 1963, was the latest comer.

Exchange rate volatility

In the pre-WW1 period, from the 1880s through 1914, the world economy enjoyed price stability and free trade under the international gold standard. Japan joined the gold standard and fixed its exchange rate to the major currencies in 1897. Soon, Japanese prices converged to the world level. But this global fixed exchange rate regime was smashed by the outbreak of WW1, and the Japanese yen started to float in 1917.

After WW1, major powers made a number of attempts to restore the prewar gold standard system without much success. Britain returned to gold in 1925 but abandoned it in 1931. The gold standard of the late nineteenth century could not be re-established partly because there was less free trade and more protectionism than before, rendering the global economy less integrated, and partly because governments now cared more about domestic macroeconomy, especially unemployment issues, than the external commitment of gold convertibility. As a result, global monetary cooperation needed for restoring the international gold standard was hardly possible.

Japan also tried to return to the gold standard at the prewar parity of two yen to the dollar. Throughout this period, "Return to Gold" (*kinkaikin* or, literally, lifting the restriction on gold export) became a national economic goal. The government seriously considered restoring a fixed exchange rate a number of times, in 1919, 1923 and 1927, but failed to do so for various reasons such as an earthquake and bank runs. Each time the government announced such policy intention, expectations drove up the yen because the actual yen was more depreciated than the prewar parity. But the yen fell back when the policy was not realized. The business community blamed domestic banks and foreign exchange traders, especially those in Shanghai, for disruptive speculation. Exchange rate instability may have further damaged the Japanese economy faced with slow growth, but it cannot be cited as the main cause of prolonged recession.

Japan finally returned to gold in January 1930 under the Minsei Party government of Prime Minister Hamaguchi and Finance Minister Inoue, for whom Return to Gold was the highest priority. But the timing coincided with the US stock market crash and the beginning of the Great Depression. Japan was forced to abandon gold after two years. The international gold standard has never been resurrected since.

Shidehara Diplomacy

As noted in Box 6.1, Japan began to emerge as a serious threat to both the West and East Asia by the end of the Meiji period. After WW1, Japan tried to allay these fears and rebuild good relationship with the West, especially the United States, and East Asia. Shidehara Kijuro (1872–1951), twice served as Foreign Minister under Minsei Party governments in 1924–1927 and 1929–1931, initiated so-called Shidehara Diplomacy pursuing friendship, reconciliation and non-military means to solve bilateral problems. Thanks to him, Japan's foreign policy in the 1920s was less belligerent compared with before or after.

In 1921, the Washington Conference for Naval Disarmament was convened in the United States, and Japan was invited to attend. The Japanese delegation went to Washington with both hope and concern. The global reduction of naval capacity was highly welcome for Japan which was facing a serious budget crisis. But Japan also feared that other powers might use the Conference to harm Japan's interests. The Conference put upper limits on principal battleships of the major naval powers. In terms of tonnage, possession of principal battleships among the United States, the United Kingdom, Japan, France and Italy was restricted proportionally to 5, 5, 3, 1.67 and 1.67 respectively. The Japanese delegation was happy to sign this agreement even though the navy wanted more battleships. In addition, through this agreement, Japan wanted to show good faith to the Western powers as a peaceful and dependable nation.

The signing of the Nine Powers Treaty had another important impact on Japan coming out of this Conference. This treaty recognized the sovereignty of China, prohibited territorial invasion of China through military means by any country and agreed to share economic interests of major powers in China under the policy of "open door and equal opportunity." Japan welcomed this treaty as it was interpreted to implicitly recognize Japan's special interests in Manchuria and Mongolia (eastern part of Inner Mongolia). The infamous Twenty-One Demands to China (Box 6.1) were also accepted, albeit with some modifications, by the international community. However, these "acceptances" were valid only so long as Japan refrained from using military force to invade China or rob interests of other powers in China.

Shidehara believed that a good relationship with the United States, Japan's most important trade partner, was critical. He also felt that Japan, as a new first-class country and a member of the Big Five, had the moral obligation to strive for global peace and prosperity. As for China, he wanted to protect Japanese economic interests by diplomatic negotiation rather than military invasion. Shidehara's idealism was evident in his parliamentary speech delivered in January 1925.

> At present, there is clearly a global movement toward solving all international issues through understanding and cooperation among concerned powers, and not by narrowly self-serving policies, excessive use of militarism or interventionism. … Japan is no longer permitted an isolated and independent existence in the Far East, interested only in its own affairs. As a major member of the League of Nations,

> Japan now bears a heavy responsibility for promoting world peace and happiness of the human race. Japan must participate in the discussions of all these important issues, even if they have only indirect influence on Japan's own interest. The fact that Japan must bear such responsibilities is beyond question. It is necessitated by the force of history. The great progress of history is making us take up these responsibilities.

However, the Japan–US relationship gradually deteriorated due to the problem of Japanese immigrants on the US Pacific Coast, especially in the States of California, Oregon and Washington (Box 6.1). Because Japanese (and to some extent also Chinese) immigrants worked very hard and had different cultures, they were discriminated against by white Americans. The rights of American citizens of Japanese origin were gradually deprived. Their schools were segregated, their freedom was restricted and their property was confiscated. In response, the Japanese government agreed to stop sending immigrants to the United States but demanded fair treatment of Japanese Americans already there. This issue soured the bilateral relationship.

Shidehara's policy of no military intervention in China was severely criticized by the military and the hardliners as "coward's diplomacy." Even the mass media echoed this sentiment and blamed Shidehara for being too soft on China. From 1927 to 1929, when Tanaka Giichi of Seiyukai Party was in power and Shidehara was out of government, Japan sent troops three times to China in an effort to prevent the Northern Campaign of Chiang Kaishek's army from unifying China. Prime Minister Tanaka also organized the Eastern Conference, a meeting among Japanese officials rejecting Shidehara Diplomacy and reaffirming aggressive policy stance toward China.

Finally, in 1931 when Shidehara was Foreign Minister for the second time, the Manchurian Incident broke out. *Kantogun*, the Japanese army stationed in China, began to invade Northeastern China in clear violation of the "open door, equal opportunity" policy of the Nine Powers Treaty. This military operation was carefully planned and executed independently from Tokyo, which made it evident that the Japanese government could no longer restrain the army. Shidehara's immediate call for peace was ignored, and the US government condemned Japanese action. Shidehara Diplomacy ended this way.

Box 7.1 Taisho Democracy

Roughly coinciding with the Taisho period of 1912–26, various social movements demanding more representation and human rights became active. This included protests against unelected or corrupt governments, women's liberation, equal rights for the discriminated underclass who were the progeny of the *eta* and *hinin* people (see Chapter 2 and Q & A section in the appendix), universal male suffrage and cultural freedom. These movements were collectively called *Taisho Democracy*.

One of the most eminent intellectual leaders of Taisho Democracy was Yoshino Sakuzo, Professor of Political Science at Tokyo Imperial University. He published many articles in popular magazines to promote his version of democracy called *minpon shugi*. It asserted that democracy could be installed and fostered even under the Meiji Constitution that bestowed sovereignty only to the emperor. Yoshino argued that establishing democratic institutions was not enough and that it was essential to constantly improve the actual implementation of constitutional government. For this purpose, he stressed the role of the elite class in guiding the mass. Yoshino also supported universal (male) suffrage. By expanding the voter base from a few rich people to the general public, he hoped that corruption and money politics would cease and politics based on broader national vision would begin. In retrospect, it must be admitted that Professor Yoshino was a little too optimistic in this expectation given the subsequent development of Japanese politics even after all adult men were allowed to vote (Chapter 9).

On the political role of the elite, Yoshino wrote:

> Some may argue wrongly that the elite class has no place in democracy. But this is not so. Evidently, if a small number of people form an exclusive class and monopolize politics independently from the people, this will produce many bad results. But if the elite humbly mingle with the general public, accept the nominal status of serving and following them but in substance guide them spiritually and for public good, they will play the role of the truly wise. … Democracy will not develop in a sound way if uninformed people literally rule. Formally, the majority must always be the basis of political activities. Yet they need intellectual leaders in their minds. They must rely on a small number of wise and capable people. A great nation will emerge when the majority is guided intellectually by the few who are wise. The elite have this responsibility in a modern state.
>
> ("Discourse on the Principle of Constitutional Government and the Way to Fully Develop its Potentiality," 1975[1916])

In 1925, the Universal Suffrage Law was enacted, extending voting rights to all males at and above 25 years of age regardless of income. But in the same year, the Peace Preservation Law was also passed to crack down on communists and anarchists. This was regarded as one step forward and a giant leap backward on a road to democracy. It should however be recalled that other major powers had similar internal security laws at that time: it was not uniquely Japanese. The extension of suffrage to women had to wait until 1945.

In 1913 and 1914, people protested against corrupt and unrepresentative governments. In 1924, three political parties joined force against the ruling government to promote universal male suffrage, military budget cuts and Shidehara Diplomacy, and they won the election. From then on, the leader of the political party having the largest number of parliamentary seats formed the government (instead of appointing an old politician or military general). When the policies of the incumbent government failed, the leader of another party replaced him. Seiyukai and Minsei Party were the two contesting parties in the late 1920s and 1930s. At election, voters often chose the party professing an economic, social or foreign policy that seemed most appropriate for the time instead of consistently supporting any one party. This two-party mechanism was not formally institutionalized in constitution or law but actually practiced, and was called *kensei no jodo* (the normal way of constitutional government).

Thus, regarding the actual evolution of politics, the great achievement of Taisho Democracy was alternate succession of party cabinets from 1924 to 1932. This practice was terminated by pressure from the military and a series of political assassinations, after which old politicians and military men were again appointed as prime ministers.

Notes

1 Later, the Japanese economy was similarly rescued out of an imminent recession following the Dodge Line stabilization measures of 1949 when the Korean War broke out in 1950. As procurement of both military and non-military goods by the US military, in combat on the Korean Peninsula, suddenly arose, Japanese industries enjoyed great business expansion and high profits (Chapter 10).

2 The name of the firm and products was changed from Toyoda, the founder's family name, to Toyota in 1936 as a result of competition for a new emblem. The latter sounded better and had a lucky number of strokes when written in katakana. The name change also demonstrated the company's resolve to shift from a personal business to a socially oriented one.

8

THE BANKING CRISIS OF 1927

Proliferation of Kikan Ginko

Industrialization requires investment, which in turn requires finance. Investment projects of zaibatsu-affiliated firms were financed by loans extended by leading banks within each group. Joint stock companies could also raise funds from the capital market. However, small enterprises not affiliated with or supplying to any zaibatsu group or large firms had no access to big banks or the stock market, and had to rely on either informal finance or loans from a small local bank. The number of such small banks increased dramatically during the 1890s from less than 400 to well over 2,000. These banks contributed significantly to the growth of numerous industrial establishments all over Japan. However, unregulated and unmonitored, they also posed serious future risks to the financial system.

Kikan ginko (literally, institution bank, which does not explain much) is a term describing a bank serving only one or a few firms. It was captured and subordinated by the parent firm and has no management independence. Naturally, such banks had many structural weaknesses which included (i) non-separation of ownership and management, in which the same boss often owned and managed the firm and the bank; (ii) no information disclosure; (iii) no portfolio diversification and (iv) no capacity to assess and manage risks and evaluate projects.

Why were *kikan ginko* created? Suppose a renowned family in a certain rural district wants to start a business. The family establishes a company but wants to keep it under its full control without going public or borrowing from someone else. To finance its activities, the family sets up a bank. As the family is well known locally, people gladly deposit their savings with the bank, believing it is safe without knowing its true financial situation. In this way, many *kikan ginko* were established all over the country. In the 1900s and 1910s, over 2,000 such banks existed which was clearly too many.

When the Japanese economy was booming during WW1, even dubious banks prospered. But when the postwar recessions started, *kikan ginko* faced a mounting bad debt problem. Since their balance sheets were not open to the public, outsiders could not judge the magnitude of the problem. As noted earlier, in the early 1920s as the war bubble crashed, the government and the Bank of Japan supported weak banks and firms with emergency loans rather than restructuring them immediately. Overcapacity and bad debt were concealed without elimination.

DOI: 10.4324/9781315444048-9

The earthquake bill problem

On September 1, 1923, the Kanto Region was shaken by a huge earthquake which recorded 7.9 on the Richter scale. Tokyo and Yokohama were very badly damaged. The main cause of destruction was fire which started at countless places. Most Japanese houses were made of wood and the quake hit just before noon when most families were preparing lunch. One hundred thousand lives were lost and another 43,000 people were missing. Residential damage totaled 700,000 units. Foreign observers praised Japanese people for remaining calm and orderly in this calamity, an observation repeated many times in subsequent disasters. The reality, however, was that many Korean people were caught and murdered by private patrol groups based on false rumors.

The Japanese Archipelago sits where four massive moving plates meet on the earth's crust. This produces earthquakes as well as volcanoes and hot springs. While scientists try to forecast areas that are likely to be hit by the next large tremors, it is practically impossible to avoid earthquakes anywhere in Japan. Earthquakes are classified into two types. The first type occurs when huge plates run into each other with one of them sinking slowly into the earth. This dynamism accumulates enormous strain which is released suddenly as an earthquake. These quakes are big, deep down and affect a large area. The second type is smaller in magnitude and impacts a smaller area but, since it is shallow, local damage could be immense. Such quakes are caused by the movement of active faults on or near the surface, of which there are many in Japan. The Great Kanto Earthquake of 1923 and the Great East Japan Earthquake of 2011 were of the first type. The Kobe Earthquake of 1995 and the Kumamoto Earthquake of 2016 were of the second type.

Back to 1923. Immediately after the Great Kanto Earthquake, the Bank of Japan extended special emergency loans to commercial banks. This was done in the form of re-discounting earthquake bills.

Firms routinely settle their accounts using commercial bills. Upon delivery of products, the buyer issues a commercial bill, or a promise to pay with agreed interest at a certain date, say, three or six months later. The supplier usually takes the bill to a bank, which provides cash after subtracting expected interest (this is called discounting). The bank may hold the bill until maturity, sell it to other banks, or take it to the central bank to similarly "cash it" (this is called re-discounting). This facility permits supplier firms to obtain cash immediately while allowing banks to earn interest by offering this service.

The Bank of Japan announced that any commercial bills originating in the earthquake-affected areas would be re-discounted limitlessly and unconditionally (i.e., without normal quality check). The Bank of Japan thus tried to sustain post-quake economic activities by supplying enough liquidity and preventing delayed business payments from paralyzing the entire financial system. This temporary rescue was justifiable for the intended purpose, but it also had a serious side effect.

Re-discounting of commercial bills with no question asked by the Bank of Japan offered a great opportunity for firms and commercial banks that had accumulated bad debt unrelated to the earthquake. They happily took advantage of this facility to exchange bad debt for good cash. If the emergency re-discounting was truly directed to firms affected by the earthquake, some firms suffering severe damage might have to close but most of them should be able to resume operation after a while, and the central bank should be able to redeem most of the earthquake bills. But in reality, even after two years, only half of the earthquake bills were settled by issuing companies. The rest was a stock of non-performing debt unrelated to the Great Kanto Earthquake with little chance of redemption. If no corrective measure was taken the central bank would incur large losses. This was called the "earthquake bill problem."

Illiquidity versus insolvency

There are two types of inability to repay which are fundamentally different and require very different solutions. One is the liquidity problem in which one is temporarily out of cash and cannot repay now, but if we wait long enough there will be a future stream of income or assets to clear the debt. The solution to this problem is delayed payment or a new loan, which is technically called debt rescheduling. The other is the solvency problem in which the borrower is unable to repay either now or later because there is no expected income or asset to be generated in the future. The only solution to this problem is cancellation or, more technically, debt forgiveness. The budget constraint is secure (i.e., expenditure and revenue match over time) in the former but it is breached in the latter.

The trouble is that, at the moment inability to repay is detected, it is difficult to tell whether the problem is illiquidity or insolvency because of uncertainty surrounding future income streams. The response of an average creditor is to assume illiquidity first, which is less serious, and pray for full repayment with added interest over time. But the generous lender will usually be disappointed, and the borrower's insolvency has to be finally admitted. All or part of the money is now lost. The solution therefore proceeds from debt rescheduling to debt forgiveness. This tendency is observed for personal advances, commercial loans, or even a sovereign debt crisis.

In their analysis of the Bank Runs of 1927, Takahashi and Morigaki describe the "fundamental causes of the financial crisis" as follows:

> Although the Japanese economy grew strongly in quality and quantity during WW1, the banking system remained pre-modern with many internal defects. When excessive speculation ended in 1920, both government and private businesses made the mistake of implementing only temporary rescue measures hoping that the next boom would bail them out. But the economic malaise was deeply rooted, and temporary measures only made things worse. In addition, the Great Kanto Earthquake of 1923 harmed our economy, and improper policies increased exchange rate instability which further aggravated the economy. Corporate profits fell significantly, bank management became chaotic and rigid within the outdated banking system, and Japanese banks, including many of the large ones, were on the verge of collapse.
>
> (Takahashi and Morigaki, 1993[1968], p. 7)

Their argument suggests a large degree of insolvency built deeply into the Japanese corporate and banking systems.

The Bank of Japan accumulated unpaid earthquake bills to the tune of 431 million yen, of which 100 million yen was deemed unrepayable. Commercial banks also held un-rediscounted bad debt. In order to "normalize" these earthquake bills, the government prepared two laws. The first law would permit bad bills held by commercial banks, up to 170 million yen, to be rescheduled for 10 years with government bonds as collateral. The second would allow the government to provide the Bank of Japan up to 100 million yen to write off its losses related to the earthquake bills. In other words, the bad earthquake bills would partly be converted into long-term debt with delayed repayment, and partly be forgiven using the government budget. Parliamentary debate on these laws began in January 1927.

The initial wave of the banking crisis

Finance Minister Kataoka Naoharu was eager to pass the earthquake bill laws, but the opposition parties, especially Rikken Seiyukai, criticized him for bailing out big banks and businesses with taxpayers' money. They demanded that the government disclose the amount of bad bills and the names of banks that held them (very little was known at that time: there were only rumors). They even argued that the government's true intention might be to help political friends. In the debating process, the size of the bad debt gradually came out—200 million yen of which half was held by the Bank of Taiwan[1] (see below). People were shocked at the size of non-performing loans.

On March 14, 1927, Minister Kataoka was pestered with questions in the Budget Committee of the House of Representatives. He was frustrated at the questioner who did not understand the nature of the problem and wanted to debate endlessly. To make the point that the situation was very serious, he announced the latest news that crossed his desk: "Today, at around noon, very regrettably, Tokyo Watanabe Bank finally went bankrupt." This was an unexpected bombshell for the financial market, as well as the people at large. Immediately, depositors queued up in front of banks to withdraw their money. Many banks in the Tokyo area closed. This was the first shock wave of bank runs. However, it was a relatively small crisis in the Tokyo area only. The worst was yet to come.

In reality, Tokyo Watanabe Bank was not bankrupt, technically speaking. It was having trouble getting liquidity but the problem was solved quickly. But the bureaucrat carrying memos to the Finance Minister forgot to cancel the first report. Some suspected that Tokyo Watanabe Bank must have been happy with the Finance Minister's "misstatement." It may have wanted to close but needed a good excuse. Now the bank management could blame Minister Kataoka instead of themselves.

Many people criticized, and still criticize, Minister Kataoka for the slip of the tongue that ignited the 1927 financial crisis. But it is very clear that, with or without his remark, the Japanese financial system faced a grave long-term problem. The true cause of the bank runs was structural, as Takahashi and Morigaki explain. We cannot blame just one individual for everything.

Suzuki Shoten and the Bank of Taiwan

Suzuki Shoten was a trading company of the *narikin* type (Chapter 7), growing rapidly during WW1 through speculative business in steel, wheat and ships. Its main office was in Kobe and its general manager was Kaneko Naokichi. In 1919 and 1920, Suzuki's turnover even surpassed those of big zaibatsu trading houses such as Mitsui and Mitsubishi. It had strong connections with Taiwan, especially the Taiwan Colonial Administration, the Bank of Taiwan, and Taiwanese sugar businesses, and was given the monopoly right to market Taiwan-made camphor.

With the bursting of the war bubble, Suzuki Shoten faced a bad debt problem like any other *narikin* business. It asked the Bank of Taiwan, its main bank, to extend rescue loans. The Bank of Taiwan was a special bank playing the double role of Taiwan's central bank as well as a commercial bank. Despite its semi-official status, it actively lent to mainland Japan, especially Suzuki Shoten (Figure 8.1). Even with Suzuki's mounting difficulty, the Bank of Taiwan was unable to terminate its relationship with the company because it was too large in the loan portfolio. This situation was described as *kusare en*, or an unhappy but inseparable relationship which is usually reserved for a love relationship. The Bank rolled over Suzuki's existing debt and provided new loans, delaying the final solution and accelerating the debt snowball. This was the *kikan ginko* problem writ large. As the saying goes, if you have a small debt to a bank and your business fails, you are in trouble; if you have a huge debt that goes bad, the bank is in trouble.

By the end of 1926, the largest part of the unsettled earthquake bills was attributable to the Bank of Taiwan (48.4 percent) and Suzuki Shoten was accountable for 70 percent of it. Thus, normalizing the earthquake bills practically meant solving the Bank of Taiwan–Suzuki Shoten problem.

On March 26, 1927, the Bank of Taiwan finally refused any more lending to Suzuki Shoten. This news sent another shockwave throughout Japan because it revealed the desperateness of the situation beyond anyone's imagination. People had expected that the government would somehow manage this problem, because the Bank of Taiwan was a special bank and Suzuki was too big to fail (this is called a moral hazard problem). No one predicted that the government would let the Bank of Taiwan give up on Suzuki. When this became reality, the second wave of bank runs started, this time in the Kansai area including the cities of Osaka, Kobe and Kyoto where Suzuki's activities concentrated.

The BOJ demands government guarantee

By 1927, the Bank of Taiwan's balance sheet was irregular. On the asset side, bad loans to Suzuki loomed large. On the liabilities side, instead of a large number of people's small deposits as with normal banks, the Bank of Taiwan relied very heavily on interbank "call" money (short-term borrowing from other commercial banks) as well as loans from the Bank

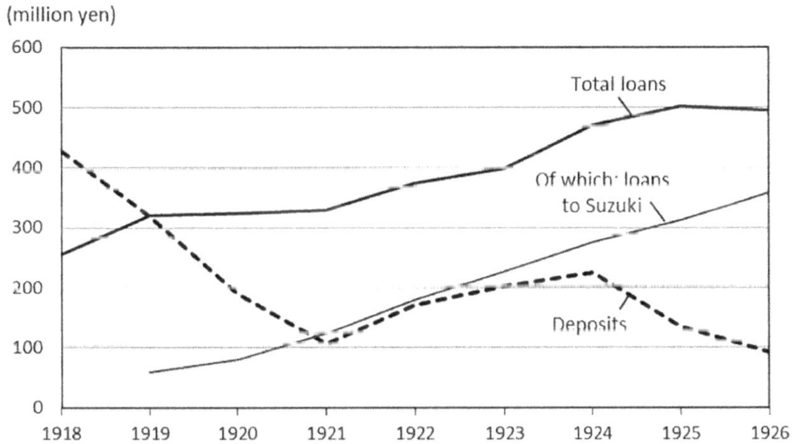

Figure 8.1 The balance sheet of the Bank of Taiwan

Source: Takahashi and Morigaki, 1993, p. 113.

of Japan. As soon as the breakup between the Bank of Taiwan and Suzuki was reported, other commercial banks immediately withdrew their call loans from the Bank of Taiwan. The only way for the Bank of Taiwan to survive was to ask for more rescue loans from the Bank of Japan.

At this time, even the Bank of Japan refused to extend additional loans to the failing Bank of Taiwan unless a new law was passed to cover the future losses of the central bank. For a long time, under political pressure, the Bank of Japan had been generously helping troubled banks. But this undermined the Bank of Japan's own financial soundness. Now at this critical moment of financial crisis, for the first time the Bank of Japan asserted independence from the government and declined to play the role of the "lender of last resort." The government was thus forced to quickly prepare a special law (actually, an emergency imperial edict because the parliament was out of session) to satisfy the Bank of Japan's demand. The edict instructed the following: (i) the Bank of Japan may extend special loans to the Bank of Taiwan without collateral until May 1928, and (ii) the government will compensate the Bank of Japan for losses related to such loans up to 200 million yen.

An imperial edict must be approved by the Privy Council and signed by the Emperor. The government expected an easy approval. But the Privy Council, an imperial advisory board dominated by conservative politicians who did not like the government's conciliatory policy toward China ("Shidehara Diplomacy," Chapter 7), unexpectedly rejected the proposed edict. This caused the Bank of Japan to stop lending to the Bank of Taiwan, forcing the Bank of Taiwan to close on April 18, 1927. On the same day, Omi Bank, specializing in cotton business and also heavily burdened by unsettled earthquake bills, also closed. The closure of these two banks started a chain reaction of bank runs all over Japan. This was the third and most severe financial panic of 1927.

On April 20, the Wakatsuki Cabinet (Kenseikai) fell and the Tanaka Cabinet (Seiyukai) was appointed. Takahashi Korekiyo, the new finance minister, tried to calm the panic psychology and financial markets. On April 22, Takahashi ordered all banks to "voluntarily" close for two days (until a moratorium was in place) and implemented a three-week "moratorium" on virtually all financial obligations. This unusual peace-time moratorium, or temporary suspension of debt repayments, was to protect banks from massive deposit withdrawals (except for small withdrawals that were permitted to cover people's living expenses). Takahashi also ordered quick printing of additional currency notes, even those with one side left blank to save printing time, to be stacked and showed off over the bank counter to reassure depositors. Calm returned, and things went back to normal when the moratorium expired—except, of course, for the banks that closed and the depositors who lost their savings.

The consequences of the banking crisis

The economic impact of the Financial Crisis of 1927 was negative but not catastrophic. The banking sector had to be restructured, but real growth and the manufacturing sector did not suffer very much. Macroeconomic statistics showed little sign of a serious downfall. The worst for the macroeconomy would come a few years later, for other reasons (Chapter 9).

The most significant consequence of the bank runs of 1927 was financial concentration. The government liquidated or merged unsound banks into about two dozen new banks. Among the 36 banks closed in 1927, fifteen banks were reopened, eight were merged, five were bankrupted, and one was still in a restructuring process after a year. In the restructuring process, unlucky people who had deposits at restructured banks on average lost

35–50 percent of their savings. The government encouraged further mergers of remaining small banks by imposing a minimum capital requirement and other regulations. Naturally, people also shifted their savings from small local banks to more well-known banks. The number of commercial banks fell from more than 2,000 in 1919 to 625 in 1932. Deposits were increasingly concentrated in the "Big Five" banks: Mitsui, Mitsubishi, Sumitomo, Yasuda and Daiichi. By 1931, they collectively accounted for 38.3 percent of total bank deposits and 29.6 percent of total bank loans (Figure 8.2).

Elimination of small *kikan ginko* was a good thing for modernizing the Japanese banking system. From another perspective, however, this reduced the supply of bank credit to small enterprises. As deposits were concentrated in big banks, these banks had more money than they could lend out. Special laws were passed for liquidity injection and increasing compensation for the Bank of Japan's losses up to 500 million yen. These created a situation of general excess liquidity and low interest rates.

In comparison with today, the financial framework of the 1920s was clearly inadequate. Information disclosure was not mandated, deposit insurance did not exist, capital adequacy ratios were not imposed and bank supervision and regulatory mechanisms were not in place. Moreover, the Bank of Japan did not fulfill its role as the lender of last resort.

But on this last point, some questions remain. Should the Bank of Japan be blamed for worsening the financial crisis because it did not provide liquidity to the Bank of Taiwan at the critical moment? We need to consider the following aspects before a final judgment is given.

First, the Bank of Japan had been forced to rescue too many banks against its will and against its own financial soundness. At some point, it had to reassert its political independence. While the immediate consequence of letting the Bank of Taiwan fall was severe, endless provision of emergency loans might not have been the right answer.

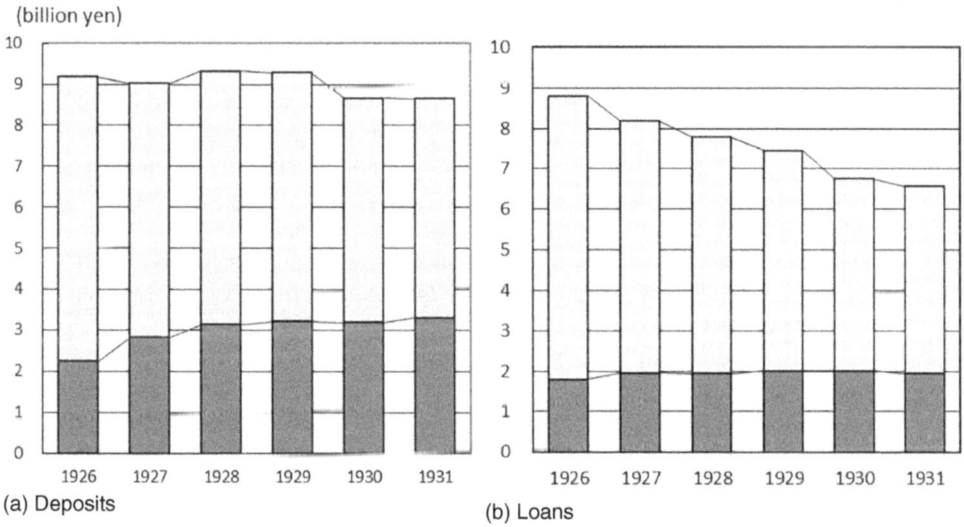

Figure 8.2 Share of big five banks

Source: Takahashi and Morigaki, 1993, p. 249.

Note: Share of Big Five is shown in dark gray. End of year data. The data of 1931 is for end June 1931.

Second, among the general public and the opposition party, political resistance to injecting public money into a few big banks was so strong. For this reason, the Bank of Japan also had to take a tough stance toward the Bank of Taiwan.

Finally, bank closures are painful in the short run but, if properly handled, they will ensure the soundness of the remaining banks and of the whole financial system in the long run.

Box 8.1 Hamaguchi Osachi and Koizumi Junichiro

Below are excerpts from Banno Junji's essay, "Hamaguchi Osachi and Koizumi Junichiro," which appeared in *Ronza*, a popular magazine, in October 2001. It compares the economic policies of the Hamaguchi government (1929–31) and the Koizumi government (2001–6). Hamaguchi's policy is also discussed in Chapter 9.

> Regarding economic structure, Japan in the 1920s faced the same problems as today [2000s]. In particular, the question of how to cope with the impact of the bursting of the WW1 bubble was very similar to the question we are now facing after the bursting of the Heisei bubble in the 1990s. In the 1920s, as at present, the economy stagnated because the policy makers avoided and delayed the resolution of the problem for fear of short-term pain.
>
> The situation of the 1920s, including the problem of how to cope with the non-performing loans and the policy decision to return to the gold standard, has many similarities with the economic problems that the current Koizumi government faces. Then as well as today, the Japanese economy, artificially supported by fiscal stimuli, was driven to a policy impasse. There was no way out except to adopt the gold standard in order to eliminate inferior firms and encourage technical innovation by efficient firms.
>
> However, the mass media's evaluation of the policies of the Hamaguchi government—as well as its Finance Minister Junnosuke Inoue who carried out austerity measures—is fairly negative. Partly because of the global depression into which the Japanese economy was plunged immediately after the return to the gold standard, today's media tend to focus only on the painful side of the economic policies of Hamaguchi and Inoue. By contrast, they happily approve the policies of Finance Minister Takahashi Korekiyo who subsequently resurrected fiscal expansionism, and argue that the Koizumi government should not repeat the mistake the Hamaguchi government made. Is this the correct lesson to take from history? …
>
> The highly regarded fiscal policy of Takahashi boils down to the issuance of government bonds to cover the war expenses of the Manchurian Incident and the active spending to help rural districts out of recession. This was called Jikyoku Kyusai (correct and rescue the situation), or more recently, Tomen no Keiki Taisaku (recovery policies for the moment). This was considered doubly effective for building infrastructure and for creating jobs … But it is hard to argue that this policy alone improved the productivity and competitiveness of Japanese firms, leading to the economic boom.

If we examine more closely, we find that the lopsided evaluation between Inoue and Takahashi comes from looking only at the macroeconomic aspects of their fiscal policies. The assessment from microeconomic aspects of how the private sector responded is totally lacking.

As I argued earlier, Japan in the 1920s desperately needed structural reforms in order to reduce the bad assets of the post WW1 period and cultivate new competitiveness. It is true that unemployment and bankruptcies surged with Inoue's fiscal policy under the Hamaguchi government. But we must also realize that, during this period, many firms implemented comprehensive restructuring and consolidation, industrial structures were reorganized, and export industries underwent management rationalization and technical progress. Only after this intensive joint effort by management and labor to improve efficiency, the Japanese economy was able to recover in the following period …

If this historical lesson is correctly learned, the Koizumi government should be able to effectively apply this lesson to the current situation. I have argued many times that today's Japan must learn from the Hamaguchi government and the Minsei Party led by Hamaguchi. Japan really needs to create another Minsei Party.

Economic reforms always come with pain. Unemployment will visibly increase and bankruptcies will surge. The economy may fail to recover soon. Under these circumstances, a political party which is willing to take responsibility and pushes reforms forward is needed. The lesson of the prewar period, as I interpret it, is that we must learn from the Minsei Party and re-create such a party today. The Seiyukai Party—in other words, the Liberal Democratic Party—can hardly carry the torch of structural reforms.

Note

1 As of end 1926, on the eve of the bank runs, the total amount of unsettled earthquake bills was 207 million yen, with the Bank of Taiwan holding 48.4 percent of it. Other banks with large shares included the Bank of Korea (10.4 percent), Murai Bank (7.4 percent) and Omi Bank (4.5 percent) (Takahashi and Morigaki, 1993[1968], p. 146).

9

THE 1930s AND THE WAR ECONOMY

The Showa Depression, 1930–32

During 1930–32, Japan experienced the deepest economic downturn in its modern history. This depression had far more serious consequences than the 1927 financial crisis (Chapter 8) on all aspects of Japanese life including economic, social and political. It was caused by the simultaneous occurrence of two factors.

Externally, Black Thursday, the Wall Street stock market crash in the United States in October 1929, and the ensuing economic depression, spread to the world and exerted a severe negative impact on the Japanese economy as well. The Great Depression thus engulfed all capitalist countries resulting in sharp price declines and surging unemployment.

Internally, the Minsei Party government (July 1929–April 1931), featuring Prime Minister Hamaguchi Osachi, Finance Minister Inoue Junnosuke and Foreign Minister Shidehara Kijuro, adopted a deflationary policy to eliminate inefficient banks and firms as well as to prepare the nation for the return to the prewar gold parity (i.e. restoring a fixed exchange rate of two yen per dollar).

Throughout the 1920s, restoration of the gold standard, which worked well to secure price stability and spur growth in the late nineteenth century, was an important economic agenda for the world as well as for the Japanese government. In Japan, the return to gold was planned a number of times but each time it had to be postponed by the occurrence of an unexpected event such as the Great Kanto Earthquake and the banking crisis. Finally, in January 1930, the gold standard was restored and the yen was re-fixed at the previous parity by the hands of Finance Minister Inoue who in preparation adopted macroeconomic austerity to deflate the Japanese economy. Inoue's argument was as follows.

> Our economy remains highly unstable because of the export ban on gold [the yen's non-convertibility to gold and the resulting exchange rate fluctuation]. We must liberalize gold export as soon as possible. But we cannot liberalize gold export without preparation. What is required in preparation? The government must tighten the budget. The people must accept this fiscal austerity and they themselves must reduce consumption. If that happens, prices will start to fall and imports will begin to contract. That will create an upward pressure on the yen in the foreign exchange … We face a recession without an end in sight. If nothing is done, we will sink deeper. In the past, Japan often overcame recessions with the help of external stimuli. But the current situation does not permit such a hope because the European economies are severely weakened by the last war.

DOI: 10.4324/9781315444048-10

> Under such circumstances, we should not hope for foreign demand to bail us out. Recovery must be generated by our hands. There is no way out except through our own austerity.
>
> (*Essays of Junnosuke Inoue*, Vol. 1, 1935)

Unluckily, Inoue's stern deflation policy coincided with the beginning of the Great Depression in the world economy. With internal and external shocks reinforcing each other, Japan was plunged into a very serious deflationary spiral with surging unemployment. Popular discontent against Inoue's policy mounted but Inoue never relented. Inoue's engineered deflation was continued for two years until the Minsei Party government was replaced by a Seiyukai government in December 1931.

In Britain, John Maynard Keynes, a Cambridge intellect and the father of macroeconomics, asserted in 1925 that his country should not return to gold at the prewar exchange rate because the equilibrium exchange rate—an exchange rate that would balance internal and external price levels—had shifted after WW1 as a result of international price divergence. He warned that the British recession would worsen if an overvalued exchange rate was chosen for fixing. Keynes calculated that the pound would be overvalued by 10 percent at the prewar parity. Similarly in Japan, Ishibashi Tanzan, an economic journalist at Toyo Keizai Shimposha, argued for a return to the gold standard at a new, more depreciated exchange rate.

However, Inoue's idea was that Japan needed forced recession. He concluded that unprofitable firms and banks survived throughout the 1920s without merger, consolidation or liquidation because the government and the Bank of Japan generously helped them. He knew very well that deflation was painful but he believed it was necessary to remove inefficient industries. Many people blamed—and still blame—him for pursuing an aggressive deflationary policy when the world was reeling from the Great Depression. But Inoue never changed his view until he was assassinated in 1932. Perhaps his idea was economically sound but the timing and degree of execution were unfortunate.

Social instability and the rise of fascism

The Showa Depression wreaked havoc on Japanese society. Its main consequences were as follows.

First, as in previous recessions, macroeconomic downturn was felt primarily in falling prices and not so much in output contraction. Estimated real growth was actually positive during this period. As prices fell, manufacturers rushed to produce more to maintain earnings, keep factories running and retain workers. But clearly, this behavior collectively accelerated the oversupply of all manufactured goods and therefore the deflation. From 1929 to 1931, the wholesale price index fell about 30 percent, agricultural prices fell by 40 percent, and textile prices fell by nearly 50 percent (Figure 9.1).

Second, rural impoverishment became severe around 1931 and continued into the mid 1930s even after the industrial sector recovered. To make matters worse, in 1934, rural communities were hit by famine. In the Tohoku (northeastern) Region of Japan, rural poverty generated many undernourished children. Some farmers were forced to sell their daughters. This ignited great anger and popular criticism against the government and big businesses which seemed to be doing nothing and caring little about this rural disaster.

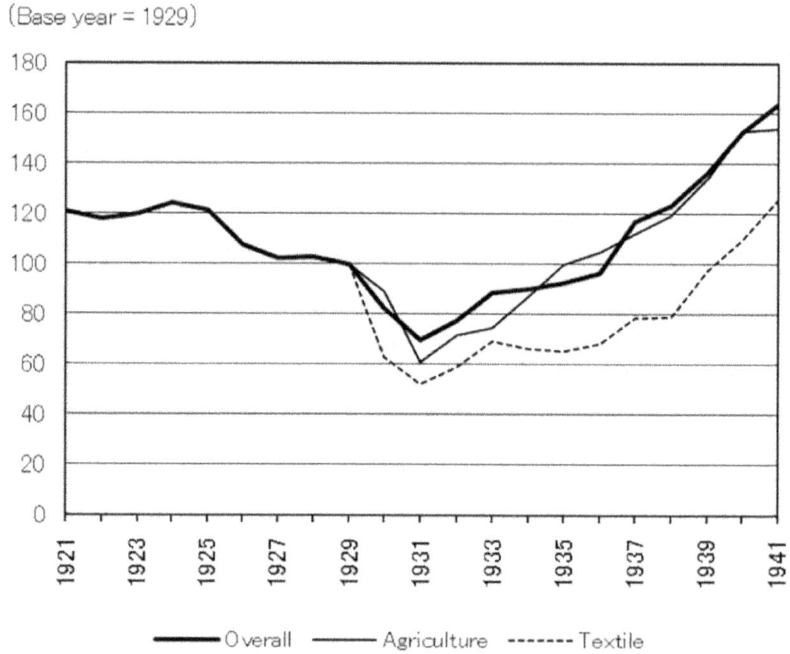

Figure 9.1 Wholesale price level

Source: Management and Coordination Agency, *Historical Statistics of Japan*, Vol. 4, 1988.

Note: No data are available for agriculture and textile before 1929.

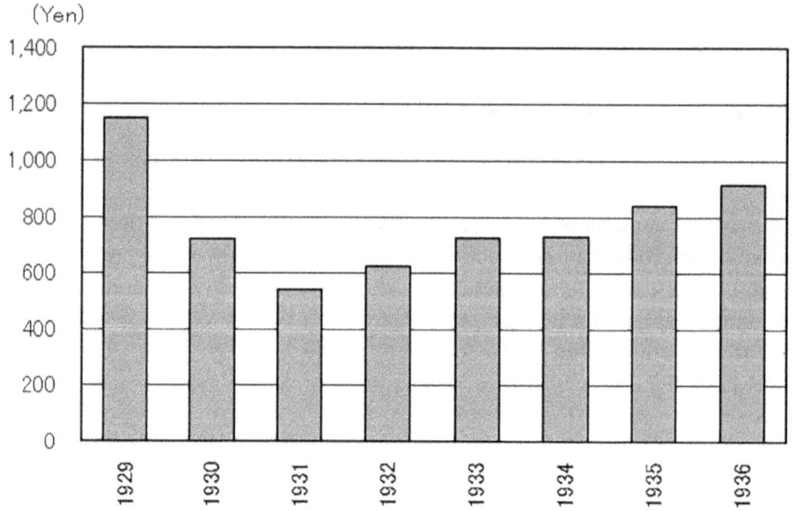

Figure 9.2 Average income of farm households (including non-farm income)

Source: Management and Coordination Agency, *Historical Statistics of Japan*, Vol. 2, 1988.

Third, cartelization and rationalization were promoted under official guidance. As free markets seemed to deepen the depression, mutual agreements on output restrictions were adopted. This practice quickly spread to virtually all material industries including cotton yarn, rayon, carbide, paper, cement, sugar, steel, beer and coal.

Fourth, the fascist movement emerged. Fascio is an Italian word used then to denote politicized military and right-wing groups with the aim of establishing a totalitarian regime. Amid economic despair, much blame was placed on party governments and their policies. Both the Minsei Party and the Seiyukai were despised. Even ordinary people, who normally hated militarism, were disappointed with the performance of "democratic" party governments and became more sympathetic to the "Reform Movement" advocated by the military and nationalists.

In the 1930s, political and intellectual preference was gradually shifting from economic liberalism to the state management of the economy. There were several reasons for this, including (i) rising popularity of Marxism; (ii) the apparent economic success of the Soviet Union which practiced state planning; (iii) the Showa Depression as evidence of failed capitalism; (iv) the view that deflation was aggravated by unregulated and excess competition and (v) general disappointment with the major political parties in economic, external and anti-terrorism policies. Many considered that the days of the American-style free market were over and that, from then on, state control and industrial monopoly would be required for building a competitive national economy.

Another aim of the military and right-wing groups was active external expansion. They criticized "Shidehara Diplomacy" which to them seemed too soft on China and too conciliatory to the United States. Their primary goal was to defend Japanese interests in Manchuria and Mongolia (more precisely, the eastern part of "Inner" Mongolia as viewed from China). However, military invasion of China would violate the agreement with the Western powers on the internationally agreed policy of "open door and equal opportunity" in China. Scrapping this agreement would carry the risk of spreading military confrontation to all China and Southeast Asia, and even to the entire world.

The Seiyukai and the Minsei Party

The Seiyukai (full name: Rikken Seiyukai) was established in 1900 by the union of Ito Hirobumi, a leading politician and the first Prime Minister of Japan, and former opposition parties that decided to cooperate with the government. Its main policies were (i) fiscal activism with an emphasis on public investment in rural and industrial infrastructure; (ii) acceptance of military buildup and expansion; and (iii) pleasing a narrow voter base (rural landlords and urban rich). It was a party supportive of a big government that allocated public money and subsidies. Seiyukai literally means "Association of Political Friendship."

The Minsei Party (full name: Rikken Minsei To) was originally called the Kenseikai (1916), which merged with another party in 1927 to become the Minsei Party. Its main policies were (i) economic austerity and industrial streamlining (a free economy and small government); (ii) return to prewar gold parity and (iii) international cooperation and peaceful diplomacy, especially with the United States. Its support base consisted of intellectuals and the urban population. Minsei literally means "People's Politics."

Japanese voters in prewar Japan did not always vote for the same party. Their allegiance switched from one party to another depending on the prevailing issue at each election (Table 9.1). The Seiyukai was a big spender and it also did not hesitate to align with the military to oust Minsei Party governments. The Minsei Party seemed more democratic and peaceful but it pursued an economic policy of belt-tightening and forced deflation. When an economic crisis was the greatest issue, people overwhelmingly voted for the Seiyukai in 1932. When uncontrolled military expansion in China was resented, they shifted support to the Minsei Party in 1936. After the voter base was enlarged in 1925, smaller "proletariat parties" (social democrats) also emerged with farmers and workers as the support base.

As explained earlier, Finance Minister Inoue Junnosuke of the Minsei Party government (1929–31) was deeply committed to the policy of deflation and returning to gold. This caused a severe depression but he never relented or regretted his position. People became greatly frustrated with his policy. Finally, the government (the second Wakatsuki Cabinet) was removed in the aftermath of the October Incident (see below) and was succeeded by a Seiyukai government (the Inukai Cabinet) on December 13, 1931.

As soon as the new government was sworn in, Finance Minister Takahashi Korekiyo completely reversed Inoue's policies. On the very first day of the new cabinet, Takahashi ended the gold standard and floated the yen which immediately depreciated. In addition, fiscal expansion financed by government bond issues (called "Spending Policy") was adopted. Monetization of the fiscal deficit, in which the Bank of Japan bought up newly

Table 9.1 Two major political parties in prewar Japan

	Seiyukai	*Minsei Party*
Establishment	Established in 1900 by Ito Hirobumi and former opposition party members as pro-government party; disbanded in 1940	Kenseikai established in 1916; Minsei Party created by merger of Keiseikai and another party (Seiyu Honto) in 1927; disbanded in 1940
In power	1900–1, 1906–08, 1911–12, 1918–22, (1924–25), 1927–29, 1931–32	(1924–25), 1925–27, 1929–31
Support base	Big businesses, landlords and well-to-do farmers	Intellectuals and urban middle class
Economic policy	Fiscal activism, big government, public investment for industry and rural infrastructure and development	Free market, small government, return to the prewar gold parity, exit of inefficient firms through austerity
Rights of working class	Not interested	Elevate the rights of farmers and workers when possible
Distinctive finance minister and his policy	Takahashi Korekiyo floated and depreciated yen, adopted easy money and fiscal expansion to recover economy, later reversed (1931–36)	Inoue Junnosuke pursued deliberate deflation policy to re-fix yen at the prewar exchange rate (1929–31)
Foreign policy	Initially peaceful (until around 1925), but later supportive of military to undermine Minsei party; sent troops to China to defend Japanese interests	Opposed military invasion of China, protected Japanese interest through diplomacy, promoted global disarmament and cooperation with the West
Problem	Opportunism to align with military undermined democracy and party politics	Sustaining severe deflation policy in the midst of global economic crisis

Note: the table shows key features of the two parties from the late 1920s to the mid 1930s. The government of 1924–25 was a coalition of the Keiseikai, the Seiyukai and the Reform Club.

issued government bonds, was tried for the first time in Japanese history. Money supply expanded and interest rates were lowered.

Thanks to this policy turnaround, the Japanese economy began to recover in 1932 and expanded relatively strongly until 1936, the last year of the non-war economy. Among major countries, Japan was the first to overcome the Great Depression of the 1930s. Fiscal and monetary expansion worked well. But the yen's sharp depreciation might be interpreted as a "beggar-thy-neighbor" policy. It was a policy that could offend other countries since Japan promoted its exports at the cost of reduced competitiveness of its trading partners.

For these achievements, Takahashi was called "Japanese Keynes." He adopted the Keynesian policy of fiscal and monetary expansion to fight an economic downturn even before John Maynard Keynes wrote his epoch-making treatise on the General Theory of Employment, Interest and Money[1] in 1936! Even today, Takahashi's policy is admired while Inoue's policy is widely criticized as stubborn and misguided. But this view can be challenged. Banno Junji, specializing in prewar Japanese politics, argues that Inoue's deflation policy, which eliminated inefficient firms and banks, provided the precondition for economic recovery of the mid 1930s. Thus, in his opinion, both Inoue and Takahashi were needed (see Box 8.1).

Around 1934, when Japanese industries were firmly on a path to recovery, Takahashi began to go back to a tighter budget, which seemed an appropriate decision. But the army and the navy continued to demand more spending despite escalating fiscal pressure. Takahashi resisted their demand and was assassinated by a military group in the February 26 Incident in 1936 (see below).

Both Inoue and Takahashi served as a Governor of the Bank of Japan before assuming the job of Finance Minister, but their personalities differed significantly. Inoue was a slim and intellectual graduate from the Imperial University. Takahashi was fat and had a nickname of Daruma, a round doll made after a famous Zen monk. He received little formal education and had a rough life when he was young. Japanese people naturally liked Takahashi who looked friendlier and who always saved Japan from economic crises.

Political terrorism and invasion of China

From 1931 to 1937, Japanese politics was gradually overtaken by the military. Many bloody incidents occurred, each undermining the foundation of party politics and democratic government. Within the army and the navy—especially the army—a few ultra-nationalist groups formed with the purpose of rejecting a party-based political system, uniting the nation under the emperor, introducing economic planning and saving the rural poor. They staged many assassinations and coup attempts. Here is a brief chronology of this dismal period.

In 1931, the Manchurian Incident (September 18th Incident) broke out in which several military officers of the Kantogun (Japanese army stationed in China), especially Ishihara Kanji and Itagaki Seishiro, started a military invasion of Manchuria (Northeastern China) by blowing up a railroad track and blaming it on the Chinese. Ishihara's theory was that Japan had to take Manchuria in order to prepare for a full war against the United States. The incident was initiated without informing the central government or the army headquarters in Tokyo. Foreign Minister Shidehara instructed Kantogun to refrain from further military action but Ishihara's group ignored this. The Chinese side adopted a non-resistance strategy, and Manchuria was soon occupied by Japanese troops. This incident clearly showed that the party government could no longer restrain the military. Separately, in the same year, there were the March Incident and the October Incident in Tokyo, two military coup attempts that were detected and aborted.

In 1932, the Blood Society, each of whose members was ordered to assassinate one politician or business leader, killed Inoue Junnosuke (former Finance Minister) and Dan Takuma (CEO of the Mitsui Group). In the May 15th Incident, young navy officers gunned down and killed Prime Minister Inukai Tsuyoshi (Seiyukai). In the same year, the State of Manchuria, a Japanese puppet state, was established. Japanese occupation of Manchuria was studied and criticized by the League of Nations, which led Japan to withdraw from the League in 1933.

The years from 1933 to 1935 were relatively "quiet" thanks to the economic recovery and fewer domestic and international incidents. But this proved to be a temporary calm before the big storm.

In 1936, the February 26th Incident, the most serious coup attempt in prewar Japan, occurred. Nationalistic army officers led their troops to stage a military coup on a snowy morning in Tokyo. They wanted to remove the incumbent government and establish a new regime. Takahashi Korekiyo (Finance Minister), Saito Makoto (Interior Minister) and Watanabe Jotaro (Army Training Director) were assassinated. The coup group occupied central Tokyo for four days. The army headquarters first approved the coup but later disowned it because the emperor angrily and unequivocally ordered the military to put down the rebellion. The coup thus failed, and radical factions within the military that staged or supported it lost political power. But other military factions continued to marginalize party governments and gained influence over Japanese politics.

During many of these incidents, the Seiyukai behaved opportunistically, often supporting the military in order to attack its rival, the Minsei Party. It was a risky tactic because the goal of radical military groups was to remove all political parties including the Seiyukai (Banno 2004). The Seiyukai also criticized the "Organ Theory of the Emperor" advocated by Professor Minobe Tatsukichi of Tokyo University, an academically well-established doctrine that justified party governments under the Meiji Constitution, to corner the Minsei Party government before an election.[2] By contrast, the Minsei Party more consistently opposed the military. Nevertheless, both the Seiyukai and the Minsei Party were seriously discredited in the eyes of the public because they were considered equally corrupt and incompetent. For farmers and workers who rejected the market mechanism and demanded economic control and pro-poor and pro-labor policies, both parties seemed too bourgeois (pro-business). In this way, the general public and burgeoning proletariat (i.e., social democratic) parties began to partially sympathize with the military. They did not welcome aggressive invasion of foreign countries, but they liked the anti-capitalist reform agenda advocated by the fascist groups.

Then, in 1937, the Japan–China War started. On July 7, Japanese and Chinese troops had a skirmish at Marco Polo Bridge near Beijing (then called Beiping). The incident was a minor one but the Konoe Cabinet in Tokyo decided to send more troops to China. Thus began a full-scale war with China, which lasted until 1945. After the Japan–China War erupted, the entire nation was mobilized for war purposes. The military took over Japanese politics, and political parties were emasculated and subsequently disbanded. This was a complete defeat and end of prewar democracy.

When did Japan cross the point of no return toward a total war? There are diverse views, but in the opinions of many, it was probably the Manchurian invasion in 1931. With this incident, Shidehara's peaceful diplomacy was abandoned and the military's influence began to increase. The forceful establishment of the puppet state of Manchuria in pursuit of Japan's interests violated the principle of "open door and equal opportunity" which was the most important agreement on China among major powers throughout the 1920s. After this invasion, Japan's international isolation was unavoidable. Party governments were too weak to reverse this trend. While some factions within the Seiyukai and the Minsei Party tried to join forces to oppose militarism, their attempts did not materialize. Counting from the Manchurian Incident, the period 1931–45 is sometimes called the "Fifteen-Year War," which is understandable from the viewpoint of international relations. However, for ordinary Japanese people, the sense of wartime did not really exist until 1937 when the Japan–China War started and a large number of controls began to be introduced to limit their civilian life.

Some argue that Japanese people and parliament in this period were suppressed by the military, and they were deprived of necessary information and the right to criticize external military activities. However, this view is not correct up until 1937. In Japanese printed media, a large number of essays and columns were found that criticized the military and its foreign invasion and called for the formation of a national anti-fascism front. In the parliament, many speakers provoked and condemned military leaders. The Social Mass Party, representing the voice of workers and farmers, increased their parliamentary seats at every election. However, the situation changed dramatically after the Marco Polo Bridge Incident of July 1931. Once a total war began, all efforts toward democracy came to nil and everything had to be reorganized for the purpose of executing the war.

The war economy, 1937–45

The military leaders thought—or at least hoped—that the war with China would be short. But in reality, it lasted for eight years. Without a realistic vision or strategy, the war front expanded endlessly and fighting escalated. Within China, the Nationalists and the Communists were fighting at first but later joined forces to resist Japanese invaders.

Until 1936, the Japanese economy basically remained market-oriented despite calls for more economic planning. But with the outbreak of the Japan–China War in 1937, national economic management was significantly transformed for war execution. One by one, new measures were introduced to control and mobilize people, enterprises and resources. Most Japanese firms remained privately owned as before but were heavily regulated in production, investment, finance, employment and so on, to contribute to the war effort.

In 1937, the Planning Board (*kikakuin*) was created. This board, directly under the Prime Minister, was responsible for comprehensive policy design for wartime resource mobilization. The brightest bureaucrats from various ministries were gathered for this purpose. Without nationalizing enterprises, it basically played the same role as state planning committees in socialist countries. Special laws for military expenditure, financial control and regulating tradable goods were implemented. The bulk of military spending was gradually shifted from the general budget to the new special account for military expenditure, and government size began to increase due to the skyrocketing military spending. In 1937, the government budget was 4.74 billion yen, of which military spending occupied 69.0 percent. This would eventually rise to 86.16 billion yen by 1944, of which military spending was 85.3 percent, and mounting fiscal deficits were financed mainly by issuing public bonds (Ito, 2007).

In 1938, the Planning Board issued the Resource Mobilization Plan, which was Japan's first economic plan. In the same year, the National Mobilization Law was also approved. The Plan and Law were put into practice over the following years as the war intensified.

In 1940, the New Regime Movement was initiated by Prime Minister Konoe Fumimaro. This movement was started in response to the Japanese invasion of Southeast Asia and Nazi Germany's victories in Europe. It was felt that a strong one-party monopoly of power was needed. All existing political parties were dismantled and replaced by the monolithic *Taisei Yokusankai* (Imperial Rule Assistance Association), an administrative organ created by the government to oversee and mobilize people for war.

In 1943, the Military Needs Company Act was adopted. Designated private companies were placed under official control. The government approved top management and production plans and imposed penalties for non-compliance. At the same time, these companies were provided with necessary inputs on a priority basis.

The primary objective of economic planners was to maximize military production with limited domestic resources and imports. Key military goods were ships and warplanes, and energy and materials to produce and operate them (toward the end of the war, as Japanese ships and sea transport capacity were destroyed, airplane production became the only priority). In order to boost heavy industries, consumption was greatly squeezed and light industries were strongly suppressed. The textiles industry, previously the leading industry of prewar Japan, was virtually eliminated and converted to military use. People were forced to live without new supplies of clothing or footwear. Steel products in structures, streets and households were stripped and used as the metal source for building more airplanes and ships. As the war continued, food rationing, forced enterprise mergers and forced factory labor were adopted in increasing intensity.

At first, the two crucial variables in wartime planning were foreign exchange reserves and the availability of energy and raw materials (and the ability to transport them by sea).

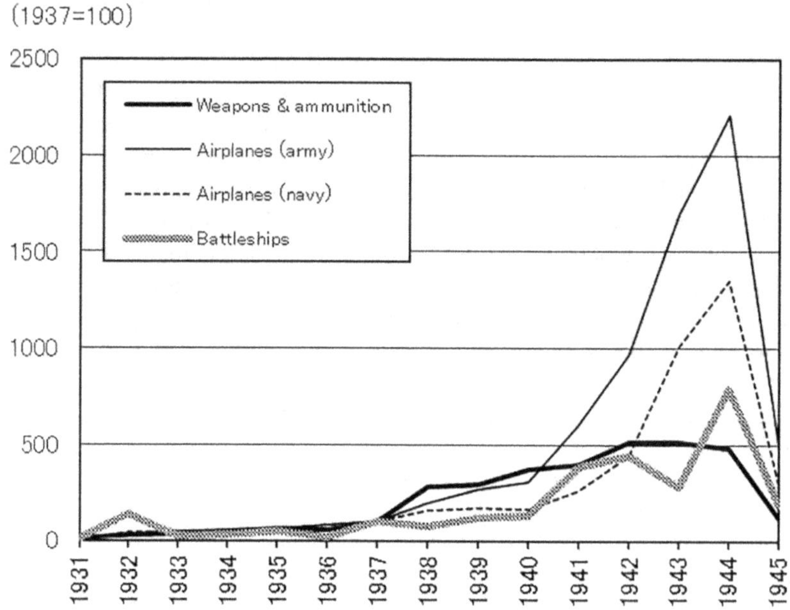

Figure 9.3 Production of military goods

Source: Nakamura (1989), p. 21.

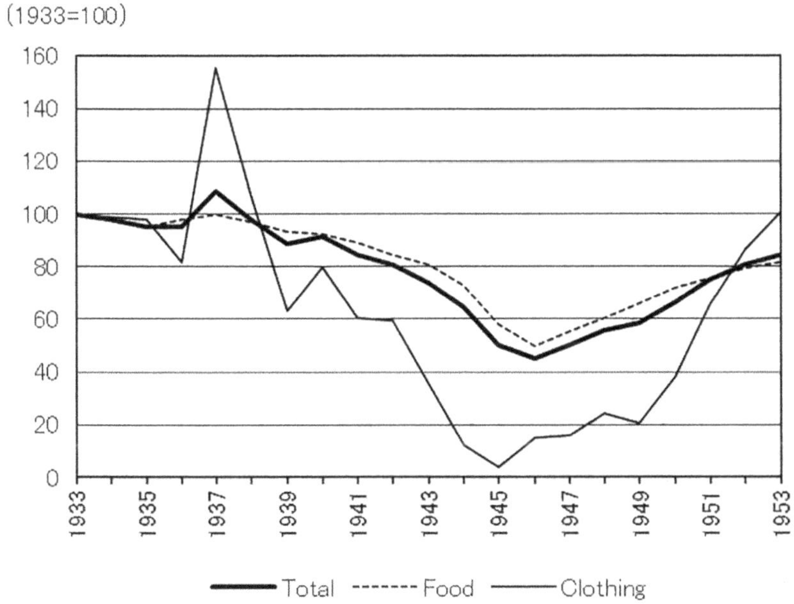

Figure 9.4 Supply of consumer goods per head

Source: Nakamura (1989), p. 22.

Until around 1940, the question was how to maximize military output subject to these two constraints. After that, because Japan could no longer trade with other countries, the problem shifted to the physical transportation of natural resources from the Japanese colonies and occupied areas in Northeast and Southeast to mainland Japan.

It was considered that the resources from the "Yen Bloc" (Korea, Taiwan, Manchuria and the rest of occupied China) were not sufficient. In July 1941, to secure more resources, the Japanese military began to invade Southeast Asia beginning with French Indochina (i.e., Vietnam). This military campaign angered the United States, prompting it to impose an oil embargo and asset freeze on Japan. If oil import from the United States were to be cut off, Japan's existing oil reserves would last only two years. At this point, Japan began to prepare for a war with the United States. Diplomatic efforts to maintain peace were attempted but failed. With the Pearl Harbor attack in December 1941, Japan started the Pacific War against the United States and its allies.

Japanese leaders did not have any clear idea regarding how to fight a war against the United States, let alone how to win it. However, they were encouraged by the brilliant victories of Nazi Germany in Europe. To them, the totalitarian states of Japan, Germany and the USSR seemed far superior to American capitalism and individualism.

Immediately after the outbreak of the Pacific War, Japan invaded a wide area of Southeast Asia but soon began to retreat under allied counter-attacks led by the Americans. Japanese ships and planes were quickly lost while the United States built an increasing number of them. From late 1944 to the end of the war, American aerial bombing, which consisted largely of incendiary bombs, destroyed virtually all major cities in Japan (except Kyoto).

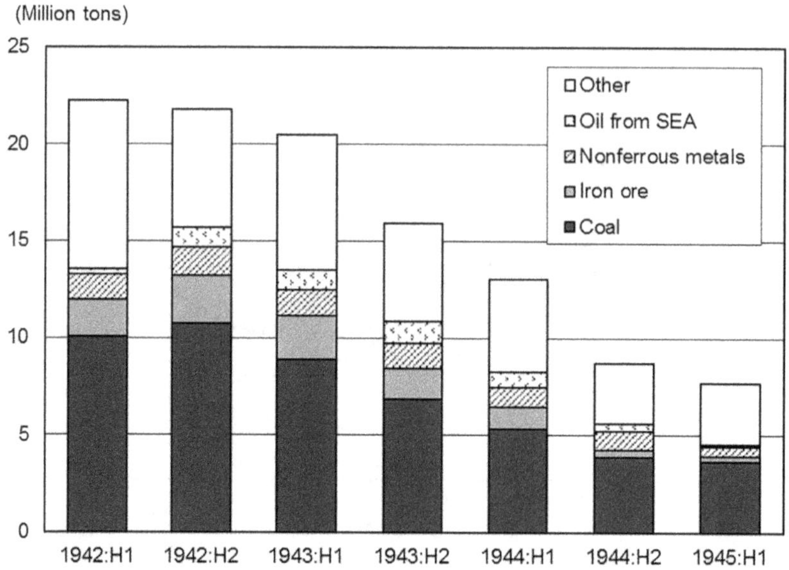

Figure 9.5 Maritime transport during the Pacific War

Source: Nakamura (1989), p. 30.

In March 1945, US troops landed in Okinawa and obliterated Japanese resistance within three months in fierce and civilian-involved fighting. In August 1945, two atomic bombs were dropped, in Hiroshima and Nagasaki, and the USSR entered the war against Japan. A few days later, Japan surrendered.

Whatever the political and social causes of Japanese militarism, the main economic reason for Japan's defeat was the collapse of its war economy due to the lack of material and energy inputs. Japan lost virtually all its means of sea transport and could not carry industrial inputs from its colonies and occupied areas to the mainland (Figure 9.5).

Collective social psychology: lessons from prewar Japan

The question of why Japan trod its aggressive military path and ended up with total war against China, the United States and most of the world is not easy to answer succinctly or convincingly to all who are interested in this question. Nevertheless, at the end of this dismal chapter, it may be useful to cite several social tendencies and reactions that led Japan, an emerging industrial power, eventually to this disastrous course. This is important for understanding not only prewar Japan but also other rising nations at any time because similar social psychology and traps seem to be at work in them albeit with different degrees and inflections.

First of all, it must be said that a nation rapidly rising in economic power becomes arrogant, militaristic and expansionist toward its neighbors. Such a nation always comes up with theories and interpretations justifying its behavior, but scientifically assessing or refuting them will not stop aggression because it comes from a deep and collective human instinct for which convenient justification is easily invented.[3]

People and various organizations—political parties, business associations, academics, media and civil organizations—initially take diverse positions on external aggression of the military, from passionate support to strong opposition. Doves and hawks coexist even within the military. Not everyone supports militarism at first.

Over time, however, as unfortunate news and events unfold, an appeal to patriotism and inflamed hatred against "unforgiveable enemies" gradually wins over pacifist voices. The government sometimes even resorts to an unwise tactic of directing blame towards foreigners, which later backfires. Mass psychology and emotion begin to rule. Oppositions continue to fight but become quieter and eventually lose.

Ignited by emotional "nationalism," the media and general public often become more belligerent than the government which wants to manage the level of external friction and prefers a diplomatic solution. Once such social momentum is unleashed, it becomes very difficult for anyone to stop. Popular sentiment becomes a constraint on foreign policy rather than its support.

Finally, the government also gives in to militarism and begins to actively prepare and execute war. Dissents are annihilated, debate ends and military objectives dominate all policies. The government turns to restrict people's freedom and suppress their living standards for the just cause of war.

Box 9.1 The origin of the Japanese system

Many of the characteristics of the post-WW2 Japanese economy originated during the war period of 1937–45. The main features of this model include long-term relationship and active official intervention as represented by such elements as:

- heavy and chemical industrialization drive
- administrative guidance (*gyosei shido*)
- the subcontracting system in manufacturing (*shitauke seido*)
- separation of ownership and management
- lifetime employment and seniority wage
- enterprise-based (not profession-based) trade unions
- financial *keiretsu* and mainbanks
- "window guidance" and the "convoy system" conducted by the Bank of Japan
- food control system
- foreign exchange budget and foreign exchange surrender requirement.

All of these policies and systems were deliberately adopted by the government in the late 1930s through the early 1940s in order to effectively execute the war. Before that, the Japanese economy was more "neoclassical," characterized by freer entry, short-term contracts and high labor mobility.

These wartime features were largely retained even after WW2 and worked relatively well in the 1950s and 1960s, when Japan was growing rapidly. However, after Japan reached high income, they became obsolete and negative, so it was argued, as barriers to quick and flexible adaptation in the age of globalization and ICT. Among the items listed above, the last one was abolished long ago but the remnants of all others still exist in the Japanese economy to varying degrees even today.

However, there is a debate among economists regarding the interpretation of the Japanese system. The majority of Japanese economists insist that Japan should go back from wartime regulation to the free market model because the relational and interventionist system was originally alien to Japan. These may have played a historical role in certain decades of the twentieth century, but the country does not need them any more—although some beneficial aspects, such as priority placed on job security, could be retained. Okuno Masahiro, Okazaki Tetsuji and Noguchi Yukio are leading advocates of this view (Okazaki and Okuno, 1993; Noguchi, 1995).

But a minority voice says that Japan needed a system based on a long-term relationship with or without war. When an economy graduates from the light industry stage featuring garments, footwear, food processing and simple assembly of electronics products, and moves to heavy industrialization and machinery production, free markets may not be the best choice. Official support and long-term trust become indispensable for industries that require large initial investments, high technology and a developed intra-firm labor market. As Japan began heavy industrialization in the 1920s and 1930s, the free economic system inherited from the Meiji period was considered inappropriate and had to change. The war provided a good excuse for accelerating this change. But even without the war, Japan had to adopt a new system anyway. Hara Yonosuke presents such a view (Hara 1996). According to him, the free economy of Meiji was unusual and foreign, and the relational and interventionist system, dating back to the Edo period and even before, is more normal for Japan.

If this view is correct, implications for today's developing countries are as follows. Light manufacturing such as garment and electronics assembly can be promoted by free trade and an open and undiscriminating FDI policy. But if the country hopes to absorb technology vigorously, have advanced manufacturing capability and climb the industrial ladder from middle income to high income, more proactive industrial promotion, featuring a strong state encouraging and assisting private dynamism, will become necessary. Japan, Taiwan and Korea all adopted this method in the past and reached high income. By contrast, no Southeast Asian economies—Malaysia, Thailand, Indonesia, Philippines, Vietnam and others—seem to have broken this "glass ceiling" and internalized their industrial power. They are trapped in middle income. If latecomer countries are now banned from taking proactive industrial measures because of the commitment to and constraints under the World Trade Organization (WTO), free trade agreements (FTAs), World Bank policy matrices and so on, their level of industrialization may forever remain low, characterized by short-term and simple contract manufacturing and processing, never reaching a higher level of technology.

Notes

1 J. M. Keynes, *The General Theory of Employment, Interest and Money*, Macmillan, 1936. Keynes criticized the classical contention that unemployment could be automatically solved through the market mechanism. Using analytical tools such as liquidity preference, shortage of investment opportunities and aggregate supply and demand, he showed the possibility of involuntary unemployment in a world where uncertainty ruled. Public investment was advocated as a remedy for this situation. Keynes' theoretical contribution revolutionized economics, which led to the creation of the discipline of macroeconomics and the system of national income statistics.

2 The organ theory of the emperor considered the state as a legal entity with a power to rule in which the emperor was its highest organ. This was the standard theory of the Meiji Constitution. The idea that the emperor's power was derived from and exercised within the Constitution was in line with the spirit of constitutional monarchy as well as the intention of Ito Hirobumi, the principal author of the Meiji Constitution. However, this theory angered the nationalists who regarded the emperor as divine and beyond the constraints of the Constitution.

3 Many political and intellectual leaders of Meiji Japan, including Fukuzawa Yukichi, Yamagata Aritomo, Kuga Katsunan and Aoki Shuzo, oscillated between the "Asia is One" anti-West doctrine and the "Japan is not Asia" doctrine that justified Japanese superiority and colonialism in the region. Banno (2013) says this is not surprising because these doctrines were used to support Japan's foreign policy for each moment—whether to resist Western advances or invade neighboring countries—and the lack of time consistency in their statements should not cause any wonder because doctrines were only the means and not the end.

10

POSTWAR RECOVERY 1945–49

Physical war damage

After the war defeat, Japan was occupied by the allied forces. In reality, the United States was the only country that ruled Japan from 1945 to 1952. The occupying force was called the Supreme Commander of the Allied Powers (SCAP) or, more commonly, the General Headquarters (GHQ). The GHQ was headed by US Army General Douglas MacArthur. The occupation of Japan was indirect in the sense that the Japanese government continued to exist and function to the degree that it often negotiated or even resisted American orders. Another feature unique to Japan was that it was occupied by only one country, unlike Germany which was geographically partitioned and governed directly by four winning forces (United States, United Kingdom, France and the USSR). This meant that Japan could avoid the risk of being divided when the Cold War began.

The United States conducted a postwar survey on the effectiveness of various military attacks against Japan during the war. It found that two factors contributed greatly to Japan's defeat. The first was a sea lane blockade as the vast majority of Japanese military and commercial ships were sunk, and the country lost the means to transport energy and materials between the mainland and the colonies or occupied areas. Without inputs, production came to a halt. This was the primary reason for the collapse of Japan's war economy.

Another factor was strategic bombing which intensified toward the end of the war. Virtually all major Japanese cities were subject to US aerial bombing. The largest air raid was launched in the eastern sections of Tokyo in the early hours of March 10, 1945 which, within a few hours, trapped and killed approximately 100,000 civilians in a field of fire. Atomic bombs were dropped on Hiroshima (90,000–120,000 immediately killed) and Nagasaki (60,000–70,000 immediately killed). However, bombing did not reduce Japan's production capacity as much as expected, though it had a strong psychological impact. The US report concluded that the sea lane blockade was more effective than the strategic bombing. It also argued that bombing should have targeted railroads rather than urban dwellings.

The Japanese government also produced a report on war damage.[1] Comparing before and after the Pacific War, it estimated that 25.4 percent of total national physical assets were lost (this includes direct damage by bombing and shelling as well as indirect loss due to scrapping, removal and inability to maintain). Most of the losses were incurred toward the end of the war. The ratios of destruction by asset type were as follows: ships (80.3 percent), industrial machinery (34.2 percent), structures (24.6 percent), industrial materials (23.9 percent), residences (20.6 percent), communication and water supply (15.9 percent), electricity and gas (10.8 percent) and railroad and road vehicles (9.9 percent).

DOI: 10.4324/9781315444048-11

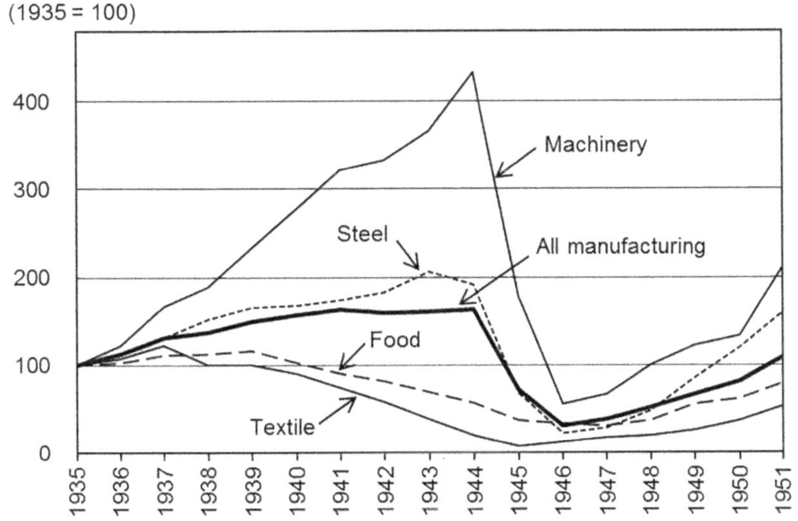

Figure 10.1 Industrial production index

Source: Management and Coordination Agency, *Historical Statistics of Japan*, Vol. 2, 1988.

Thus, two-thirds of machinery stock and most railroads survived despite heavy air raids. However, surviving factories and railroads were inoperative due to the lack of energy and materials. In 1945 and 1946, output collapsed to only 20 percent of the wartime peak, or 30 percent of the prewar peak which was recorded between 1934 and 1936. The lack of inputs was the reason, not the lack of capacity.

Shortage and inflation

Economic planning was continued even after the war ended and up until 1949. In a crisis situation, previously for executing war and now for resuscitating the economy from severe shortage, economic control had been used to complement paralyzed private sector activity. As during the war, necessities were rationed and the government directed production and procurement of key inputs. Prices were controlled, subsidies were provided and the economy was still tightly regulated. However, compared with wartime, controls became less effective because of the emergence of a large number of black markets.

Shortages were most severe and living standards were lowest in 1946, one year after the end of the war. As food became extremely scarce, it was feared that many would starve to death. Average calorie in-take per head hovered around 2,000 calories/day during 1934–44 but it plunged to 1,793 calories/day (88 percent of 1934–36) in 1945 and 1,449 calories/day (71 percent of 1934–36) in 1946 before recovering to nearly 2,000 calories/day by 1949. The urban population fared much worse than this average number shows while the rural population did not suffer very much from food shortage (Shimizu, 2007). As soldiers and civilians returned home from war fronts and former colonies, unemployment became a serious problem. Joblessness was expected to reach 10 million. However, neither mass starvation nor massive unemployment materialized, because the idle population was absorbed largely in informal and agricultural sectors. These sectors provided temporary jobs and a food sharing mechanism.

Many urban residents worked in the informal sector to survive.[2] They also had to travel to rural areas in super crowded trains to exchange their remaining property, such as kimono and clothing, for food with farmers. Because food rations were so small, everyone was forced to violate the law and go to illegal markets to survive. It is reported that Judge Yamaguchi Yoshitada of the Tokyo District Court was so law-abiding that he refused to disregard the Food Control Law. He ate only rationed food. In October 1947, he died of starvation.

To cope with output collapse and unemployment, the Japanese government printed money to finance subsidies while imposing price controls. This strategy could not be sustained for long. Monetization of fiscal deficits created triple-digit inflation from 1946 to 1949. Black market prices rose even faster, especially in the early period. This was the highest inflation that Japan ever experienced in its history.

Foreign trade was strictly controlled and any international transaction had to be approved by the GHQ. Private foreign trade was prohibited. For each commodity, the GHQ decided the dollar price and the yen price separately, creating different exchange rates for individual products. Thus, Japan between 1945 and 1949 had a multiple exchange rate system. Exchange rates for exports (150–600 yen per dollar) tended to be more depreciated than exchange rates for imports (125–250 yen per dollar).

The volume of international trade was also very limited. Apart from controlled trade, the United States provided generous humanitarian and economic aid to Japan amounting to cumulative $1.95 billion during 1946–50, which helped to ameliorate the shortage of food, medicine and consumer goods. The Japanese economy was barely standing with two artificial supports, namely government subsidies and American aid. These supports had to be eventually removed before Japan could walk on its feet again.

The basic problems of 1946

Immediately after the war defeat, two young officials, Okita Saburo and Goto Yonosuke, organized a study group to discuss ways to rebuild the Japanese economy from the war damage. Actually, the study group was under preparation toward the end of the war. Okita and Goto were electrical engineers stationed in China, but they knew Japan would soon lose the war. They returned to Tokyo to organize a study group.

The first meeting of the study group was held on August 16, 1945, one day after Japan's defeat. The topic was the impact of the Bretton Woods Agreement concluded a year earlier and the creation of the International Monetary Fund and the World Bank. Following this, study meetings on various topics were organized every week with the attendance of prominent officials and academics. Okita and Goto served as the secretariat summarizing the key points of each meeting and drafting a report. The study group began informally but was later officially recognized as the Special Survey Committee of the Ministry of Foreign Affairs. The interim report was produced in late 1945 and the final draft was delivered in March 1946. With minor revisions, the final report was published in September 1946.

The report, "The Basic Problems of Japan's Economic Reconstruction," is an excellent specimen of Japanese development thinking.[3] It has 193 pages in two parts. The first part analyzes new global circumstances and the historical and geographical position of defeated Japan. War damage is carefully examined and some positive aspects are also noted. The second part contains proposals for promoting industries and targeting exports, sector by sector. Real sector issues dominate, while monetary and fiscal problems are discussed only briefly. The report urges Japan to have a comprehensive and concrete recovery strategy whose core content must be industrialization, technology improvement and a dynamic transformation of trade structure. Priority industry must be analyzed carefully, and realistic and concrete promotion programs must be devised. Comparative advantages in textile and agriculture are now lost because of the expected emergence of the rest of Asia. Japan must aim at skilled labor-intensive industries.

Here are some direct quotes from the Report (the two page numbers refer to Japanese original and English translation respectively).

- The major causes for such reproduction on a regressed scale are found in the sluggish domestic production of coal and in the shortages of raw material imports. (p. 63/p. 66)
- In capitalistic free competition many Japanese industries will be overwhelmed by gigantic modern foreign industries, and Japan's industrial structure will thus be deformed. This will make it necessary to adopt State policies that will keep at least basic industries intact. (p. 81/p. 85)
- A national posture will have to be assumed in which all the people do not seek an affluent consumer life but are content with minimum standards of living, consume conservatively, and increase savings—thereby contriving to recover economic power and not seeking financial assistance from the outside world for consumption purposes. (p. 85/p. 88)
- A comprehensive and specific year-to-year reconstruction program will have to be formulated in order to revive the Japanese economy from the extreme destitution in which it finds itself now. The waste of economic power that would result from allowing laissez-faire play to market forces will not be permitted in order that all the meager economic power remaining may be concentrated in a direction toward reproduction on an enlarged scale and that the process of reconstruction may be expedited. (p. 92/p. 94)
- The principal role in Japan's economic reconstruction will have to be played by manufacturing . . . Therefore when the Japanese political and economic systems have been democratized and their aggressive character wiped out, the nation's heavy industries should be allowed to grow to a considerable extent . . . As Japanese heavy industries are certain to be subjected to international competition in the future on the one hand, and because the benefit of adequate governmental protection as experienced in the past will become difficult to obtain on the other hand, they will have to cultivate—through the rationalization of management and the elevation of technological levels—the ability to withstand the competition from foreign goods in terms of production costs as well. (pp.111–112, 114)

Strategic orientations of this report—real-sector concerns, long-term industrial goals, selecting priority sectors, serious attention to concrete details, desire to produce new dynamic comparative advantages, and so on—are common to Japan's development cooperation philosophy even today. And it is quite different from the strategy often advocated by the IMF and the World Bank that puts macroeconomic stabilization, liberalization, openness and good governance before pragmatic discussion of leading sectors for output recovery and growth. For example, when Professor Kaneda Tatsuo submitted policy recommendations to Kyrgyzstan (Kaneda, 1992), when Professor Ishikawa Shigeru wrote a diagnostic report on Vietnam (JICA, 1995), when the Japanese government made a new proposal to Africa (JICA and JBIC, 2008) and when the present author advises the Ethiopian government

(GRIPS Development Forum, 2016), the logical sequence is very similar to that of the Basic Problems report. While initial conditions and targeted industries may differ from one country to another, procedure to identify and study them remains common.

Many people were inspired by the Basic Problems Report even though its recommendations were not formally adopted by the government. Indirectly, however, the idea that "limited resources must be selectively used for restarting an expansionary reproduction cycle" was put into practice via the Priority Production System directed by Professor Arisawa Hiromi, one of the members of the study group (see below).

Stopping inflation

Inflation peaked in 1946 and persisted in triple digits until 1949 (see Figure 10.2). The cause was clear: monetization of the fiscal deficit. The fiscal deficit in turn was generated by the following two policies. First, subsidies were directed mainly at industrial inputs such as coal, steel, copper and fertilizer but some were targeted at consumer goods, especially food. Price controls were imposed, and the government provided production subsidies (called "compensation for price gaps") to cover the losses incurred by private producers. Second, the Recovery Financial Fund (*fukkin*) loans were poured into designated priority industries, in particular the coal industry. They were provided by the Ministry of Finance financed by issuance of government bonds (fukkin bonds). Most of the bonds were directly purchased by the Bank of Japan, which increased money supply.

Economists debated, and still debate, the merits and demerits of these policies. From the viewpoint of stopping inflation, massive subsidies and policy loans were clearly undesirable

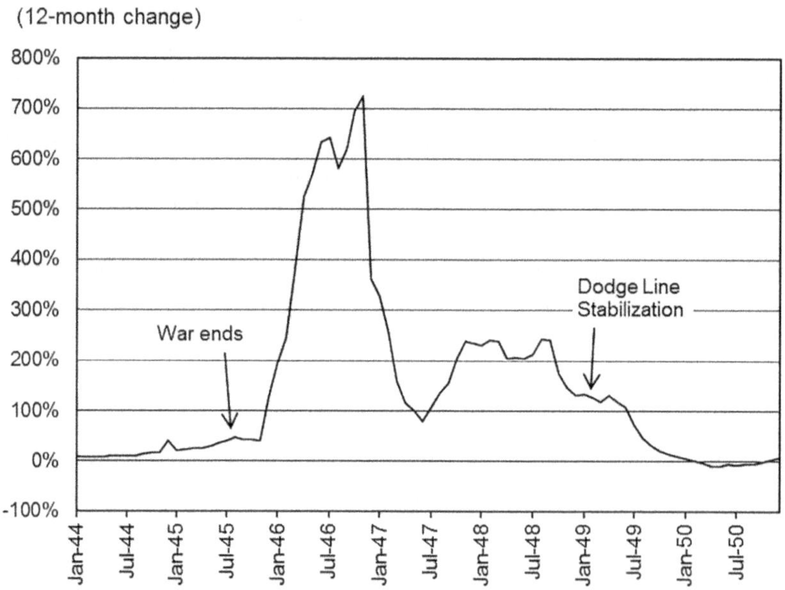

Figure 10.2 Retail price inflation in Tokyo

Source: Management and Coordination Agency, *Historical Statistics of Japan*, Vol. 4, 1988.

and had to be terminated as soon as possible. But from the viewpoint of real sector recovery, a delicate balance had to be struck between fighting inflation and sustaining output. Cutting these subsidies and loans immediately might have killed all remaining industrial activities.

The first attempt to stop inflation was the deposit blockade of 1946. The government suddenly announced that (i) everyone now had an upper limit of 500 yen per month for the withdrawal of bank deposits; and (ii) circulating paper notes would be annulled unless they were deposited at the bank. Thus, people were forced to keep their money at the bank while inflation continued. This reduced money supply to one-third and slowed inflation temporarily. But people naturally felt betrayed by the government and the credibility of monetary policy was lost. Soon, inflation accelerated again because the root cause—subsidies and fukkin loans—was not removed.

After the failure of the deposit blockade, different approaches to disinflation were proposed and hotly debated. Contested ideas included the following.

1 *Accepting inflation*—in July 1946, Finance Minister Ishibashi Tanzan stated that budget deficits and high inflation were acceptable as long as they prevented further output decline and unemployment. According to him, the present inflation was caused by supply shortage rather than excess demand. Macroeconomic policy must support producers and workers. A sound budget in such a situation meant accepting fiscal deficits and high inflation.
2 *Shock approach*—in January 1948, Kimura Kihachiro, a socialist Member of Parliament, argued quite the opposite. He considered price stability as the precondition for output recovery. As long as inflation continued, hoarding of goods in anticipation of higher prices would never cease. This would reduce supply and raise prices even more. A bold anti-inflation policy was required to stop this vicious circle. The United States government in Washington also shared this view.
3 *Gradualism*—the Economic Stabilization Board, as well as General MacArthur of the GHQ, feared that big-bang stabilization would devastate Japanese industries and lead to social crisis. They hoped to lower inflation step by step using subsidies, fukkin loans and American aid, and reducing these support measures over time.
4 *Conditional shock approach*—Professor Arisawa Hiromi of Tokyo University recognized that an anti-inflation policy would reduce output temporarily. But he also knew that inflation had to be eliminated to end speculation and hoarding. He proposed that *output should be raised by the planning method to 60 percent of the prewar level, then a strong anti-inflation package should be adopted.* Output would probably fall back to about 30 percent of the prewar level, but people could somehow endure this level, which actually prevailed in 1946. If the anti-inflation policy was implemented too soon, without such initial output recovery, the shock would be too severe.

The policy that was eventually adopted turned out to be close to what Professor Arisawa proposed.

Priority Production System, 1947–48

The Priority Production System (PPS) refers to a policy of concentrating scarce resources in a few strategically important sectors to jump-start an economy. Although it is called a "system," it is actually a policy based on planning method. Recovery of key sectors is expected to have positive spillover effects on the entire economy.

Arisawa was a member of the personal advisory group of Prime Minister Yoshida Shigeru. In July 1946, General MacArthur said that he would allow Japan to import a small number of goods.[4] Yoshida ordered bureaucrats to prepare a wish list for imports, but the list they produced was too long. Yoshida asked his advisors to shorten it. The following five items finally remained: steel, coal (anthracite), heavy oil, rubber and buses.

MacArthur would not allow Japan to import heavy oil, an item in short supply globally. But Arisawa urged Prime Minister Yoshida to renegotiate with the GHQ, by promising that if Japan was permitted to import heavy oil, the Japanese government would ensure that 30 million tons of coal would be produced. Heavy oil was an input to steel production, and steel was needed to rehabilitate coal mines. For Japan, coal was the only energy source available domestically. If enough coal was produced, surplus could be distributed as an energy input to other industries.

MacArthur agreed to let Japan import heavy oil under this condition. Arisawa, who proposed the idea, became the chairman of the subcommittee responsible for producing 30 million tons of coal.[5] Arisawa's method was meticulous. He summoned the general directors and chief engineers of all coal mines in Japan to gather necessary information. Based on available coal deposits, veins, extraction speed, working hours and so on, he calculated the supply capacity. On the demand side, he estimated the possible coal use by the Americans, power companies, railroads and industries.

"Dig 30 million tons of coal" became a national slogan. The Minister of Commerce and Industry visited the Joban Mine to cheer workers and be photographed. In the streets of large cities, the daily output of coal was posted. An evening radio program sent words of thanks to hard-working coal miners all over Japan. The government secured inputs for coal mines using subsidies and fukkin loans, and offered special housing for coal miners. Although the delivery of imported heavy oil was delayed, the production goal of coal was more or less realized. Domestic coal production in 1947 was 29.32 million tons. The output of key industries other than coal fell slightly short of targets in 1947. The economy began to rebound. The PPS was continued in 1948 and most targets were achieved in that year. But inflation was still high.

US policy in occupied Japan

Japan was under US occupation from 1945 to 1951. Japan regained independence after the San Francisco Peace Treaty was signed in September 1951 and became effective in April 1952. During the occupation period, US policy toward Japan shifted significantly.

Initially, the objective of occupation was demilitarization of Japan. The United States wanted to cripple the Japanese economy so it would never be able to produce military goods again. No heavy industry was to be allowed, and remaining machines were to be stripped and shipped to the rest of Asia as reparations in kind. However, these policies were not actually implemented. The GHQ was also keen to introduce democracy in Japan since the lack of democracy, such as business monopolies, absence of workers' rights and exploitation of poor farmers, was considered to have propelled Japan's militarism. The following three democratic reforms were executed by the order of the GHQ.

- *Zaibatsu breakup*—big businesses were accused of helping militarism during the war. Group companies were broken up into separate entities. However, this policy was later reversed and a new type of industrial group, called *keiretsu*, emerged. Keiretsu is a collection of business establishments without a holding company.[6]
- *New labor laws*—the new laws guaranteed workers' rights to organizing labor unions, collective bargaining and basic working conditions.
- *Land reform*—the initial plan of 1945 was rejected by the GHQ and a more radical plan of 1946 was adopted. It was implemented mainly in 1947 and 1948 affecting 6 million families, of which 2 million were losers. All farmland holdings above 1 ha (4 ha for Hokkaido) were confiscated and sold to actual tillers. The sales price was low and high inflation quickly eroded its real value. This increased the land ownership of farmers from 54 percent to 91 percent, which was good from the viewpoint of justice and equity, but land was now divided into too many small plots, which was bad for efficiency. Family farming on a small scale has become the dominant trait of Japanese agriculture ever since.

In addition, a new constitution was drafted and implemented on May 3, 1947 under the pressure and guidance from the GHQ. Japan now celebrates May 3 as a national holiday. Compared with the Meiji Constitution of 1889, the following features are noteworthy:

- Sovereignty rests with the people.
- The emperor is a symbol of Japan with no political functions.
- Renunciation of war and non-possession of military forces (Article 9).
- Guarantee of basic human rights.
- Separation of power among legislative, administrative and judicial branches.

In particular, Article 9 is unique to Japan and has caused many heated arguments ever since. The full text of Article 9 runs as follows:

> Aspiring sincerely to an international peace based on justice and order, the Japanese people forever renounce war as a sovereign right of the nation and the threat or use of force as means of settling international disputes.
>
> In order to accomplish the aim of the preceding paragraph, land, sea, and air forces, as well as other war potential, will never be maintained. The right of belligerency of the state will not be recognized.

Although the possession of armed forces is explicitly prohibited by this Article, Japan later established the Ground, Maritime and Air Self-Defense Forces (SDF) in 1954. The government explained that the constitution did not rule out self-defense, and that the SDF was a minimal power and not military forces. Hardliners want to revise Article 9 so Japan can legally own military forces without an acrobatic interpretation of the constitution.[7] Others want to keep Article 9 as it is and abolish the SDF.

Around 1947, US occupation policy shifted dramatically because of the start of the Cold War. The US government now wanted to strengthen Japan as a capitalist ally and an anti-communist base. Besides that, generous economic aid to Japan was becoming too burdensome for American taxpayers. Remilitarization and the economic recovery of Japan, including rebuilding of heavy industries, were promoted. Socialist and labor movements were discouraged. The establishment of the SDF mentioned above was also in line with this revised US strategy.

It must also be noted that a policy gap existed within the US government. Washington demanded free markets and big-bang macroeconomic stabilization in Japan as soon as possible, but General MacArthur and his GHQ staff in Tokyo, who were dubbed "New Dealers," a group of people who supported official intervention at the time of the Great Depression in the 1930s, preferred gradualism with appropriate state roles.

Dodge Line stabilization of 1949

This debate within the US government was ended when Washington sent Joseph Dodge to Tokyo in early 1949. Dodge was the president of Detroit Bank and a strong believer in the free market economy. He ordered the following austerity measures to terminate inflation. His policy package was called the "Dodge Line":

- stop fukkin loans;
- abolish all subsidies and raise public utility charges;
- strengthen taxation and cut expenditure;
- achieve a "super-balanced budget"—the primary balance should be zero, which means the normal budget should be in surplus;
- unify multiple exchange rates at 360 yen to the dollar.

In addition, Professor Carl C. Shoup, an American fiscal expert, was also dispatched to Japan to introduce a new tax system. His advice was adopted in 1950. It was a system with heavy reliance on direct taxes, especially income and corporate taxes, that became a key feature of the Japanese tax system for a long time to follow.[8] As a result, Japan had no broad-based indirect tax, such as VAT or general consumption tax, until 1989.

The Dodge Line stabilization was very successful in stopping inflation. But as feared, the negative shock on economic activity was severe and people expected a serious recession following austerity measures. Indeed, output soon began to decline. The Bank of Japan ignored the instruction of Dodge and supplied liquidity to ameliorate the coming recession. Professor Arisawa, the inventor of PPS, also felt that stabilization measures were adopted too soon. He hoped that Dodge should have waited another year, until 1950.

We do not know how serious this recession would have been because another big event intervened. The Korean War broke out between North Korea, backed by China, and South Korea, backed by the West, in June 1950 and lasted until 1953. It was one serious incident of the Cold War turning hot. Whatever the political implications of this war might have been, its impact on the Japanese economy was positive. The US forces regarded Japan as a supply base and procured great amounts of military and non-military goods and services such as metals, machinery, textiles, construction, and maintenance and repair services for automobiles and machinery. For Japanese industries, this was tantamount to a sharp increase in external demand, just as the great export boom experienced during WW1. The recession caused by austerity measures ended quickly and the Japanese economy began to expand. Minor inflation also returned, but price stability was restored when the Korean War ended.

The Dodge Line stabilization also had important systemic implications. The Japanese economy had been under state planning since 1937 and economic control was maintained during the postwar recovery period of 1945–49. The achievement of price stability and the abolition of price controls and subsidies finally allowed Japan to return to a market economy. Japan was now ready for economic deregulation, and the role of government could be reduced. However, this by no means meant a return to a completely free economy as many elements of official intervention remained even after the end of planning (Chapter 11).

Among academics, Joseph Dodge is sometimes appreciated for ending inflation and restoring economic freedom, and sometimes criticized for implementing a shock therapy (although its undesirable effect was cancelled by the Korean War). But most Japanese people then would have thanked him rather than blamed him.

Box 10.1 Arisawa Hiromi and Okita Saburo discuss postwar recovery

Below is an excerpt from a dialogue that took place in 1986 between Arisawa Hiromi (1896–1988) and Okita Saburo (1914–1993), two gentlemen who were deeply involved in the postwar recovery policies as explained in the main text (quoted from Arisawa, 1989, pp. 33–34).

Okita: What was your opinion on the nationalization of the coal industry [proposed around 1946–47]?

Arisawa: As for me, I never thought of nationalizing it.

Okita: Wasn't it at the time of Minister of Commerce and Industry Mizutani Chosaburo, when a law on the nationalization of coal mines was proposed?

Arisawa: I never thought of nationalization. As a matter of fact, Japanese coal mines were already operating under government's directives. Therefore, coal mines were virtually under state control. Germany nationalized coal production, and I discussed the matter extensively in many articles. But I had no intention of nationalizing our coal mines. Of course, if some unexpected situation arose, nationalization would have been an option. But what was the point of nationalizing only coal?

Okita: Around that time, there was a debate over the so-called *Chukan Antei Ron* [intermediate stabilization, which means gradual disinflation] between you and Mr. Kimura, a socialist Member of Parliament. Your idea was to stop inflation after the government permitted output to recover to a certain level relative to the prewar size. But Mr. Kimura regarded disinflation as the prerequisite for output recovery. That was the key point in the debate. You wrote in an article that the two views differed in the prioritization of policies. It certainly was a big difference, from the viewpoint of your "economics of transition."

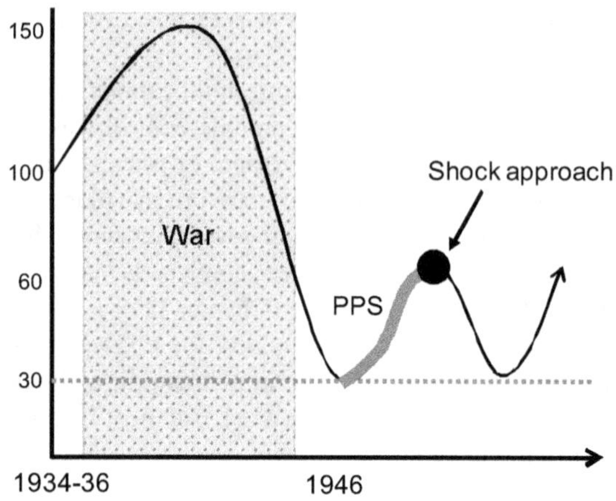

Figure 10.3 Priority Production System in theory (production index)

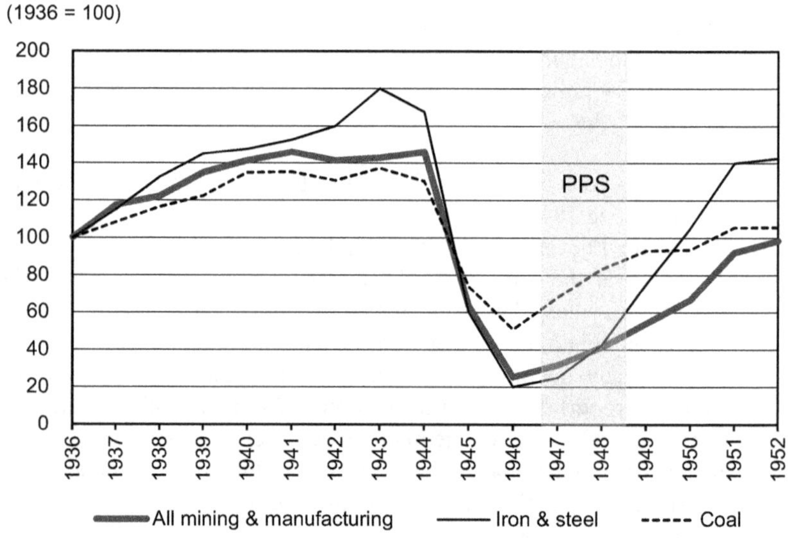

Figure 10.4 Priority Production System in practice (production index)

Source: Management and Coordination Agency, Historical Statistics of Japan, Vol. 2, 1988.

Arisawa: Regarding the disinflation policy, my view at that time was to adopt the Priority Production System first to let the production recover to 60 percent of the prewar level, then stop the inflation by bold measures. If big-bang disinflation were introduced before output recovery, it would have plunged the Japanese economy into a tremendous confusion, so it should not have been done. In either case, inflation stabilization would cause the output to decline. The crucial point was how deep we would sink. Bold stabilization measures were unavoidable, but the timing must be chosen wisely, at a time when the Priority Production System proceeded further and the output reached 60 percent of the prewar level.

My view was that bold stabilization would surely cause output to decline. Under the worst scenario, the output might even decline to a half. I insisted on a recovery to 60 percent of the prewar level, because if you had that level, the subsequent output decline would take it to 30 percent of the prewar level. Since output actually fell to that level immediately after the war and people could somehow survive, to me that was the minimum acceptable level.

Before Mr. Dodge arrived in Japan, I went to see Mr. Fein, financial advisor of the GHQ's Economic and Science Bureau. His position was that Japan needed a big-bang anti-inflation program. I told him that it was too early to implement it. He tried to persuade me into early stabilization, but I never relented. The logic I have just explained was behind my insistence.

Notes

1 Economic Stabilization Board, *A Comprehensive Report on the War Damage of Japan Caused by the Pacific War*, 1949.

2 The informal sector refers to the collection of jobs that are not officially registered or permitted, such as street peddlers, personal service providers and household works in contrast to legally sanctioned enterprises and cooperatives. Since it operates in a grey zone between legal and illegal, its status remains uncertain, being subject to official round-ups and confiscation, and without protection of workers' rights or contract enforcement. For the same reason, there is little incentive for physical asset formation. An informal sector tends to emerge in a country in crisis or whose market economy is underdeveloped or temporarily paralyzed.

3 This report is now available in English translation—see Saburo Okita, ed., *Postwar Reconstruction of the Japanese Economy*, University of Tokyo Press, 1992.

4 During the war, the Japanese government guaranteed compensation for any losses incurred by individuals or firms engaged in military production. In July 1946, the GHQ ordered the cancellation of this guarantee which drove a large number of firms into bankruptcy and default. Prime Minister Yoshida appealed to General MacArthur on the difficulties caused by this decision, to which MacArthur responded by allowing Japan to import certain products to ameliorate the situation.

5 In parallel, the Ministry of Commerce and Industry was contemplating a similar plan. Some argue that the idea of PPS originally belonged to the Ministry, not Arisawa, but the truth is difficult to tell.

6 *Zaibatsu* is a group of large companies operating in many sectors that are owned by one holding company dominated by an influential family. *Keiretsu* is a looser collection of companies without a holding company at the top, whose member companies are related to each other through cooperation in finance and technology, mutual shareholding, staff rotation, monthly lunch meetings of general directors and the like. In postwar Japan, holding companies were prohibited by the anti-monopoly law until 1997 when they were again permitted. A pyramidal subcontracting structure in the automobile and motorcycle industries is also called a system of *keiretsu* companies.

7 More recently, the second Abe Cabinet (2014–) is working toward a more active military role of Japan in self-defense and international contribution. In July 2014, the Right of Collective Self-defense (the SDF to assist US forces under enemy attack) was approved by a cabinet decision. In July 2015, parliament passed a bundle of laws to allow the SDF to go abroad (until then, ad hoc laws were created for individual operations in different countries). Prime Minister Abe also talks about the possibility of constitutional amendment.

8 Prior to the Shoup reform, the tax system was revised in 1937, 1938, 1940 and 1947. Wartime Japan was moving toward strengthening direct taxes with its share in central government revenue rising from 22.8 percent in 1935 to 53.9 percent in 1940. This should be construed as an effort to raise sufficient revenue for war execution under the situation of suppressed consumption and disappearance of international trade. The Shoup reform in 1950 continued in this direction but his strong influence in firmly installing a direct tax-based system in postwar Japan can hardly be disputed. This is so even when many individual items in Shoup's advice were weakened in the tax revision of 1953.

11

THE HIGH GROWTH ERA

From devastation to high income

After the postwar recovery (1945–49) and the Korean War (1950–53), the Japanese economy entered a period of high growth. From the mid 1950s to the early 1970s, average real growth was approximately 10 percent. This high and sustained growth—interlaced by short recessions—greatly transformed the Japanese economy and society. In 1945, most of the major Japanese cities were destroyed by US bombing. In the 1950s reconstruction was under way and Japan rejoined the international community. In the 1960s as growth further accelerated, Japan built fast trains and hosted the Summer Olympic Games. By 1970, Japan overtook West Germany in economic size and became the second largest economy in the capitalist world after the United States. This was the second time Japan accomplished miraculous growth from the very bottom to the top. The industrial revolution of Meiji took half a century, but this miracle took only about two decades (Figure 11.1).

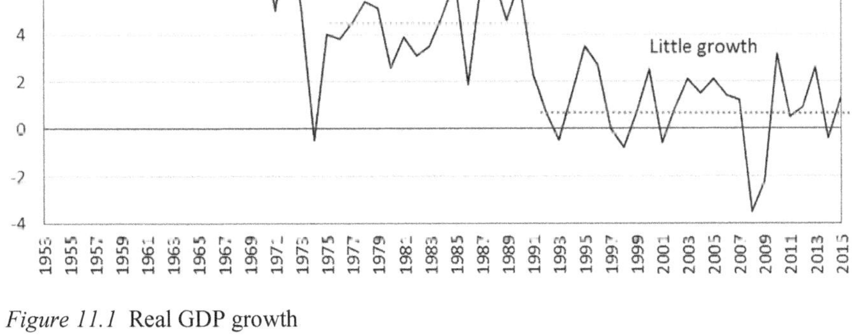

Figure 11.1 Real GDP growth

Source: Cabinet Office website.

Note: Fiscal year based growth (April to March). Gaps exist in the definition of GDP in 1981 and 1995 due to revisions of the System of National Accounts.

DOI: 10.4324/9781315444048-12

It should be noted that post-WW2 growth momentum did not stop until Japan reached high income. While problems and short-term business cycles were encountered along the way, no structural impediment emerged that was serious enough to stall Japan's growth at middle income. This is in sharp contrast to the situations seen in many emerging and developing economies today that seem to have been stuck in "middle-income traps." Productivity increase was high, continuous and institutionalized. Consumption and investment were strong. The macroeconomy and the speed of global integration were well managed. Negative aspects of high growth, such as pollution and urban congestion, were overcome eventually if not immediately. Externally, US-led global economic growth and stability combined with fixed exchange rates and trade liberalization worked very favorably with Japanese exports.

Post-WW2 Japan chose to be under the American nuclear umbrella for national security. Japan regained independence with the signing of the San Francisco Peace Treaty in 1951 and its implementation in 1952. At the same time, the Japan–US Security Treaty was concluded in 1951 (and renewed in 1960), and Japan became a faithful US ally in the Cold War.

There are many issues to be discussed in this remarkable period. The remainder of this chapter will focus on rationalization, shifting policy focus, global reintegration, macroeconomic management, private dynamism, industrial policy and social transformation.

Rationalization

During the period of 1945–49, economic planning of the war years was basically retained, and Japan was practically a closed economy. The principal policy objective at that time was quantitative recovery. Recovery was pursued at any cost, ignoring efficiency. Generous subsidies, fukkin loans and US aid were provided (Chapter 10).

By the early 1950s, the Japanese economy entered another phase. An upward trend in economic growth had been secured thanks to the Priority Production System and other support measures. High inflation was stopped thanks to the Dodge Line stabilization. Shortages and black market prices began to disappear. Private international trade resumed. As a result, Japan reached a stage where it could finally end planning, heavy subsidies and tight controls initiated in 1937 and restore the market mechanism as a central economic force. However, this was not necessarily an installation of a free market economy as many past legacies, such as exchange control, import protection, foreign currency surrender requirement and administrative guidance, were to be removed only gradually, as explained below.

There was a global inflation associated with the Korean War and, due to proximity to the war front and involvement in war procurement, Japanese inflation was higher than the world average (Figure 11.2). Between 1949 and 1951, Japanese wholesale prices (covering industrial inputs) rose 64 percent and consumer prices rose 8.5 percent. In the same period, wholesale prices in the United States and the United Kingdom increased only 16 percent and 11 percent, respectively. The new fixed exchange rate of 360 yen to the dollar was considered appropriate when it was established in 1949. But with the appearance of Korean War inflation differentials, the yen became overvalued and Japanese industrial inputs overpriced. Coal and steel, the two priority goods previously targeted by the Priority Production System, were among the most expensive. The "problem of high prices of coal and steel" emerged, reducing the competitiveness of all other industries that used them as inputs. Japanese industries now had to strive for efficiency and competitiveness. The days of physical expansion under generous support and international isolation were over, and the challenge for cost reduction and higher quality began.[1]

To cope with difficulties caused by the overvaluation in the early 1950s, three policy options were theoretically possible: (i) yen devaluation; (ii) deliberate deflation through macroeconomic austerity and (iii) productivity improvement. At this time, the private sector and the government of Japan jointly chose the third option. Firms were determined to reduce cost and restore competitiveness by investing in newer and better technology. Option (i) was not even considered because it was just after Japan had unified exchange rates and joined the global fixed exchange rate system in 1949 as part of the overall reconstruction strategy. Japan felt it politically and diplomatically embarrassing to leave the newly installed global economic system so soon. Option (ii) was partly adopted by maintaining a relatively tight macroeconomic policy stance, nudging Japanese enterprises to adopt new technology without waiting for an official bailout. But this tightness was not as devastating as the austerity measures introduced by Finance Minister Inoue in the late 1920s to the early 1930s (Chapter 9).

Gorika, a Japanese word for rationalization, means improving productivity through investment in new technology and machinery and reorganizing production and management for efficiency. This became the hottest economic issue in the early 1950s. The government recognized the need for gorika and issued a cabinet decision, an official report and incentives for gorika. During the Korean War boom, many companies accumulated profits as American military procurement soared. Such retained profits were the main financial source for introducing new technology and machinery, which were supplemented by tax, tariff and depreciation allowance privileges to promote such investment. However, labor unions often opposed rationalization because they feared this slogan would be used as an excuse for laying off workers and imposing hard working conditions.

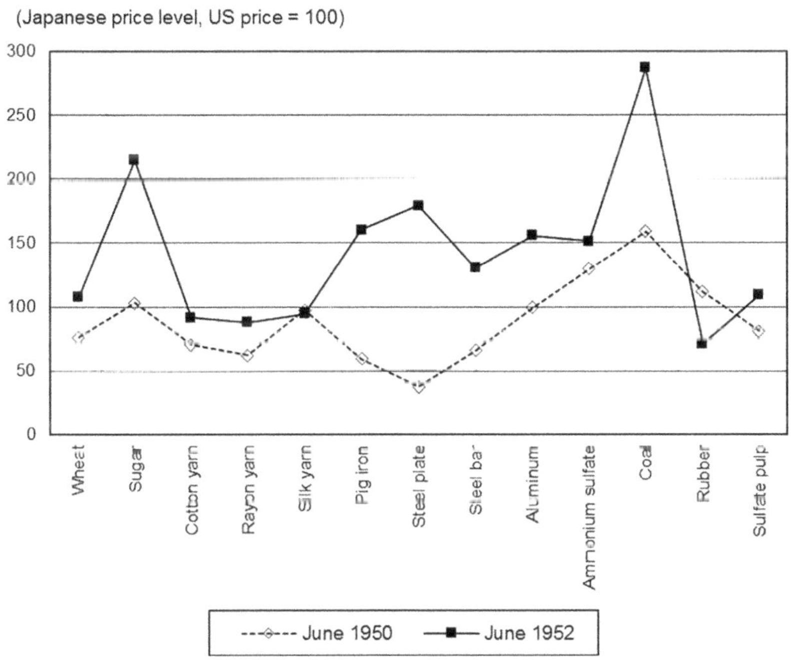

Figure 11.2 Japanese industrial prices relative to US prices

Source: Kosai (1995), p. 56.

Some industries succeeded in rationalization but others failed. Between coal and steel, the former turned out to be a loser and the latter a winner. Both contributed to a rise in overall productivity—the coal industry by disappearing and the steel industry by becoming more competitive. The coal industry was especially hard hit because the world energy source was shifting dramatically from coal to oil, which was then cheaper. Unlike coal which was abundant at home, Japan had little domestic supply of oil. It had to import 90 percent of oil in the early postwar period, and the ratio would subsequently rise to as high as 99.7 percent.

The steel industry adopted integrated steel making in place of fragmented old processes. Shipbuilders introduced the latest methods including arc welding, block construction, photo marking and automatic gas cutting. The fertilizer industry diversified gas sources and product types, and shifted to synthetic organic chemistry. Artificial fibers such as nylon and vinylon also began to be produced. Power companies were reorganized geographically, hydraulic power plants were built with the latest construction equipment and World Bank loans were mobilized to erect large-scale thermal power plants. In assembly-type industries such as automobile and electronics, new technologies were adopted and innovations were made. Toyota modernized its factories beginning in 1951 and Sony produced transistor radios in 1953.

The policy stance of the government was also crucial in promoting rationalization. As Korean War procurement ended and imports surged, Japan began to face intermittent recessions and balance-of-payments crises in 1951–54. The Bank of Japan raised interest rates, and the government budget and the fiscal investment and loan program (FILP)[2] were tightened. The intention of these policies was to lower inflation to near zero (finally!) and encourage industries to reduce costs further. This was quite different from the policy stance adopted after the end of the WW1 export boom in the 1920s. At that time, the main policy objective was to rescue weak firms and banks. In the 1950s, by contrast, Japanese enterprises were asked to become more efficient or leave. When an artificial boom ends and the business condition worsens, an appropriate degree of macroeconomic tightness is perhaps needed to prepare for the subsequent period of sustained high growth.

Another important fact about the early 1950s was the creation of new policy instruments suitable for the age of active industrial policy for guiding and supporting private dynamism instead of compulsory state planning. To replace the price controls, subsidies and fukkin loans of the early recovery period, the government introduced a foreign exchange budget (for allocating scarce foreign exchange), capital control, regulation for technology import, privileges and incentives for priority industries, establishment of new policy banks such as the Japan Development Bank, the Long-term Credit Bank and the Export–Import (Exim) Bank for supplying long-term investment funds, as well as a number of laws for promoting rationalization as mentioned above. Equipped with these policy tools, the government in general and the Ministry of International Trade and Industry (MITI—see below) in particular were now ready to assist industrial development. Some even argue that the high growth of postwar had Japan already begun in the early 1950s. However, it is more appropriate to regard these years as a preparatory period for high growth to come in the mid 1950s and beyond.

From politics to economics

The year 1960 was a dividing year in postwar Japan. A major labor dispute at Mitsui Miike Coal Mine, located in Kyushu and operated by the Mitsui Group, came to a climax.

The management announced a lay-off program of workers targeted at labor union leaders to carry out rationalization. In protest, coal miners, their families and sympathizers occupied hopper facilities. The company in turn locked out workers. This was considered an ultimate fight between all capitalists and all workers in Japan, in which the miners lost eventually. Another big event in 1960 was a renewal of the Japan–US Security Treaty. The Kishi Nobusuke Cabinet of the Liberal Democratic Party (LDP) tried to force it through parliament despite nationwide protests. A huge demonstration was staged around the parliament and one female student was killed. But the treaty was renewed and the Kishi government subsequently resigned for causing the mess.

With these two events, the days of direct ideological confrontation in Japan between capital and labor as well as between allegiance to the United States and the Communist block were over. Japan was to stay in the capitalist camp and labor was to cooperate for economic growth. The new LDP government of Ikeda Hayato refocused national attention from politics to economics by launching the "Income Doubling Plan." He proposed to double Japan's Gross National Product (GNP)[3] in ten years which required an average annual growth of 7.2 percent. Japan actually grew faster than this and Ikeda's goal was achieved within six to seven years, far sooner than expected.

From 1955 to 1970, labor productivity in the manufacturing sector annually rose 10.0 percent, wages at large and medium firms (employing 30 workers or more) rose 10.2 percent, and wages at small firms rose 10.9 percent. As living conditions improved greatly for almost everyone, social stability and labor discipline were maintained. Virtually all Japanese people came to feel that they belonged to the middle class. Under these circumstances, political radicalism gradually gave way to a more cooperative management–labor relationship. There were some remnants of student and left-wing movements calling for violent revolution into the early 1970s, but they lost the support of the general public.

Reintegration into the world economy

In 1951, US occupation ended and political independence was restored, which became effective in 1952. The milestones of Japan's reintegration into the world economy included membership of the IMF and the World Bank in 1952, membership of the General Agreement on Tariffs and Trade (GATT, the predecessor of WTO, although Japan was not immediately given full rights), and membership of the United Nations in 1956. A little later, in 1963, Japan became the GATT Article XI country which prohibited the use of import restriction for balance-of-payments reasons, and the system of foreign exchange allocation was also terminated. In 1964, Japan was admitted to the Organization for Economic Co-operation and Development (OECD) and assumed the IMF Article VIII status, which means Japan was no longer permitted to use exchange restrictions on current-account transactions (i.e., for import protection). Also in 1964, Japan hosted the Tokyo Olympics. For any emerging nation, hosting Olympic Games boosts national pride and enhances its standing in the international community.

Meanwhile, trade liberalization proceeded gradually and in steps. As discussed above, the Dodge Line stabilization and the return to the market mechanism in 1949 did not immediately remove all controls. On the contrary, many measures continued to regulate markets, and one of them was import protection. Japan's trade barriers had been high during the 1920s and 1930s, and international trade was nonexistent during the Pacific War (1941–45) and severely restricted under the US occupation (1945–51). When private trade was restored in the 1950s, tariff protection remained high. However, the Japanese government was determined to lower tariffs in an effort to rejoin the world economy and implement the GATT Kennedy Round that required comprehensive tariff reduction by all member countries. Transition to a more liberal trade system was also necessitated for political and diplomatic reasons.

Japan's trade liberalization mainly in the 1960s had the following features. First, it was executed gradually and in a well-planned manner with prior announcement. Second, tariff reduction was closely linked with promotion measures to strengthen competitiveness. Third, the government used international commitments to avoid domestic political capture. Removal of import barriers was carried out under the strong "ownership" (policy initiative) of the Japanese government in consultation with the business community. Since trade liberalization plans were pre-committed and regarded as non-negotiable, producers had to make efforts in improving efficiency rather than lobbying for an extension of protection. Official support was provided according to actual performance, such as export volume, rather than political connection. Producers competed fiercely with each other, but competition was managed by the government so as to prevent elimination or bankruptcy of any firm. Murakami (1984) termed such officially guided coexistence of competition and cooperation among leading producers as "compartmentalized competition." Postwar Japan employed trade liberalization as a device to force domestic industries to become competitive, which is an ideal way to combine industrial policy and international integration. But its success required a very high institutional capacity including the competency of MITI to conduct arms-length intervention and deep trust and close communication between the government and the private sector. For most developing countries, this is not an easy task.

Although trade barriers were thus gradually reduced, capital control was not abolished during the high growth period. It was removed step by step from the 1970s onwards. The most important step in liberalizing capital transactions was the Foreign Exchange Law of 1980, which belongs to a later period than the one we are discussing.

Japan joined the World Bank in 1952 and borrowing started in the following year. It soon became the World Bank's second largest borrower after India. Japan continued to borrow from the World Bank until 1969 using all loans for building industrial infrastructure such as power plants, highways and the Shinkansen (bullet trains). Unlike current global development policy, no part of the loans was directed toward education, healthcare, rural development or other social-sector programs. In a procedure called "two-step loans," World Bank funds were made available first to the Japan Development Bank, which on-lent them to proposed industrial projects. It is also worth noting that World Bank loans covered less than 1 percent of Japan's total domestic investment demand. Japan in the high growth period financed its enormous investment demand almost entirely from domestic savings. There was virtually no receipt of FDI, let alone portfolio capital (investments in Japanese bonds and stocks), from abroad. Though development funds were generated at home, Japanese firms were extremely eager to import advanced technology from abroad, and the government strongly supported it.

Macroeconomic management

During the 1950s and 60s, macroeconomic management had the following features.

The government budget was generally sound and in surplus. In addition, the size of government relative to GNP gradually declined, especially during the 1950s (Figure 11.3). Monetization of fiscal deficits was prohibited. In fact, no government bonds were issued in postwar Japan until 1965. For this reason, there exist no statistics on government bonds or their interest rates prior to that time.

The fixed exchange rate of 360 yen to the dollar was maintained from 1949 to 1971. The Bretton Woods exchange rate system permitted occasional realignments of exchange parities when "fundamental disequilibria" existed.[4] Britain, West Germany and France made use of this clause, but Japan never considered changing its exchange parity. Some people argued that the yen became increasingly undervalued in real terms because Japanese productivity rose faster—and thus Japanese costs became lower—compared with other industrial nations. However, it must be recalled that Japanese productivity and wages were rising at similar high speeds, about 10 percent per year each, during the high growth period, which is exactly what should be expected in a world of well-functioning fixed exchange rates (McKinnon and Ohno, 1997). An emerging nation in the process of rapid industrial catchup naturally expands its global market not only because of cheapness of its products but more because of increasing product diversity, improved quality and aggressive marketing which wins the hearts of world consumers. Exchange rate adjustments alone can hardly reverse the dynamism of a rising nation driven by productivity and deep structural change. This was true for postwar Japan as well as China in more recent decades.

Monetary policy of the Bank of Japan was constrained by its commitment to the Bretton Woods fixed exchange rate system. Technically, this is called the "endogeneity" of monetary policy in a fixed exchange rate regime. A fixed exchange rate does not automatically happen; it must be supported by the central bank which uses its policy instruments to keep the rate at the pre-set level. In postwar Japan, this policy constraint exhibited itself in the following manner.

Because there was no free international capital movement during the high growth period, a balance-of-payments deficit essentially meant a trade deficit (imports exceeding exports). When the Japanese economy overheated and imports surged, the Bank of Japan tightened domestic financial markets by raising short-term interest rates as well as through "window guidance" (telling commercial banks to reduce new loans). This made it difficult for firms to

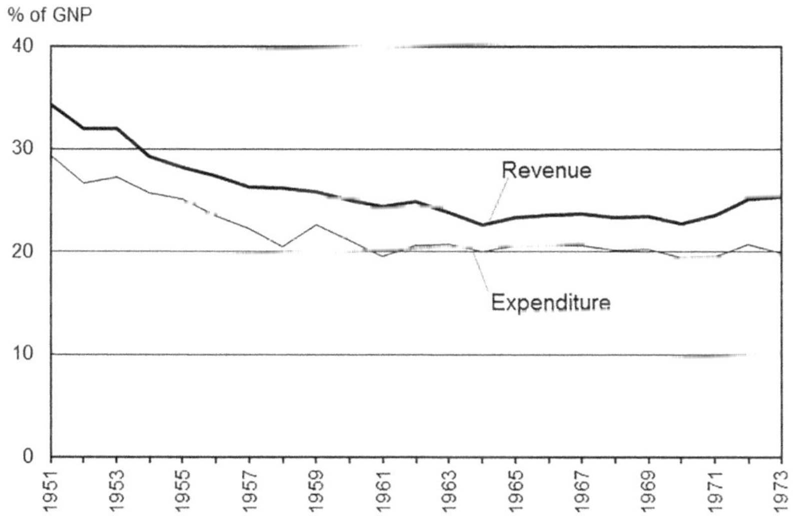

Figure 11.3 Central government revenue and expenditure

Source: Management and Coordination Agency, *Historical Statistics of Japan*, Vol. 3, 1988.

borrow from banks. Since Japanese firms in this period depended heavily on bank loans for business expansion, this had an immediate negative effect on investment. As the economy cooled down, imports fell and the balance-of-payments pressure eased. Every time the economy grew too strongly, the Bank of Japan resorted to this policy. This was called the "ceiling of the balance of payments" or "stop–go policy" which was the standard policy procedure until the mid 1960s (Figure 11.2).

In sum, the Bank of Japan chose domestic macroeconomic tightening (monetary contraction) for balance-of-payments adjustment. In contrast, West Germany adopted a quite different mode of macroeconomic adjustment. The Deutsche Bundesbank frequently intervened in the foreign exchange market and occasionally even adjusted the Deutsche Mark exchange rate in an upward direction. As a result, West Germany accumulated international reserves through purchasing dollars, while Japanese international reserves remained small until the mid 1960s (after that, the Bank of Japan also intervened aggressively in foreign exchange and rapidly accumulated dollar assets).

Under the Bretton Woods international monetary system, Japanese wholesale prices (representing industrial inputs) were quite stable. From 1951 to 1971, the wholesale price index rose at an annual rate of 0.7 percent. This remarkable price stability was a global phenomenon also observed in the United States and West Germany. The early post-WW2 period was thus a time of historically unprecedented global price stability. Japan "imported" this stability from the United States by maintaining a fixed exchange rate and gradually liberalizing trade. Consumer prices rose slightly faster, at an annual rate of 4.4 percent. This was called "creeping inflation" and considered a problem, but it is impossible to have zero inflation on all prices when productivity—and cost—diverges across different sectors.[5] During the same period, nominal wages rose 10 to 11 percent, nominal GDP rose 14.5 percent, and money supply (measured by M1) rose 15.9 percent per annum. Meanwhile, real GDP grew an average of 9.4 percent per annum. These were impressive macroeconomic achievements.

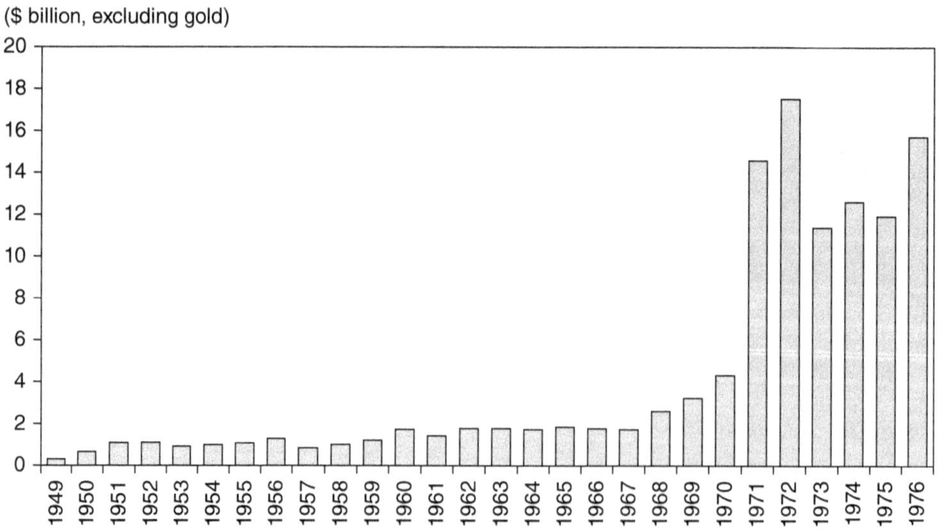

Figure 11.4 International reserves

Source: International Monetary Fund, *International Financial Statistics*, various issues.

Private dynamism

The postwar high growth was the result of re-ignited private dynamism that existed in the Japanese economy for a long time but was suppressed during the wartime. Given the artificially low starting point due to war defeat and supported by favorable international conditions, the Japanese private sector developed very rapidly both in quality and quantity. In this section we will take a look at *monozukuri* and *kaizen* which forged Japan's unique manufacturing and served as factors behind strong investment, consumption and productivity growth during the high growth period.

Monozukuri, which literally means "making things," is a term used to describe a specific value upheld by the majority of Japanese craftsmen as well as modern manufacturing firms. It is a sincere attitude toward production with pride, skill and dedication. It targets perfection, innovation and customer satisfaction as the ultimate goal of business enterprise, often disregarding company books and balance sheets. It is a spiritual quest similar to sword practice or a tea ceremony rather than a sheer profit-making venture. Japanese firms are surely after profits but they try to pursue them by conforming to monozukuri principles, not by any means. Allegiance to monozukuri spirit can instruct and discipline Japanese managers and engineers without any commandment from God, laws or government authorities. This attitude can be traced back to the Meiji, Edo and even earlier periods. In postwar Japan, excellent manufacturing firms were established or run by people full of monozukuri spirit including Matsushita Konosuke (the founder of Panasonic), Honda Soichiro (the founder of Honda), Ibuka Masaru and Morita Akio (the co-founders of Sony), as well as countless, but less famous, leaders of small and medium enterprises.

Even today, monozukuri spirit is alive and well in a vast majority of Japanese firms. Its characters, which become particularly visible when they go overseas, include the following. First, Japanese firms abroad are more manufacturing-oriented than Chinese, Korean, Singaporean or American firms which are more active in trade, property development, finance or professional services. Over half of Japanese overseas investors are manufacturers, and many others provide producer-supporting services such as business loans, logistics and industrial parks. Second, they routinely pursue zero defect, cost reduction and on-time delivery (called quality-cost-delivery (QCD) requirement). Third, the Japanese aim at long-term business relations and prosperity; they are usually the last to arrive in frontier countries but, once invested, they will not leave even with difficulties—whether political turmoil, recession, flooding, terrorism, or street violence. Fourth, because of this long-term orientation, most firms are willing to train local workers and teach local suppliers beyond the immediate need of operation, even at the risk of losing trained engineers through job hopping and talent poaching. Fifth, Japanese firms on average have a better record of complying with local laws and regulations regarding contracts, safety, labor rights, environment and so on even when they are unreasonable or inconsistent.

As one of the efforts toward respectable monozukuri, postwar Japan invented *kaizen* (meaning "improvement") which is a way of continuously improving efficiency at *gemba*—factories, shops, offices or farms where work actually takes place—through teamwork and without spending any money on new equipment. The purpose of kaizen is to eliminate *muda*, or any waste that does not add value whether it is overproduction, waiting, transport, processing, inventory, movement or defects ("seven muda" of the Toyota Production System). Kaizen usually starts with such mundane instructions as "Keep the factory floor and toilets clean," "Remove all unnecessary tools and materials" and "Place necessary things in marked positions for easy pickup," which are collectively taught as "Five S" (Seiri, Seiton, Seiso, Seiketsu and Shitsuke, translated as Sort, Straighten, Shine, Systematize and Standardize; other English renditions also exist). These are easier said than done but can produce miracles in productivity and cost reduction when everyone's mindset has been transformed and order and cleanliness rule the workplace. After learning Five S, firms normally proceed to quality control circles (QCCs), equipment layout, *mieruka* (visualization), suggestion system, automation, total quality control (TQC), total quality management (TQM), total productive maintenance (TPM) and other tools of productivity enhancement (GRIPS Development Forum, 2009).

Japan's kaizen movement began in the late 1950s when a new quality control method was imported from the United States. The management theories and lectures of Professors W. E. Deming and J. M. Juran had enormous impact. They were quickly assimilated and modified to create a uniquely Japanese way of efficiency improvement. Unlike the American original which relied heavily on statistics collection, the adapted method emphasized process orientation, worker participation and hands-on pragmatism. Kaizen spread rapidly to Japanese companies, large and small, to form the foundation of monozukuri. The movement was propelled by the dynamism of Japanese firms craving concrete instruments for achieving rationalization and competitiveness. It was assisted by three non-profit organizations—the Union of Japan Scientists and Engineers, the Japan Productivity Center and the Japan Management Association—which sponsored lectures, foreign tours, awards and other measures (Kikuchi, 2014). Subsequently, kaizen spread abroad as Japanese manufacturing firms expanded their production bases to the rest of the world. Kaizen is now one of the most common tools of Japanese industrial cooperation in developing countries.[6]

Quantity, not just quality, also supported economic growth in the 1950s and 1960s. Investment demand of Japanese firms was very strong in order to realize rationalization, modernization, scaling up and industrial linkage. Heavy industries greatly expanded as investments in mechanical sectors such as automobile, shipbuilding and electrical equipment induced investments in material and energy sectors such as steel, petrochemicals and thermal and nuclear power generation. Computers and numerical control were introduced to manufacturing, telecom, banking and transport services. High-rise buildings, highways and Shinkansen lines (fast trains) began to be constructed. Because corporate saving and share issue were hardly enough to satisfy extremely strong investment demand, bank loans became the dominant mode of raising investment funds. To respond to huge loan demand, commercial banks often lent out more than their deposits and covered the gap by borrowing from the Bank of Japan in a situation dubbed as "overloan." Gross capital formation hovered around 30–40 percent of GNP, peaking at 40.5 percent in 1961. Large firms merged to become even larger to enjoy scale merit and prepare for the removal of import protection. Zaibatsu groups, disbanded under US occupation, re-formed to become *keiretsu*, characterized by mutual cooperation without a holding company as a command post (see Chapter 10).

High growth was also accompanied by vigorous private consumption. Postwar recovery, land reform and high productivity growth enhanced people's income and desire for better material life. Even if workers were currently poor, they could look to a much better future for them and their children as wages rose about 10 percent per year. Households purchased popular consumer durables such as black-and-white TVs, refrigerators and washing machines in the late 1950s ("Three Sacred Treasures"), and color TVs, coolers (air-cons) and cars in the late 1960s ("Three Cs"). Motorization advanced rapidly as private cars overtook taxis in 1964, trucks surpassed railroads in freight transport in 1966, and car registration reached 10 million in 1967. As markets and production expanded, costs and prices declined, which further stimulated demand. The mass production system also generated a white-collar middle class who purchased these goods. This virtuous circle continued until the early 1970s.

There is still an argument about the true cause of high growth in the 1950s and 1960s. Some say that vigorous investment was the key. Others insist that it was export-driven. Still others, including Yoshikawa (1997), believe that the most important force was robust consumption. However, it is very difficult to single out one factor as the only cause since all variables were interrelated. Private consumption was certainly the largest component of expenditure GNP, at 50–60 percent, yet the engine of growth cannot be ascertained just by size.

MITI and industrial policy

The Ministry of International Trade and Industry (MITI) was created in 1949 by merging the Ministry of Trade and Industry, the Coal Agency and the International Trade Agency. Later in 2001, it was renamed to the Ministry of Economy, Trade and Industry (METI). Despite the name change, its broad authorities and functions remained essentially the same. MITI, the Ministry of Finance and the Economic Planning Agency (dissolved in 2001) formed the government trio to promote industrialization but the authority of MITI was broadest and most powerful.

From the mid 1950s to the early 1970s, MITI played a role in Japanese economic development, but economists still debate what exactly its role was. Was high growth achieved because of MITI or despite it? Some insist that MITI's policies were crucial for rapid growth while others argue that they were counterproductive, only to be overpowered by strong private dynamism. Still others say that MITI policies were neutral and insignificant. It is easy to cite Japanese industries that prospered without official promotion such as consumer electronics, cameras, motorbikes, pianos, watches and calculators. Others such as coal, aluminum refining, nuclear fusion and mainframe computers failed even with official support. But it is not so easy to draw a negative conclusion about MITI from this, because growth potential differed across industries and also because MITI often assisted "sunset" sectors, such as coal and aluminum refinery, for smooth downsizing and transfer of labor to other sectors.

As for the automobile industry, there was both rejection and acceptance of official intervention. MITI tried to merge automobile firms prior to trade liberalization because Japanese carmakers seemed too small and too numerous to compete effectively with the American Big Three. But car companies refused MITI's meddling, remained separate and did very well subsequently (see Box 11.1 on Honda at the end of this chapter). At the same time, it should be recalled that the automobile industry was protected with high tariffs in its early stage of development, and protection was lifted only gradually and when Japanese firms became competitive enough. The government also effectively supported numerous small-sized component suppliers which ultimately strengthened large car assemblers.

There are econometric studies on the effectiveness of MITI policies, but results remain inconclusive. Some studies ask whether targeted industries on average achieved higher growth than those without support while controlling for other factors. But for the reasons mentioned above, such a test cannot properly assess MITI's policy objective and outcome. Using statistical methods to estimate the impact of industrial policy is generally difficult because convincing "counterfactual" evidence (how Japanese industries would have developed without MITI's intervention) does not exist. The tentative conclusion of this book, based on a large number of facts and cases, is that private dynamism was the primary engine but policy also played a useful role in the postwar high growth period. This conclusion is basically the same as for Meiji industrialization much earlier.

Many of the industrial promotion measures adopted by the Japanese government were no different from those widely practiced elsewhere in the world. They included preferential taxes and subsidies; low-interest policy loans; assistance for technology import and R&D; small and medium business promotion; entry restriction and licensing for certain sectors; coordination of output, investment and exports; building infrastructure and industrial zones and areas; and geographic planning. While these were similar to policies adopted in other countries, MITI implemented them far more effectively than others. In addition, MITI also had a set of softer instruments for sharing information and encouraging, nudging and coordinating actions among various stakeholders. They included the creation of visions and targets; *shingikai* (deliberation councils); close links with and active use of business associations; administrative guidance and human networks through personnel rotation and *amakudari* (assumption of high posts in private firms under MITI's supervision after early retirement from MITI).[7]

MITI's policy is sometimes explained as targeting industries whose markets were expanding and whose productivity would rise rapidly (the "income elasticity criterion" and the "productivity criterion"). But this explanation is a bit too simple and obvious. Certainly, all governments would like to do this if it were possible. The real question is how MITI successfully collected relevant information, avoided wrong choices and mobilized private firms to action. In selecting priority industries, MITI did not rely on rigid formulas or econometric models. It fully utilized soft and often informal channels listed above to talk to businesses. What is most amazing is the fact that crucial information and agreements naturally emerged in MITI's daily contacts with the private sector. MITI also knew the diverse intentions of individual firms and mediated among them. It can even be said that MITI and private firms chose "winners" jointly for promotion. Industrial targeting of this type, backed by intense public–private interaction, is quite different from the often-criticized "picking the winner" strategy by a government with limited knowledge on industrial trends or firms' intentions, which usually leads to a disaster.

Among MITI's information mechanisms, deliberation councils and bottom-up decision making are worth special mention. As a collective decision making body, deliberation councils can be set up at various levels including central government and ministries as well as local governments. MITI used, and still uses, deliberation councils actively to draft policies. They are orchestrated by MITI which selects a chairperson and invites relevant stakeholders from businesses, academia, media, consumers, NPOs and so forth. The most important deliberation council of MITI is the Industrial Structure Deliberation Council that formulates long-term industrial policy orientation. It also sponsors a large number of deliberation councils on specific industries and issues. For long, they have functioned well as a collective decision making process. However, some criticize deliberation councils as a rubber stamp device because MITI picks the agenda, participants and procedure, and sits as an overseeing secretariat.

Unlike many governments and ministries whose decisions are generated at the top, MITI's policy making was—and is—bottom-up. It typically starts with MITI's junior officials gathering and analyzing data, drafting reports and conducting intensive hearings with stakeholders, especially the business community. Collected information is used as an input for subsequent discussions in a relevant subcommittee and deliberation council under MITI.

Throughout the process, deputy division directors (officials in their mid-thirties) serve as the hub of information flows both inside MITI and between MITI and the private sector, thus having a considerable voice in shaping the final outcome (Okimoto, 1989).

Regarding concrete policy actions, SME promotion and strengthening part and component suppliers can be cited as examples of successful interventions.

Japan's SME promotion dates back to the early postwar years with the establishment of the SME Agency in 1948. Starting from business consultation, many support measures were subsequently added. By now Japan has one of the most sophisticated systems of SME support in the world serving as a model for Taiwan, Korea and other countries. The key policy objective has shifted over time from protection of weak SMEs against exploitation by large companies to creation of self-standing and globally competitive SMEs, as the number of excellent SMEs increased and the recognition that SMEs were the source of Japanese industrial strength rather than a problem spread. Accumulated measures are summarized in the *Guidebook for Using SME Support Measures*, an annual free publication to help SME owners locate appropriate policy measures. It covers priority measures of the year, management support, financial support, accounting and tax support, commerce and local economy support, sector-specific support, and inquiry and consultation windows over 340 pages (2016 edition). Note that these are measures under the SME Agency only. Many more measures are available from local governments, business associations and NPOs, commercial and local banks, JICA and JETRO.

Shindan (enterprise diagnostics and advice) and shindanshi (officially certified business consultants) are the critical mechanisms guiding SMEs to improve operation and introduce available policy support. In 1952, MITI began to certify outstanding consultants and actively mobilize them in SME support. In 1954, the Japan SME Management Consultants Association (J-SMECA) was founded as a professional association of shindanshi, headquartered in Tokyo with a branch in every prefecture of the country. Shindanshi must pass theoretical and practical examinations and registration must be renewed every five years. In 1962 SME University was founded in Tokyo for shindanshi training, with eight more campuses added over the years, where economics, finance, accounting, management, business operations, IT and SME policy were taught with continuous updating and emphasis on the actual practice of business consultation. In 2016 the number of registered shindanshi was about 23,000 which is annually increasing. Many shindanshi also work as industrial experts in developing countries.

SME loans have been provided by the Development Bank of Japan (DBJ), the Exim Bank, commercial banks, local banks and credit unions. For financial institutions, reports submitted by shindanshi were an important information source in evaluating projects and providing loans to SMEs. Loans and management advice of DBJ were often combined with technical advice by MITI's Machinery Industry Bureau. Even when applications for DBJ or SME loans were rejected, financial institutions told firms how to improve them for the next round in what Professor Suehiro Akira calls the "Return Match Game." In this way, management advice, technical support and financial access were integrated, and the government and financial institutions actively coached SMEs instead of just serving as a neutral judge.

To enhance "supporting industries," which is a Japanese term for part and component suppliers, MITI enacted the Law on Temporary Measures for Promoting Machinery Industries in 1956 and the Law on Temporary Measures for Promoting Electronics Industries in 1957. These "temporary" five-year laws were extended a few times to improve SMEs that produced intermediate inputs for large automotive and electronics assembling firms.

Incentives included low-interest loans from DBJ and other banks as well as customs duty exemption and accelerated depreciation of approved equipment, which were made available for designated processes and products such as machining, molding, forging, welding, gears, nuts and bolts, bearings, valves and so on. Other than technical support, these laws also contributed to the modernization of management of SMEs and their business associations. Many industrial experts believe that these laws, though long expired, effectively defined and executed key policies for supporting industry promotion, and should therefore be carefully studied by industrial officials of developing countries that are considering introducing similar policies.

MITI was very eager to incentivize importation of technology and advanced equipment, but Japan was generally reluctant to open its market for FDI for fear of foreign manufacturing dominance. Like Korea but unlike a vast majority of today's developing nations, postwar Japan did not welcome or rely on the domestic presence of foreign manufacturers as it wanted to rebuild an industrial base by Japanese firms alone. For the same reason, issues such as local contents requirement and requirement for technical transfer or export–import balance were not raised in postwar Japan. As Japan opened its trade and investment gradually and in steps along with GATT commitments, MITI used this "national emergency" as an excuse to press Japanese producers to quickly upgrade technology and enhance competitiveness, and policies were mobilized to help firms that did this. This can be viewed as an ideal way of combining a global integration process with domestic industrial promotion, although not all governments can do this because it requires high policy competency.

Social transformation

Before the high growth period, the basic lifestyle of the Japanese people in terms of food, clothing and housing changed very slowly. Before WW2, most people ate traditional food such as rice, miso soup, pickled vegetables, fish and natto beans; drank green tea and sake; wore kimonos, geta (wooden sandals) and zori (another kind of sandals); and lived in wooden houses divided by sliding paper doors. People slept on tatami mats with futons. But all this changed dramatically during the 1960s. Bread, coffee and Western food became common. Few people now wore kimonos except on New Year Holiday and other special occasions. Concrete and steel-built apartments with blinds and curtains became popular. Urbanization progressed. Large families were replaced by nuclear families. Individualism began to replace group orientation. Among all periods of Japanese history, the postwar high growth era brought the greatest changes in lifestyle.

For a long time (except during WW2), the labor surplus persisted and wages remained depressed in Japan. But high growth brought a critical change. Around 1960, labor surplus turned to labor shortage. The so-called "turning point" in the Arthur Lewis model was finally reached.[8] The job offer/job seeker ratio stayed around 1 until 1959 but began to rise in 1960 until it reached 6 to 7 for middle and high school graduates in 1970. The unemployment rate also declined from over 2 percent to nearly 1 percent during the 1960s. As the labor market tightened, young workers were highly demanded by urban industries as "golden eggs." Special trains and ships were organized to transport fresh graduates from middle and high schools in rural areas to big cities as new workers. They worked hard in urban SMEs and service sectors and supported Japan's high growth, but employment opportunity at large companies with high salary and job security were closed to them. This "dual structure," in which good jobs were reserved for university graduates while others had to endure harsh conditions, was a serious socio-economic problem of the postwar Japanese economy. Similarly, SMEs working under a large company to supply components were squeezed by unreasonable demands for cost reduction, prompt delivery and unstable orders. Up until 1960, wage levels at SMEs were only about half or less of those at large firms, but this gap narrowed over time due also to acute labor shortage, reaching 60–70 percent of large firms by 1970.

Despite this dual structure, from an international perspective, it must be admitted that postwar Japan succeeded in achieving fast growth and income equality simultaneously. There was no major social group in Japan that felt so aggrieved economically as to resort to violence or social disruption. Surely, there were some unhappy workers and a few radical students but they hardly represented the voice of the mass. Instead, *Ichioku Sochuryu* (all 100 million belong to middle class) was the sentiment of the day, and statistics bear this out. According to the World Bank's combined and standardized Gini data, which measures the degree of income inequality ranging from zero to one, the Gini coefficient of Japan declined from 0.37 (moderate) in 1962 to 0.33 (quite equal) in 1972—compared with the Chinese Gini that remained about 0.3 (quite equal) in the 1960s and 1970s but shot up to 0.48 (highly unequal) by 2007. Among East Asian miracle economies, Japan, Korea and Taiwan experienced equal or equalizing income during their high growth periods while China, Thailand, Philippines and Malaysia had unequal or polarizing income during fast growth. More recently, Indonesia and Vietnam seem to be joining the latter group.

Income equalization in postwar Japan was the result of many factors. Spontaneous labor migration from rural to urban areas mentioned above, whether permanent, temporary or seasonal, had a strong effect of converging income under the circumstances of general labor shortage and rising wages. Policies of supplying public housing, schools and transport infrastructure in expanding cities as well as strengthening and protecting SMEs also contributed. Politically, the Liberal Democratic Party which ruled from 1955 (see below) secured rural votes by offering subsidies, public investment and agricultural price control and protection in favor of farmers. Tokyo taxes were channeled to build railroads, highways, ports and airports in rural constituencies. Some of these measures may have caused inefficiency but they certainly equalized income and stabilized society.

During the high growth period, environmental destruction associated with rapid motorization and industrialization became intolerable. Rivers and sea coasts were black with sludge and fish died. Skies were grey with car and smokestack fumes, and incidents of respiratory diseases soared. Grass-roots movements arose against corporate irresponsibility and official negligence, which culminated in four principal lawsuits against pollution hazards as shown in Table 11.1. All of these lawsuits ended with the victory of the plaintiff consisting of affected residents.

The Japanese government and business community, which initially turned blind eyes to environmental damage, gradually had to acknowledge the seriousness of the problem. The Basic Environment Law was enacted in 1967 and the Environmental Agency was established in 1971. Policy finally shifted from growth-first to environmental protection. Air and water quality gradually improved. Environmental technology was researched and energy conservation was targeted. After many decades, Japanese cities with highways, steel mills and petro-chemical complexes are now relatively clean with low CO, CO_2, SO_X, NO_X and PM levels. A high price was paid, but Japan finally overcame the economic growth–environment dilemma. Many Japanese firms and local governments have developed technology and systems to cope with environmental problems which they want to market inside and outside Japan.

Table 11.1 Four major pollution lawsuits of postwar Japan

	Cause and symptoms	*Accused*	*Final ruling*
Minamata Disease (Minamata City, Kumamoto Prefecture)	First reported in 1956. Water contaminated by organic mercury causing numbness, speech disturbance, narrowing of vision field, mental disorder, loss of muscle coordination and other neurological disturbances.	Chisso Corporation	The plaintiff won in March 1973
Itai-itai Disease (Jintsu River, Toyama Prefecture)	First reported in 1955. Water pollution by cadmium causing severe pain. "Itai-itai" means "it hurts, it hurts."	Mitsui Mining and Smelting Company	The plaintiff won in August 1972
Niigata Minamata Disease (Agano River, Niigata Prefecture)	First reported in 1965. Water pollution by organic mercury, with same disturbances as Minamata Disease.	Showa Denko	The plaintiff won in September 1971
Yokkaichi Asthma (Yokkaichi City, Mie Prefecture)	Petrochemical complexes from the late 1950s causing air pollution by SOx and other substances. Major symptoms included sore throat, coughs, respiratory organ troubles, vertigo, nervous diseases and eye irritation.	Mitsubishi Petrochemicals, Showa Yokkaichi Sekiyu and four other companies	The plaintiff won in August 1972

In Japan, inequality and environmental destruction, which are two common problems in rapidly industrializing society, were prevented by appropriate policy interventions albeit with much delay and damage in the case of the environment.

In the political sphere, two conservative parties merged to become the Liberal Democratic Party in 1955, which has since dominated Japanese politics except for a few short breaks. The LDP lost the prime minister's seat from 1993 to 1996 and from 2009 to 2012 but subsequently regained it. The situation in which the strong and conservative LDP overpowers weak opposition parties has been called the "1955 Regime." In many aspects, the LDP is much like the Seiyukai Party in the prewar period. Its support base is rural. The LDP distributes public money for rural investment and farm subsidies. With the coming of Prime Minister Kakuei Tanaka (in office during 1972–74), the LDP's ruling style characterized by rural money politics for winning votes became firmly established, and it still continues today. Many LDP politicians want to continue building Shinkansen (bullet trains), airports and highways despite the severe budget crisis.

In comparison with prewar politics punctuated by dramatic power shifts and frequent crises, the postwar political structure in general and the 1955 Regime in particular have been more static (Banno, 2004). The absence of an opposition party that can challenge the ruling party, such as the Minsei Party in the 1920s and 1930s, partly explains this. In a situation where no serious political competition existed, LDP-led Japan assured national security by becoming a faithful US ally and staying within the US nuclear umbrella, and confined domestic agenda to such issues as growth, trade negotiations, environmental protection and social welfare while suppressing ideological dissent or capitalist–labor confrontation. This led to a political regime in which serious debates and power shifts rarely occurred.

Box 11.1 Honda Soichiro: a postwar business hero

Postwar Japan produced many business heroes. Among them, Honda Soichiro (the founder of Honda Motor Company), Matsushita Konosuke (the founder of Panasonic) and Ibuka Masaru and Morita Akio (the co-founders of Sony) are among the most well known. They were all engineer-inventors who started in a tiny factory with a great vision and desire to produce new and better products to conquer the Japanese—and world—market. They encountered many failures and hardships but persevered until great success was reached. They were driven by unquenchable *monozukuri* (making things) spirit, not by the desire for a high salary, quarterly profits or balance sheets. After building a business empire, each became a philanthropist and made contributions in education, culture, environmental protection or economic diplomacy.

Honda Soichiro (1906–91) was the son of a blacksmith in Shizuoka in Central Japan. From early on, he learned the skills of bellowing, using furnaces and casting metal from his father. The boy was crazy about mechanical things. When his father opened a bicycle shop, Soichiro was happy to assist him as a repairman.

After finishing at secondary school, Soichiro worked at an automobile repair company. After six years, when Soichiro was twenty-one, he was promoted to direct the company's Hamamatsu branch. But he was not satisfied with just repairing automobiles, and he started to experiment and produce new parts. In those days, virtually all cars were imported or produced by American carmakers in Japan, and domestic production of automotive parts was an important goal for the industry. Soichiro tried to self-produce piston rings, a crucial engine component, but it was not easy. After realizing that experience must be supported by theory, he went to Hamamatsu Technical College to study metallurgical and mechanical engineering for three years.

After the war defeat, in 1946, Soichiro established his own company to produce motorbikes which later became Honda Giken Kogyo (Honda Motor Company). Honda's first motorbikes, the Dream (146cc) and the Cub (50cc), were instant hits. Around 1954, Honda faced a crisis due to fierce competition and technical problems with its products, but the crisis was overcome by the efforts of Fujisawa Takeo, the company's competent marketing manager.

Soichiro wanted to join—and win—the Tourist Trophy (TT), an international motorbike race in Great Britain. He organized a special team to manufacture a very powerful motorbike for this race. In 1959, Honda participated in the TT for the first time. Two years later, in 1961, Honda won a sweeping victory by grabbing the first to fifth prizes in both 125cc and 250cc classes. Around the same time, Honda introduced the Super Cub, a popular 50cc motorbike with an efficient engine. It became an even bigger hit with Japanese and world consumers.

In the 1960s, Honda began production of automobiles. This move was prompted by the MITI's plan to consolidate Japanese auto makers to only a few to compete with American Big Three. If this policy was implemented, newcomers such as Honda would be excluded so Soichiro rushed to enter this game before this happened. The first popular small car, N360, sold well but was later criticized as a defective product.

In 1970, a tough environmental law was enacted in the United States requiring automobiles to drastically reduce emissions. Honda became the first car company in the world to clear this standard in 1972 by inventing the Compound Vortex Controlled Combustion (CVCC) engine. This proved that Honda had frontline technology in automobiles as well as in motorbikes. Honda's move also stimulated other Japanese auto manufacturers to produce fuel-efficient, low-emission cars.

Here are some words of Honda Soichiro:

"The General Directors of this company have all been unruly and unpredictable, including myself. So all of you must work very hard to sustain the company." (Addressing the company gathering at Honda's 35th Anniversary, 1983.)

"All General Directors raised issues with me. Any General Director who doesn't do this is useless." (Recalling the time when GD Kume and GD Kawamoto both advocated a water-cooled system when Soichiro insisted on an air-cooled system, in developing the CVCC engine.)

"Don't be a victim of the company. You must work in order to enjoy your own life." (To new recruits.)

"Everyone dreams and hopes for a success. I believe a success comes only 1 percent of the time, supported by the 99 percent of failures. The final success is attained by challenging the new world with pioneer spirit and after the repeated use of failures, reflection and courage." (At the time of receiving an Honorary Doctor's Degree from the Michigan Institute of Technology, 1974.)

"It's OK. Your greasy hand is good. I very much like the smell of grease." (When a worker tried to shake hands with Soichiro but, realizing his own greasy hand, quickly withdrew it.)

(Sources: Miyamoto, 1999 and Honda Soichiro Study Group, 1998)

Notes

1 The Economic White Paper of 1956, published by the Economic Planning Agency. Economist Goto Yonosuke remarked a famous phrase, "We are no longer in the Postwar Phase." This meant that an "easy" recovery from an artificial bottom created by the war was over, and growth from now on had to be generated by conscious efforts in productivity and economic transformation. However, many mistook this message as implying that the hardest time was over and a bright future was upon them.

2 The fiscal investment and loan program (FILP) is a mechanism in which people's small funds collected through state institutions and credit mechanisms, such as postal savings and pension contributions, were mobilized for investments and loans having a public nature such as housing, small enterprise promotion and regional infrastructure. During the high growth period when more funds were paid in than withdrawn, the FILP grew to a size as large as about the half of the general budget and was used for various projects in close coordination with the general budget.

3 In those days, Gross National Product (GNP), or values produced at home and abroad by "domestic residents" (those who were in Japan for six months or more), was the popular indicator of economic size instead of Gross Domestic Product (GDP), or all values created within Japanese territory regardless of official residence or nationality of firms or individuals, which is commonly used today. The main differences between GNP and GDP are treatment of wages, interests and dividends earned abroad. In the case of Japan, GNP and GDP are roughly the same.

4 The Post-WW2 Bretton Woods international monetary system was established by the Bretton Woods Agreement in New Hampshire, United States in 1944 and managed by the International Monetary Fund, an institution also created by the Bretton Woods Agreement. It was a US dollar-centered fixed exchange rate system under tight capital control, with the possibility to adjust exchange rates under certain conditions.

5 Different inflation in different sectors does not necessarily imply disequilibrium. If wage and other factor prices are the same across all domestic businesses, sectors with high productivity growth can achieve cost reduction relative to sectors with low productivity growth. Japanese consumer prices rose while wholesale (industrial) prices remained stable because productivity grew faster in machinery, automobile, electronics, and so on, than food, housing and services purchased by consumers. This phenomenon is technically proven in the Balassa-Samuelson Theorem in international economics.

6 A question frequently raised about kaizen is whether it works in societies quite different from Japanese which features teamwork, patience and collective decision making. The question is understandable, but the fact is that kaizen is already practiced widely in Southeast Asia, India, Western and Eastern Europe, America, Latin America and Africa, each of which has a very different culture from Japanese but produces similar immediate and remarkable results in productivity improvement and cost cutting. There is no society in which muda elimination, when done properly, fails to produce wonders in workplaces.

7 For more on MITI's policy measures, see Johnson (1982), Itoh et al. (1988), Komiya et al. (1988) and Okimoto (1989).

8 The Lewis model divides the economy into the traditional sector (rural agriculture) and the modern sector (urban industries). It assumes labor surplus in rural areas, which prompts labor migration from villages to cities as the modern sector expands and requires more labor. When this process progresses sufficiently, a new phase, called the *turning point*, is reached at which surplus labor disappears and a wage hike becomes necessary to employ more workers.

12

ECONOMIC MATURITY AND SLOWDOWN

Japan's high growth came to an end in the early 1970s. Annual growth fell to an average of about 4 percent in the 1970s and 1980s, and further down to near zero in the 1990s (see Figure 11.1 in the previous chapter). The government called this "stable growth." Why did growth slow down in the early 1970s?

One important fact that we should keep in mind is that growth slowdown in this period was common to all industrial countries in North America and Western Europe. The reasons for slowdown must have therefore been at least partly global though domestic factors may also have played a role. Moreover, inflation accelerated in all industrial countries in the 1970s. This also points to a globally common cause. Let us look at the domestic and international causes of Japan's slowdown respectively.

The end of catching up

On the domestic side, transition to lower growth was natural and inevitable because the Japanese economy had caught up with the US and European economies and matured. During the catching up process, a developing country can (selectively) import technology and systems that exist in the developed world. But when you become part of the developed world, you can no longer copy others but must create something new in order to grow. Naturally, clearing your own path is harder and slower than following someone else's path.

Measured in income per head (in actual dollars, not purchasing power parity—or price-adjusted—dollars; see below), the gap between Japan and the United States was 1 to 14 in 1950, 1 to 6 in 1960 and 1 to 2.5 in 1970. This narrowing of bilateral income difference was the result of Japan's much faster growth compared with the United States. In the 1970s, the fluctuating yen–dollar exchange rate began to disturb this income comparison. The income ratio was 1 to 1.3 in 1980 and 1 to 0.93 in 1990, which means Japanese income was temporarily higher than US income in that year. But since Japanese prices were in general much higher than in the United States, this does not necessarily mean Japanese people had attained a higher living standard than Americans in 1990.

To make adjustments for different price levels, the concept of purchasing power parity (PPP) is used. The same amount of money can buy much in countries with low prices and only a little in countries with high prices. For example, consumers in Vietnam, where prices are low, could enjoy much higher living standards than consumers in Japan, where prices are high, if they had the same income measured in a common currency. The real income of Japanese consumers must therefore be discounted by the extent that Japanese prices are higher than

DOI: 10.4324/9781315444048-13

Vietnamese. This adjustment is necessary to correctly compare income and living standards across countries. Measured by this PPP criterion, Japan's per capita income surpassed that of Italy in 1966 and that of Britain around 1975. Japan did not overtake the United States, West Germany or France but came close to them by the mid 1970s. Thus, it can be said that Japan was firmly in the highest income group by the 1970s.

Another way to measure income is by affordability of consumer durables (Figure 12.1). It took 10.7 months of average Japanese salary to buy a new car (the basic model of Toyota Corolla) in 1966, but workers had to work only 4.0 months to buy a similar car in 1974. In 1991, a new car could be had after 2.4 months of work. By the mid 1970s, virtually all Japanese households were equipped with washing machines, refrigerators, vacuum cleaners, telephones and color TVs. Automobiles and air-conditioners were not as widely owned as these items because they were not considered necessary or useful for some households.

The oil shocks of 1973–74 and 1979–80

On the external side, there were two major economic shocks in the 1970s that were common to all countries: the oil shocks and the beginning of general floating of major currencies.

The price of crude oil was low and stable, at around $2–3 per barrel, for a long time in the post-WW2 period. However, in the autumn of 1973, the Organization of Petroleum Exporting Countries (OPEC) decided to raise it dramatically to $11 per barrel and reduce oil export to industrial countries by about 10 percent. The oil price was again raised to about $30 per barrel in 1979–80. Both of these price increases were associated with political and military situations in the Middle East with the first oil shock resulting from the Fourth Middle Eastern War and the second from the Iranian Revolution.

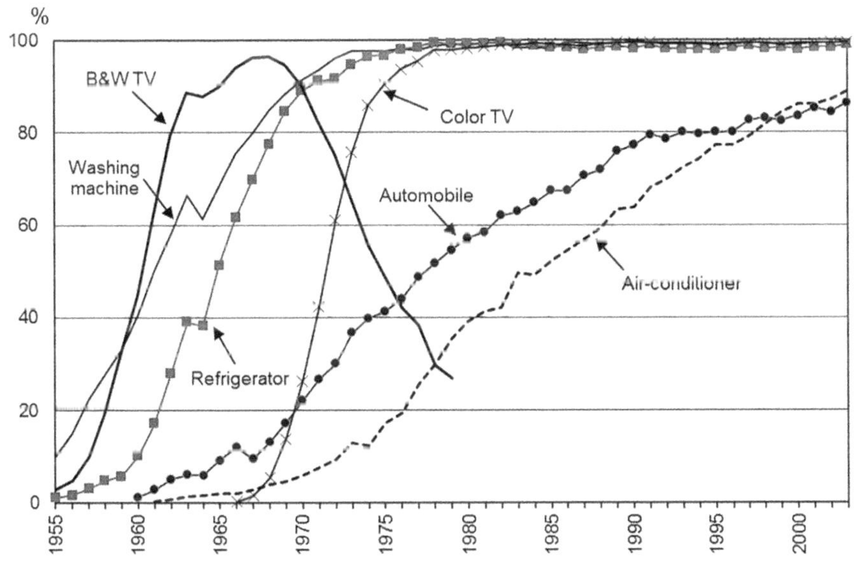

Figure 12.1 The ratio of households owning consumer durables

Sources: Cabinet Office, Trends in Household Consumption, 2003, and others.

Many of the advanced countries depended heavily on imported oil with the average import ratio of 67 percent of domestic demand. Among them, Japan's foreign oil dependency was particularly high at 99.7 percent. The first oil shock caused both wholesale prices and consumer prices in Japan to surge beyond what could be explained only by the oil impact (see Figure 12.2). Between these prices, wholesale prices rose faster. Japanese people panicked and tried to hoard as many daily necessities as possible, including toilet paper, detergent and kerosene. But this stocking behavior collectively generated empty shelves in supermarkets, despite the fact that the flow supply was sufficient to cover the flow demand. Seeing empty shelves, people panicked even more. Shortages spread from consumer goods to industrial inputs. Speculative hoarding by traders and brokers was suspected of further accelerating the price increase, which was then called *kyoran bukka* (crazy prices). Workers demanded high wage hikes. In 1974, Japan registered its first negative growth in the post-war period of –0.5 percent (slightly different numbers exist due to subsequent revisions). "Stagflation" was the term that economists used to describe the simultaneous occurrence of business recession and high inflation.

Compared with the first oil shock of 1973–74, the second oil shock of 1979–80 had a relatively minor impact on the Japanese economy. Inflation rose but not very much, and the economy continued to grow.

On close examination, Japanese money supply was increasing rapidly prior to the first oil shock and inflation already began to accelerate in the early 1970s. Monetary expansion was caused by the Bank of Japan's foreign exchange intervention to support the dollar. It aggressively bought dollar assets and sold yen assets, typically Japanese government bonds, which artificially increased demand for dollars (see the next section for why the Bank of Japan did this). The injection of yen assets into the economy had the effect of pushing up money supply. Moreover, fiscal policy was also very active at the time of the first oil shock. Prime Minister Tanaka Kakuei's "Japanese Archipelago Rebuilding Plan," announced in 1972, called for massive public investments to build highways and Shinkansen (fast trains) to connect planned industrial areas across Japan with urban centers. Such fiscal activism

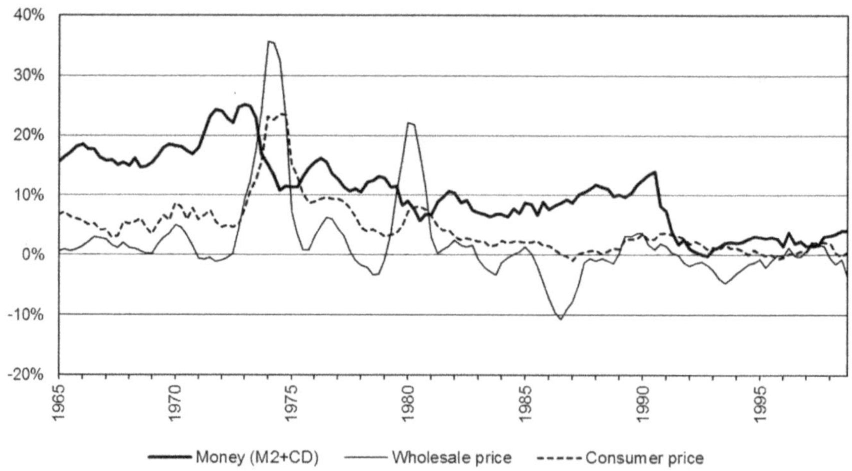

Figure 12.2 Money supply and inflation (increase over 12 months)

Source: International Monetary Fund, *International Financial Statistics*, various issues.

stimulated the economy, and land speculation became rampant along proposed routes of large-scale transportation projects. These monetary and fiscal policies were already nudging Japanese prices upward when the OPEC crisis hit.

After the first oil shock and "crazy prices" erupted, Tanaka's "Rebuilding Plan" had to be abandoned. Monetary policy was also gradually tightened. The Bank of Japan was severely criticized for being expansionary and fueling inflation in the early 1970s. In response, it converted to "monetarism"—a school of macroeconomics that taught that money and only money was the cause of inflation, always and everywhere. The Bank of Japan began to target monetary growth to avoid future inflation.

As part of structural reform, the government tried to reduce national energy consumption and promote "rationalization" (i.e. downsizing and closure) of energy-intensive industries including paper and aluminum refining. The national campaign was launched to turn off unnecessary lights, set the room temperature lower in winter and higher in summer, and discourage commercial neon signs. However, serious energy saving would require an overall improvement of energy efficiency, not just turning off lights more frequently. This would take time because new technology and large investment were required. Japan's effort to economize energy relative to the size of economic activity turned out to be brilliantly successful in the long run. By the early 1980s, Japan became the most efficient energy user among industrial countries. The Japanese automobile companies also succeeded in mass producing energy-efficient cars, many of which were exported to overseas markets, especially to the United States (see the story of Honda at the end of Chapter 11).

Many papers and books were written on the nature and cause of the oil shocks in the 1970s. There were two distinct and diametrically opposed interpretations, and it must be admitted that the final verdict has not yet been reached even today. Economists such as Jeffrey Sachs, Michael Bruno and Barry Bosworth took the position of the supply shock view. Hans Genberg, Alexander Swoboda and Ronald McKinnon advanced the global monetarist view.

The supply shock view was an obvious and more popular view that argued that the oil shocks were supply shocks caused by OPEC's political power. Consider an upward-sloping aggregate supply curve and a downward-sloping aggregate demand curve in a standard macroeconomics textbook.[1] As the oil price is jacked up artificially, the resulting cost inflation moves the aggregate supply curve up and to the left, causing higher prices and lower output, namely, "stagflation." If trade unions additionally succeed in an aggressive wage hike, inflation will rise even further. According to this view, inflation is generated by supply-side factors and its solution must also be sought on the supply side, for instance, by coping with energy shortage and real wage rigidity.

The global monetarist view is quite different and insists that high inflation of the 1970s was caused by global monetary expansion, which in turn was caused by the breakdown of the Bretton Woods fixed exchange rate system. As the Japanese and European central banks tried to buy up dollars to prevent sharp appreciation of their currencies against the dollar during 1971–73, the money supply was increased in all major economies. Global excess liquidity ignited commodity price inflation even before the first oil shock occurred. The oil shock was the final phase and not the cause of high inflation, which was created by the oversupply of global money. OPEC is always aggressive, but its attempt to raise oil prices succeeds only when there is too much liquidity in the world that sustains oil inflation. Thus, in this view, stagflation in the 1970s should be explained by a monetary factor. More specifically, it was the result of the built-in instability and eventual collapse of the international monetary system of the early post-WW2 period.

Floating of major currencies

From 1944 to 1971, the world was on the dollar-based and US-centered Bretton Woods system of fixed exchange rates. It achieved unprecedented global price stability, high growth and trade liberalization in the 1950s and the early 1960s. But the system began to strain in the mid 1960s.

The fate of the system critically depended on the macroeconomic policy of the United States. As the US government adopted an expansionary policy stance to finance welfare spending, the war in Vietnam and the space race with the Soviet Union, inflation emerged and spread to the world in the 1960s. The United States was producing higher inflation than the rest of the world wanted to import. Despite fixed exchange rates, the dollar was under downward pressure and corresponding upward pressure on gold and European and Japanese currencies developed. As gold reserves at the Federal Reserve System (US central bank) dwindled, the US government introduced two-tier pricing of gold for foreign governments and free markets separately.

Finally, in August 1971, President Richard Nixon announced that the dollar was no longer to be fixed to gold or other currencies. This ended the Bretton Woods system and major currencies began to float immediately. President Nixon also imposed temporary price controls and stiff import surcharges. These were supposed to fight inflation and ameliorate the balance-of-payments crisis the United States was facing. Surprised Japanese officials and media called this the "Nixon Shock." To avoid appreciation of home currencies (the loss of export competitiveness), the Bank of Japan and central banks in Europe intervened massively in the foreign exchange market to buy and prop up the dollar.[2] This dramatically increased money supply in each country.

Between 1971 and 1973, there was an international effort to re-establish a fixed exchange rate system at new levels (with a more depreciated dollar). In December 1971, the monetary authorities of major countries gathered in Washington DC to set new exchange rates (the Smithsonian Agreement). The yen was set at 308 to the dollar. But these rates could not be maintained for very long. In early 1973, under another bout of heavy speculative attacks, the Smithsonian rates were abandoned and major currencies began to float again with no prospect of returning to fixed rates. Floating exchange rates have continued well into the twenty-first century.

Monetarist economists—such as Milton Friedman—predicted that freely floating exchange rates would move smoothly and help international adjustments. However, it was soon discovered that floating currencies in reality were volatile and injurious to national economies. In 1985, the Group of Five (G5)—the United States, Japan, West Germany, France and the United Kingdom—jointly intervened to lower the too-high dollar (the Plaza Agreement). But it fell too much. In 1987, the Group of Seven (G7)—G5 plus Italy and Canada—again intervened to stabilize the dollar (the Louvre Accord). Such joint interventions have been tried occasionally when needed to correct extreme currency movements. Among major central banks, the Bank of Japan has been particularly averse to excessive yen appreciation and often intervened unilaterally to buy up the dollar. This has resulted in rapid accumulation of international reserves to the highest level in the world. Meanwhile, from the 1970s, European countries cooperated toward the creation of a regional monetary union, which produced the euro in 1999 and its paper notes and coins began to circulate in 2002.

The Japanese economy is highly vulnerable to the fluctuation of the yen–dollar exchange rate for several reasons. First, the yen is a lone floater as there is no yen zone in Asia—unlike the euro area in Europe or a large number of dollar-using nations in the world for the United States. Second, most of Japan's trade and virtually all of its financial transactions are conducted in dollars. Third, Japan, as a large creditor country, has accumulated a huge amount of unhedged dollar assets in the form of US government bills and bonds, whose values depreciate whenever the dollar falls. Fourth, Japanese industries exhibit relatively low exchange pass-through (domestic prices change little when the yen rises or falls) and Japanese manufactured products contain high domestic value-added (domestic materials and components). When the yen appreciates, their costs also rise with the yen almost proportionately, leading to the loss of competitiveness. When this occurs, Japanese output and investment stagnate, prices and wages are suppressed, and financial strain is created. This is called *endaka fukyo*, or high yen-induced recession.

Delayed systemic reform?

Some argue that the Japanese economic system of the 1950s and 1960s, based on long-term relations and active official intervention and featuring the main bank system, lifetime employment, seniority wages, cooperative management–labor relations, administrative guidance and the like, became obsolete by the 1970s. According to them, this system functioned reasonably well while the country was in the catching up phase, but it was no longer appropriate when Japan became a mature industrial society. Japan should have shifted decisively toward a more market-based, less officially guided system during the 1970s. But two major global shocks of oil price hikes and the beginning of floating currencies intervened, which kept the Japanese government too busy coping with these macroeconomic problems instead of launching systemic transformation. Moreover, trade friction with the United States and Europe intensified (see below) which further diverted policy attention. As a result, the Japanese economy failed to cast off many legacies of old times such as over-regulation and the lack of incentives for innovation. This has become an institutional barrier for Japan's further development.

Noguchi (1995) criticizes Japan's current economic regime which promotes production rather than consumers' welfare, suppresses competition and uses social policies to reduce popular dissent and dissatisfaction as the "1940 regime," a system created to execute war but has no place in today's Japan. Similarly, Ota (2010), who served as the Minister of Economy and Fiscal Policy in 2006–8, strongly supports economic deregulation and fiscal discipline. She condemns any attempt to revive old-fashioned fiscal activism and random subsidies.

However, there is another view that cautions against admiring and uncritically adopting an American-style free economy. Advocates such as Hara (1996) assert that long-term trust and official support are two ingredients that are critical in any society that wants to move from an early light manufacturing and simple assembly phase to a fuller, more technology-based heavy industrialization. The free market of Meiji had to inevitably evolve into a more relational and guided market economy as Japan mastered heavy and mechanical industries in the mid-twentieth century, with or without war. All latecomer countries of yesterday and today need such modification to their domestic economic system so development will proceed smoothly and without social crisis. Disapproving all relational and state-guided systems as obsolete is too simplistic and without a historical perspective, especially when the world now clearly recognizes the instability and harm that unregulated global markets can bring through asset bubbles, speculative waves, currency attacks and income gaps.

Therefore, Japan's transition to a freer market economy, if it is to be done, must be done carefully and selectively without throwing away desirable Japanese features such as long-term perspective, teamwork, monozukuri spirit and the balanced sense of efficiency and equity together with the bath water.

Trade friction with the United States

Japan's main external problem in the 1950s to mid 1960s was how to reduce emerging trade deficits. Phrases such as "the ceiling of the balance of payments" and "stop–go policy" (Chapter 11) reflected this problem. Around the mid 1960s, however, the problem changed 180 degrees. Japan now had to reduce the rising trade surplus as a top priority. A trade surplus was politically undesirable as it angered the United States, especially the US Congress and industrial lobbies. In the 1980s, Japan began to record the largest trade surplus and the United States had the largest trade deficit in the world, year after year. Furthermore, the size of Japan's surplus and that of the American deficit were similar. Japanese saving was used to finance American overspending, and that became the largest financial flow in the world economy.

After the oil shocks of the 1970s, the Japanese economic structure moved away from heavy and energy-using sectors to lighter and more mechanical sectors. Industrial activities shifted from *Ju-ko-cho-dai* (heavy-thick-long-large) products such as steel, cement and petrochemicals to *Kei-haku-tan-sho* (light-thin-short-small) ones. In the process, electronics and automobiles emerged as two major export items. Japan was leading the world with such products as semi-conductors, cameras, calculators, TV sets, video machines, Walkman music players and energy-efficient cars. Productivity tools developed since the 1950s, including the Toyota Production System, were embraced with renewed zest to strengthen Japanese competitiveness once again under the new global reality of higher energy prices and floating exchange rates.

The history of Japan's trade friction with the United States—and, to a lesser extent, with Western Europe—is long and highly politicized. It began in the 1960s, when Japan was exporting cheap textile products (the "one-dollar blouse") to the US market. In response to American complaint, Japan was forced to adopt "voluntary" quotas on textile export. From then on, a stream of Japanese products came under attack: steel, TV sets, machine tools, automobiles, video players, semi-conductors and so on. From the 1980s, in addition to pressure to export less, the United States began to demand that Japan buy more from America including farm products such as oranges and beef, automobile parts and construction and financial services. Moreover, US trade negotiators argued that the Japanese economic system was inefficient and closed to imports, and thus must be reformed. What started as complaints on individual products ultimately spread to the universal criticism of the economic system of America's major trading partner.

The idea that the American trade deficit was caused by Japan's unfair trade practices, and that its reduction required bilateral diplomatic negotiations (not automatic market mechanisms), was behind the tough stance of the US trade negotiators. A too cheap yen was also regarded as part of the problem, so currency adjustments were also negotiated. Every five to seven years when the US trade deficit with Japan became politically intolerable, the United States demanded two things: (i) the yen must appreciate; and (ii) Japan must buy more from and sell less to the United States. This occurred in 1971–73, 1977–78, 1985–87 and 1993–95. Each time, trade tension rose between Japan and the United States, and the yen was sharply appreciated as the US Treasury Secretary, and sometimes even the President, talked up the Japanese currency. Such American economists as Paul Krugman, Fred Bergsten and Laura Tyson provided theoretical support to this approach.

But was this view correct? Other economists strongly rejected the tough trade-cum-currency negotiation approach as seemingly obvious but economically wrong. Komiya (1994) and McKinnon and Ohno (1997) argued that neither trade talks nor exchange rate adjustments could "correct" bilateral trade imbalance and, if implemented, they would only cause additional problems (the Hypothesis of the Syndrome of the Ever-Higher Yen). This view was certainly in the minority in the United States but had broad support among Japanese businesses, officials and economists.

McKinnon and Ohno (1997) argued that the US trade deficit was a long-term structural problem caused by the savings shortage of both the American government and households. Trade and currency negotiations with Japan or any other trading partner could hardly remove the true cause of this US-made problem. The fundamental solution must come from the American side by spending less and saving more, and mobilizing domestic policies to encourage this trend. Japan's external opening to the world (not just to the United States) would do it good, but this would have little impact on Japan's trade balance which is determined by the relative savings–investment position of each country at the macro level.[3] Japan and the United States should conclude bilateral agreements to solve trade disputes at the micro or sectoral level (or take them to the WTO) and refrain from using the yen–dollar exchange rate for commercial policy purposes (see Box 12.1 at the end of this chapter for Komiya's similar argument).

In the 1990s, the Japan–US bilateral policy pattern further evolved. In the mid to late 1990s, the US economy was soaring with an IT boom and an asset bubble while the Japanese economy was stagnant due the bubble collapse (Chapter 13). The usual US demand to open up Japan and appreciate the yen was in recess, even though the Japan–US trade gap was very large. It was feared that a further destabilization of the already weak Japanese economy would damage the world economy and backfire against the United States.[4] In particular, the collapse of Japanese financial systems would have an adverse effect on the international financial system. In the late 1990s, some Japanese officials and economists even hoped for a sharp depreciation of the yen to boost the lackluster economy, as fiscal and monetary stimuli had all failed. But this was not actually implemented, not only because the authorities did not have the power to dictate a floating currency but also because the move would anger the Americans. In the meantime, the US government continued to send very ambiguous signals on the desired movement of the dollar. It repeated that the strong dollar policy would be maintained but the exchange rate should be determined by the market.

Another important fact is that China overtook Japan as the largest trade surplus country vis-à-vis the United States around 2000 and, as a consequence, trade friction similar to what Japan experienced in the past had emerged between China and the United States (Figure 12.3). As long as the American savings shortage remained the same, some other country would be obliged to provide a sufficiently large trade surplus with the United States (i.e. a loan to America), if Japan were not to do it. As predicted, the United States strongly demanded an appreciation of the Chinese renminbi (RMB) to "correct its gross undervaluation" and diminish Chinese competitiveness. Since China was still a middle income country with significant capital control, the situation was not exactly the same as Japan. China also had skirmishes with the United States over human rights, intellectual property rights, cyber-attacks and the like which Japan did not have. But the American complaint pattern over unfair trade practices

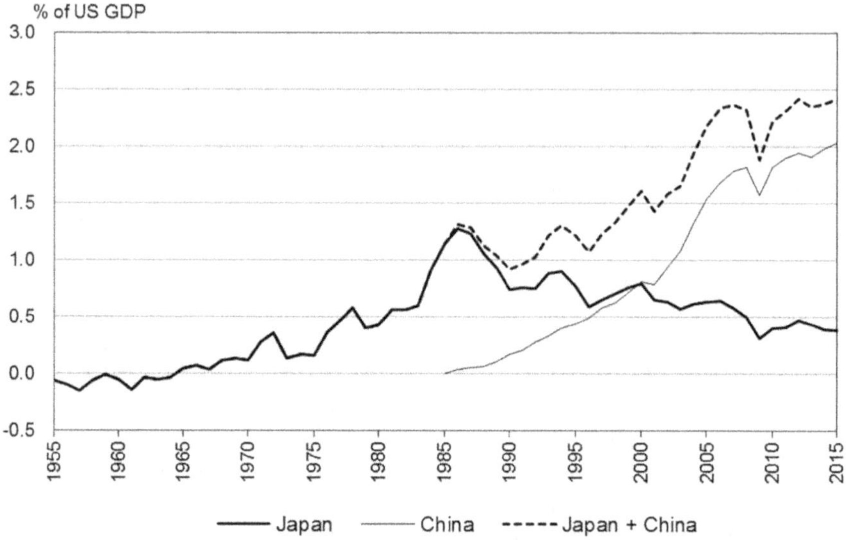

Figure 12.3 US bilateral trade balances with Japan and China

Sources: US Bureau of Economic Analysis, *National Economic Accounts*, and US Census Bureau, *US International Trade Data.*

and an undervalued currency remains basically the same. Thus, China now faces more of the blame from the United States than Japan.[5] Earlier, Japan was criticized because it was too strong. Since the 1990s, Japan has been weak and stopped drawing much attention from foreign governments. This change is described as "Japan bashing" turning to "Japan passing." The Japanese like self-depreciation and are very sensitive to how others perceive them.

In July 2005, China revalued the RMB by two percent and officially moved from the fixed exchange rate system to the basket currency system with unannounced basket contents. However, the actual mode of currency management did not change very much. The RMB still remains virtually pegged to the dollar and its speed of crawl has been controlled and very slow—it rose slowly until mid 2015 when it began to fall. In light of China's unbending inclination toward state control and gradualism, this is quite expectable.

Fiscal expansion and consolidation—and expansion again

During the high growth period of the late 1950s to 1960s, the central government budget was generally sound. It was in surplus and no government bonds were issued until 1965. However, in the mid to late 1970s, fiscal expansion to stimulate the economy was re-activated, financed by the issuance of new government bonds. These bonds were initially of ten-year maturity but bonds with shorter maturities were later added. Public debt quickly accumulated.

The seriously worried Ministry of Finance launched an initiative for fiscal consolidation in the 1980s. A tighter budget and bold expenditure cuts were planned. Fiscal and administrative reforms were proposed and partly carried out. For this purpose, two recommendation reports were drafted with somewhat different policy directions.

The Second Ad Hoc Commission on Administrative Reform (*Dai Ni Rincho*, 1981–83), an official advisory body chaired by former Keidanren President Doko Toshio, recommended expenditure cuts without resorting to tax increases. His recommendations also included greater international contributions through increased ODA and military spending, reduction of healthcare costs and private-sector initiatives. Mr. Doko himself was a man of self-discipline and modest living. He ate only a small dried fish for breakfast, setting an example of cost reduction for the government to follow.

Subsequently, the Maekawa Report was prepared in 1986–87 by the Advisory Group on Economic Structural Adjustment for International Harmony, a private group advising Prime Minister Nakasone. The Group was headed by former Bank of Japan Governor Maekawa Haruo. It recommended expansionary fiscal and monetary policies to boost domestic demand, economic deregulation and reduction of the trade surplus to avoid further friction with the United States. His low interest rate policy was later criticized as causing an asset bubble. Additionally, Professor Komiya Ryutaro severely criticized Maekawa's recommendation for trade surplus reduction, arguing that the surplus was a macroeconomic phenomenon that should be left to market forces (see Box 12.1 below).

Thanks to the efforts of the Ministry of Finance and the emergence of an asset bubble in the late 1980s, fiscal balance gradually improved. However, the situation would radically change in the 1990s. With the bursting of the asset bubble in 1990–91, the Japanese economy was plunged into a long recession. A series of fiscal stimuli were tried in increasingly large amounts and public debt began to accumulate again (Chapter 13).

Box 12.1 Prof. Komiya and the Japan–US trade friction

Professor Komiya Ryutaro (1928–) is one of the most prominent and out-spoken economists in Japan. After graduating from Tokyo University, he conducted research at Harvard University, Stanford University, Aoyama Gakuin University and others. He was a professor as well as the Dean of the Faculty of Economics at Tokyo University. He also served as the President of the Research Institute of Economy, Trade and Industry (RIETI), the MITI's policy think tank.

Professor Komiya's main research area has been international economics. In addition to theoretical works, he has written many books that openly criticized the policies of the Bank of Japan as well as the Japanese and US governments. In 1983, he co-authored a two-part book that mercilessly blamed the behavior of the Bank of Japan when the world transited from the fixed exchange rate system to general float in the early 1970s (Komiya and Suda, 1983). In his 1994 book, *Economics of Trade Surplus and Deficit*, he flatly dismissed the idea that Japan's trade surplus was generated by the closed nature of Japanese markets. He argued that the trade gap was fundamentally a macroeconomic phenomenon of the savings–investment balance. He asserted that, unless the United States adopted internal policies to increase its own saving rate, no trade negotiation or exchange rate manipulation would "resolve" the trade gap issue. He also reproached the Maekawa Report as completely wrong-headed. This view is quite close to the Hypothesis of the Syndrome of the Ever-Higher Yen of McKinnon and Ohno (1997) presented in the main text.

Here are some extracts from his 1994 book.

- Let me reflect on why I am writing this book. My current position is roughly as follows. For more than a decade since around 1983, Japan's huge current account surplus and America's huge deficit—or Japan's trade surplus with the US—have been a cause of economic "friction" between the two countries. Against this trade surplus of Japan, the US has aggressively demanded that we reduce the surplus and open up the Japanese market.
  To me, first of all, these demands for reducing the surplus and opening the markets—or more precisely, the ideas behind these demands—seem extremely illogical and unreasonable. Japan's response to the United States in the so-called Maekawa Report in 1986 was also highly inappropriate.
  Second, from the viewpoint of economics, the debate over the bilateral current account imbalance is full of elementary mistakes. Stupidity and nonsense rule over this debate. And I believe it is my mission as an economist to correct such mistakes and nonsense.
  Third, I consider myself an internationalist and not a nationalist, and I am proud of it. But I cannot endure a situation where Japan is unduly criticized by the international community based on misunderstanding, prejudice and malice. I want to refute such criticisms and correct these misguided ideas. (pp. 3–4)
- Recently, there is a re-emergence of the idea that yen appreciation can reduce Japan's trade surplus. But this idea is fundamentally mistaken. The exchange rate can adjust only the cyclical part of the surplus, if at all. In a floating exchange rate system, the (real) exchange rate is endogenous [determined by the interaction of many variables] and cannot be manipulated to an arbitrary level. (p. 106)
- In general, the impact of the real exchange rate (in other words, the terms of trade) on savings and investment is ambiguous . . . As a first approximation, I propose to presume that the terms of trade has no direct relationship with the trends of S [saving] and I [investment] in each economy . . . Existing theoretical and empirical studies on savings have not considered the effects of changes in relative prices or the terms of trade on the trend of savings, because such an inquiry is theoretically a very remote one. (pp. 180–181)

Notes

1 In the diagram measuring the price level vertically and income horizontally, a downward-sloping aggregate demand curve is derived from the IS–LM analysis, representing the demand side of the national economy. An upward-sloping aggregate supply curve is constructed from the supply side reflecting the production function and the labor market. An equilibrium is found where these two curves intersect. An oil shock, if it is to be regarded as a supply shock, shifts the aggregate supply curve upward to the left. The equilibrium point moves in such a way that the price level rises and income declines.

2 For eleven trading days following the Nixon Shock, the Bank of Japan intervened heavily in the currency market to fight off massive speculative attacks, thereby losing 4 billion dollars of foreign reserves. Then, it gave up and let the yen appreciate. European central banks gave up much sooner before losing foreign reserves significantly.

3 Denoting exports by X, imports by M, savings by S and investment by I, the current account is expressed as $X - M = S - I$ and this is an identity relationship. In words, the current account must by definition be equal to the gap between a nation's savings and investment. While the current account is the sum of the merchandise trade balance, the services account (including cross-border payments of wages and interest) and the transfer account (official grants and private remittances), the difference between the current account and the trade balance was small and stable for Japan. For this reason, the two concepts are used interchangeably in this chapter as in most practices.

4 In executing economic policies, the US government traditionally abhors an upward movement of long-term dollar interest rates and a decline of the Wall Street stock index, both of which are supposed to dampen investment and consumption and reduce economic growth. Lower economic growth bodes ill for the next election. When such a risk is suspected, the US often softened or postponed its demands on the Japanese side.

5 In January 2017, President Trump re-intensified criticism against Japan and China as unfair surplus countries with undervalued currencies. His criticism is far more extreme than before but his mindset is fundamentally the same as traditional trade negotiators.

13

THE ASSET BUBBLE AND PROLONGED RECESSION

Post-bubble stagnation and the debate over reforms

Japan experienced an asset bubble in the late 1980s. After the bubble collapsed in 1990–91, the Japanese economy was plunged into a long period of deflation and recession. Growth became near zero and sometimes even negative. For the first time in the postwar period, general price levels declined persistently. Economic statistics remained gloomy and, more importantly, consumers and producers became pessimistic. Some said that Japan was still a very high income country. Others said that sources of the next growth were being prepared under the disguise of recession, and pointed to some companies that were doing very well. But overall, it can hardly be denied that Japan's economic performance in the 1990s and the early years of the twenty-first century was less than hoped for.

The 1990s became Japan's Lost Decade. Naturally, the main argument among Japanese economists was why this recession persisted and what should be done to end it. More specifically, the key question was whether or not bold structural reforms and deregulation measures, which were supposed to revive economic dynamism, should be undertaken at a time when the overall economy was very weak. Some argued that painful reforms were necessary precisely when we faced a recession. Others argued that structural reforms should not be carried out under poor economic conditions. Instead, they argued that fiscal and monetary stimuli should be mobilized for lifting the economy before such reforms were attempted. The debate continued well into the twenty-first century with variations and added aspects. The policy actually adopted was that of fiscal activism and aggressive monetary injection into the macroeconomy with forced zero or negative interest rates, interlaced with occasional and modest postures for fiscal consolidation.

The business situation picked up in some years thanks to strong demand in the United States and/or China and a transitory yen depreciation, but growth impetus was never sufficient to put the Japanese economy on a robust development path (see Figure 13.1). In other years there were shocks originating abroad—the Asian financial crisis in 1997–98, the IT bubble crash in 2001, the global financial crisis in 2007–8, which was particularly severe and pulled Japanese growth well into the negative range, and the Euro economic and political crises starting from 2011. Japan also faced internal problems including the banking crisis culminating in 1997–98, the Kobe Earthquake in 1995, the Great East Japan Earthquake and the Fukushima nuclear accident in 2011, and intermittent political instability. While most other Asian economies, especially China, were growing strongly,

DOI: 10.4324/9781315444048-14

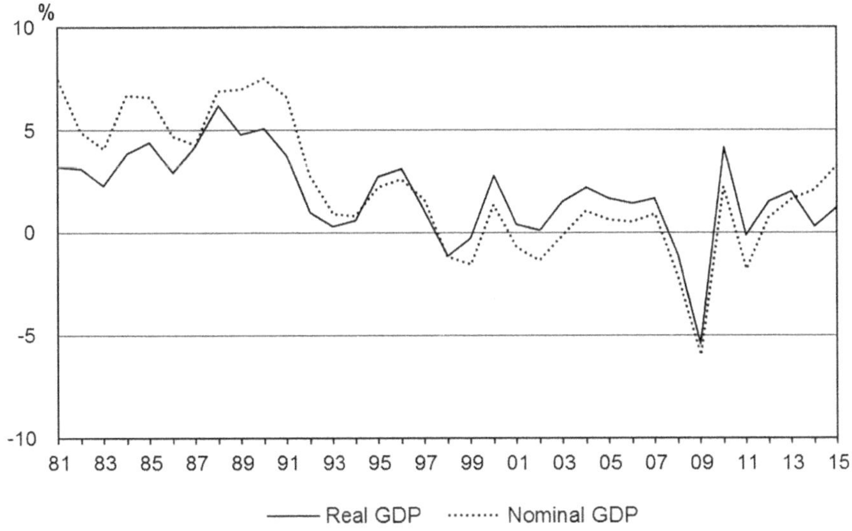

Figure 13.1 GDP growth

Source: Cabinet Office.

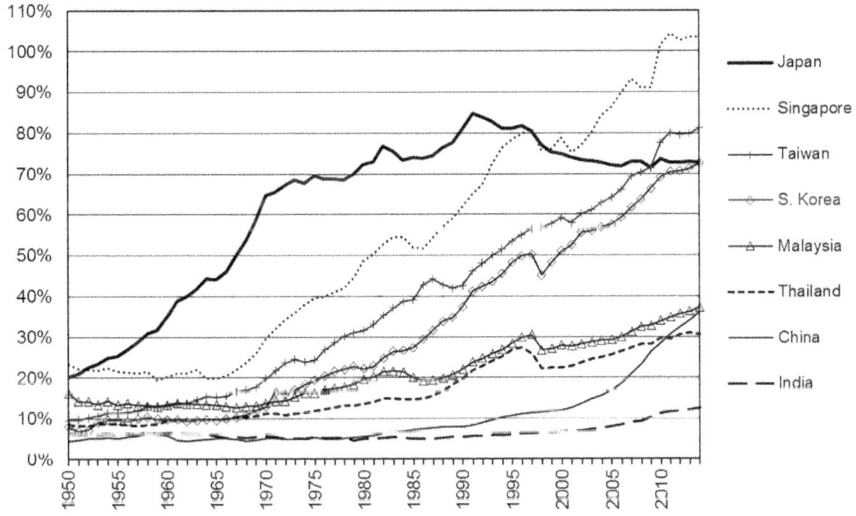

Figure 13.2 Real income per head relative to the United States

Sources: Angus Maddison, *The World Economy: Historical Statistics*, OECD Development Centre (2003); updated to 2014 using International Monetary Fund, *World Outlook Database*.

Japan's real income per capita steadily declined relative to its neighbors (see Figure 13.2), and so did its economic and political clout in the region. Japan's Lost Decade turned into the Lost Quarter Century.

The occurrence of the asset bubble

Japanese stock prices began to rise in the early 1980s and peaked in 1990 at more than five times the 1980 level. Then, it started a long period of decline with medium-term fluctuations (Figure 13.3). Japanese land prices also rose throughout the 1980s until they more than doubled. The turning point for land prices came a year later, in 1991. Since then, the land price index has continued to decline. Urban land prices rose more and fell harder in comparison with rural land prices (Figure 13.4). There are two explanations of why this asset bubble emerged.

The first was a structural one associated with bank deregulation. Previously, Japanese banks were tightly regulated by the Ministry of Finance. There was little incentive to innovate, but

Figure 13.3 Nikkei 225 stock index average

Source: Bank of Japan Time-series Data Search.

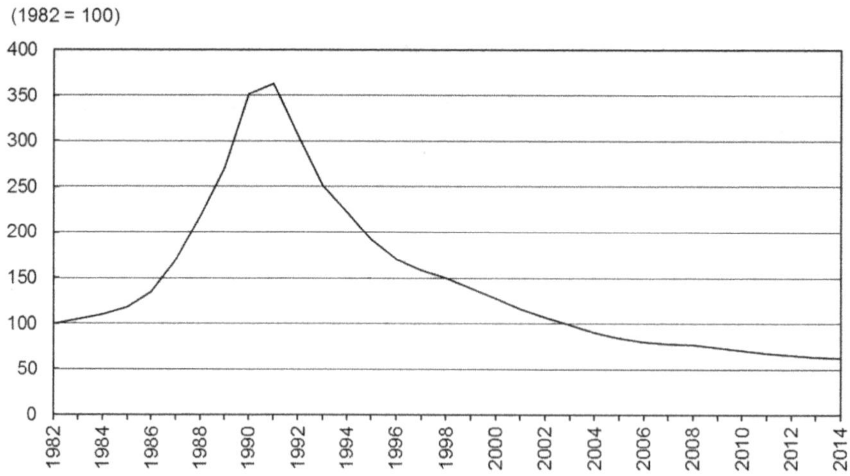

Figure 13.4 Urban land price

Source: Japan Real Estate Institute.

as long as banks followed official instructions, they were assured of adequate profit margins and protection against bankruptcy. This rigid regime was removed in the early 1980s in an effort to liberalize the Japanese financial sector under the pressure of globalization and a rising stock of government bonds. As competition began, extra bank profits associated with protection vanished. At the same time, large corporate customers moved away from domestic bank loans to other funding such as retained profits, corporate bond issuance and access to international financial markets. As Japanese banks lost lucrative corporate customers, they rushed to find new—untested and more risky—borrowers and projects such as small and medium business loans and property investments, especially urban office buildings and rural resort development. But they lacked the capacity to properly assess and monitor these borrowers and projects. When the economy was booming in the late 1980s, they over-lent. Careless business strategies and potential problems were concealed. When the bubble ended, loans that banks had made became a huge mountain of bad debt (Yoshitomi, 1998).

The second cause was monetary; easy money in the late 1980s generated and sustained the asset bubble. The yen appreciated sharply in 1985, which triggered the Bank of Japan to lower short-term interest rates and increase money supply. This was the Bank of Japan's traditional policy response to a high yen which aimed at stimulating export and investment to offset the negative impact of yen appreciation. Many later blamed then Bank of Japan Governor Sumita Satoshi, who implemented this policy, for easing too much and for too long. But because domestic price inflation was close to zero at that time, the Bank of Japan could not find a good reason to tighten money and end the asset boom everyone was enjoying. There was a signaling problem—when asset prices rise but goods prices remain stable, is monetary policy too generous or not? The data shows that the annual growth of broad money (M2+CD) accelerated to more than 10 percent during 1987–89. In retrospect, this was too high for an economy growing at about 4 percent. Succeeding Bank of Japan Governor Mieno Yasushi, who assumed the office in December 1989, deliberately tightened money and raised interest rates to end the bubble, and it did collapse quickly. Some criticized Mieno for his brutality, but can an asset bubble go on forever? It had to end some time, and usually the sooner the better.

These two explanations are not mutually exclusive. Bank deregulation explains why reckless projects began to be financed and monetary expansion explains why the bubble continued for so long. These were structural and macroeconomic reasons that complemented each other to produce the rise and fall of the asset bubble.

During the rising phase of the bubble in the late 1980s, many queer phenomena were observed. Those who owned land became very rich while those without land faced little chance of buying their home, which increased the sense of inequality and social injustice. Enriched people bought luxury goods and consumed lavishly, travelling all over the world to snap up landmark towers and art objects in a situation similar to the narikin boom during WW1 (Chapter 7). Students chartered a luxury cruiser to organize a graduation party in the Bay of Tokyo. Discotheques became popular with the youth where girls displaying large fans danced on the stage. Since vacant land was more valuable than built-up land, the *yakuza* (Japanese mafia) was hired to illegally demolish buildings and forced owners to sell the land. Sometimes the yakuza drove a truck into a house to destroy it.

Too many office towers were built in urban areas, which remained empty or unfinished for many years to follow. A large number of amusement parks and resort hotels were also developed. Among them, the only hugely successful one turned out to be Tokyo Disneyland while others subsequently got into financial trouble. Some were transferred to new owners for restructuring, including Huis ten Bosch (Dutch theme park in Nagasaki), Phoenix Seagaia Resort (seaside complex in Miyazaki), and Alpha Resort Tomamu (winter sports resort in Hokkaido). Thanks to the building boom, a large number of male construction workers from the Middle East, especially Iran, came to Japan. Some of them had work permits but others did not. Every weekend they gathered in Ueno Park in Tokyo to enjoy themselves and exchange information.

But after the bursting of the asset bubble, these phenomena all disappeared.

The Lost Decade

GDP statistics and other business indicators such as industrial production, machine order, housing starts and wage and unemployment reveal that business conditions were not uniformly poor during the first decade following the end of the bubble. The Japanese economy declined three times, in 1992–93 immediately after the bubble collapse, in 1997–98 following the consumption tax hike[1] and the banking crisis, and in 2001 amid the US and global IT recession. However, economic performance in intervening periods was not so bad. There were times when the Japanese economy appeared to improve. In 1996, Japan's real growth registered 3.5 percent which was the highest among the G7 countries. But each time the recovery was short-lived. Not surprisingly, small businesses faced greater difficulties than large enterprises in sales, corporate finance and other aspects. Banks no longer lent to SMEs.

The big question is, why did the Japanese economy remain so weak for so long after the bubble burst? Economists debated but no consensus view emerged. One explanation was purely cyclical. Since the bubble created large overcapacity, it would take time to reduce the capital stock and inventory to normal levels. But a decade seems too long for such stock adjustment. Another explanation was related to non-performing loans held by financial institutions. Because banks failed to get rid of bad debt, and because the government did not introduce proper measures, financial intermediation was impaired which hurt the real economy. This vicious circle continued until a bold action to clean up the banks' balance sheets was taken toward the end of the decade (see below).

Another popular explanation was that Japan's economic system had become obsolete. Japan's long-term relational systems, such as lifetime employment, seniority wage, keiretsu groups, sub-contracting, administrative guidance and so on, might have worked well during the 1950s and 1960s, but they became ineffective in the age of rapid change and globalization. Some argued that Japan must face a third major transformation (the first was Meiji revolution and the second was post-WW2 reforms). But others cautioned that Japan should not adopt the American system uncritically because many Japanese systems were still useful—see Box 9.1. Yet another explanation pointed to the long-term changes in Japanese society. The nation had a rapidly aging population and snowballing government debt. People became uncertain about the future regarding income and jobs, the rising tax burden and the sustainability of medical care and pension schemes. This pessimism slowed down consumer spending and business investment.

Externally, the emergence of China as the factory of the world and other newly industrializing economies, and the "hollowing-out" of Japanese manufacturing (the exodus of factories and jobs to other countries), were cited as a great threat.

It is highly probable that Japan's long stagnation was the combined result of all these problems in mutual interaction even though the exact weight of each is difficult to determine. But if one ultimate cause behind these problems is to be named, that must be the lack of political will and leadership. Japan did not have a prominent leader who could identify key national issues, explain the situation to the people in honest and persuasive language, design and implement long-term solutions, and assume full responsibility for this. Japan's problems listed above are not particularly colossal or intractable in comparison with problems faced by other countries. The uncertainty and anxiety permeating in Japanese society must be explained by the low quality of leadership rather than the size of the problems. Japanese people just did not believe that their leaders had the courage and capacity to cope with these "normal" problems. This was the situation prevailing in the first Lost Decade. Unfortunately, the political and economic landscape did not improve significantly in the following decades.

Financial crisis and monetary policy

In the post-bubble period, Japan's monetary authorities faced two challenges. The first was coping with non-performing loans, which took as long as a decade to clean up. The second was reviving the macroeconomy, which remains unfulfilled even to this date.

In the early 1990s after the asset bubble collapsed, Japanese financial institutions that previously lent recklessly to SMEs and property development projects got into trouble. The declining land and stock prices seriously hurt the balance sheets of commercial banks and *jusen* (nonbank institutions specializing in real estate loans). Japanese financial institutions often required land as loan collateral and engaged in mutual stock holding, but the values of both assets plummeted. Bad debt further rose as the recession continued and corporate bankruptcies increased. As non-performing loans accumulated, many Japanese banks faced difficulty in observing the Bank for International Settlement (BIS) capital adequacy requirement, which said that a bank's capital must be at least 8 percent of its risk assets, properly weighted, if it was to engage in international business. If this ratio fell below 4 percent, the bank was not allowed to conduct even domestic business and had to close.

In 1995 and 1996, the mounting bad debt at jusen became a political problem. But this was only the beginning. Toward the end of 1997, the fear of commercial bank defaults was widespread. When Yamaichi Securities and Hokkaido Takushoku Bank went bankrupt, the fear turned into reality. In the following year, the Long-Term Credit Bank and the Securities and Credit Bank also fell. For survival, remaining banks scrambled to improve their BIS ratios by reducing risky assets. This was done by lending less, especially to SMEs. This led to a credit crunch in the real economy, causing more bankruptcies and further worsening the quality of bank assets. This vicious circle continued from late 1997 to early 1998. Japanese banks were considered untrustworthy, and the "Japan premium," an additional charge to Japanese banks when they borrow internationally, surged. People wondered which bank would fail next. Worried savers shifted their deposits from seemingly risky banks to bigger and safer ones and postal savings.

In response to the 1997–98 banking crisis, the government created the Financial Supervisory Agency in October 1998 and the Financial Restructuring Commission in December 1998. They were merged to become the Financial Services Agency in 2000. The government also prepared "public money" up to 60 trillion yen (12 percent of GDP) to deal with the bad debt problem, recapitalize banks and manage the closure of weak banks. As a result of financial deregulation and crisis, Japanese banks also began to merge. In the 1970s and 1980s under the old regulated regime, the number of commercial banks was very stable at eighty-six, among which twenty were relatively large. They began an active merging process in 1999 that ultimately produced three Mega Banks—Mitsubishi UFJ, Mizuho and Sumitomo Mitsui—by 2006.

The Bank of Japan responded to the 1997–98 banking crisis by providing ample liquidity. Subsequently, it adopted a "zero interest rate policy" in April 1999 in an effort to revive the overall economy. This meant that the short-term interbank rate (the call rate), which the Bank of Japan directly controlled, was lowered to zero except for a very small technical margin. The Bank of Japan tried to end this abnormal policy in August 2000, but as the economy further worsened it was forced to return to zero interest. The official discount rate was also reduced to a very low level, from 6 percent in 1990 to 1.75 percent in 1993, and to 0.10 percent in 2001. The financial panic subsided in early 1998, but general recession persisted into the 2000s.

Even with the zero interest rate policy in place, pressure on the monetary authorities to do more to stimulate the economy did not let up. Some argued for a more drastic increase of money supply by any means. To do so, the Bank of Japan was advised to purchase more risky assets including bank and corporate bonds, foreign bonds and mortgage bonds. Traditionally, it bought and sold only government bonds for safety reasons. Another group of economists proposed inflation targeting. According to them, the Bank of Japan should announce a positive inflation rate for the next two to three years and be responsible for it. This was considered necessary to change people's expectations about future inflation. Paul Krugman (Princeton University), Alan Meltzer (Carnegie-Mellon University), Ito Takatoshi (Tokyo University) and Itoh Motoshige (Tokyo University) supported this idea. But others, including Bank of Japan economists Okina Kunio and Ueda Kazuo, were skeptical. They argued that, even if the Bank of Japan tried, there would be little impact on expectations because the monetary transmission mechanism was broken. Worse, if people's expectations suddenly shifted for whatever reason, after too much liquidity was injected, the resulting inflation would become uncontrollable.

Anomaly in Japan's monetary transmission mechanism deserves special attention. Normally, the central bank controls monetary base (deposits by commercial banks at the central bank, plus cash) which influences money supply and commercial bank lending, the two important intermediate targets for macroeconomic management. This in turn impacts on production and investment. This is the monetary transmission mechanism by which a central bank stimulates or restrains overall economic activity. However, the relationship between monetary base on the one hand and money supply and commercial bank lending on the other became unstable in post-bubble Japan. As Figure 13.5 shows, these variables moved more or less in tandem in the 1980s. But a disconnect emerged after the bubble collapse in 1990–91. Monetary base was pushed up by the Bank of Japan gradually but in increasingly large doses. But even a massive injection of monetary base did not lead to any visible increase in money supply, and commercial bank lending remained flat or even declined. When interests were zero or negative, there was no penalty (foregone interests) for holding dead cash so banks did just that. Excess deposits by commercial banks at the central bank ballooned without turning into business loans or investment. Japan's monetary transmission mechanism is broken. Unless this is fixed, pumping more money into the financial system will add little impetus for growth.

Another issue related to monetary policy was a call for yen depreciation. Some insisted that aggressive monetary expansion coupled with an official statement to welcome a weak yen would depreciate the yen, improving Japan's international competitiveness and stimulating export and domestic business. The government and the Bank of Japan sometimes appeared to endorse this strategy, and the yen actually depreciated moderately when such policy intention was announced. But currency depreciation is a controversial beggar-thy-neighbor policy in which Japan gains at the cost of other countries. If the United States, China or any other large trading partner opposes the yen's weakening, this policy will have to end. Moreover, exchange rate adjustment is unable to solve the long-term structural problem of any country, and often diverts attention from the real cause of economic weaknesses (Chapter 12).

For a long time, the Bank of Japan intermittently intervened in the foreign exchange market to curb yen appreciation when it was deemed excessive. Since 2011, however, it

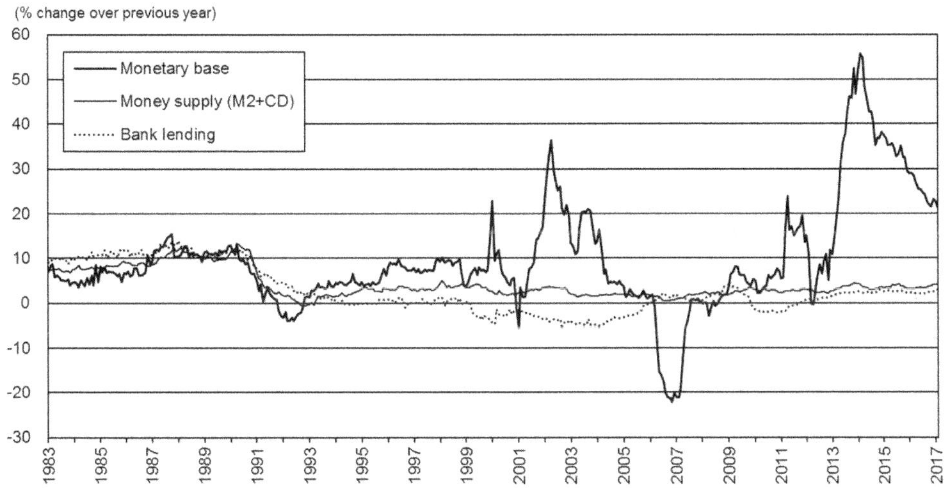

Figure 13.5 Monetary base, money and bank lending

Source: Bank of Japan Time-series Data Search.

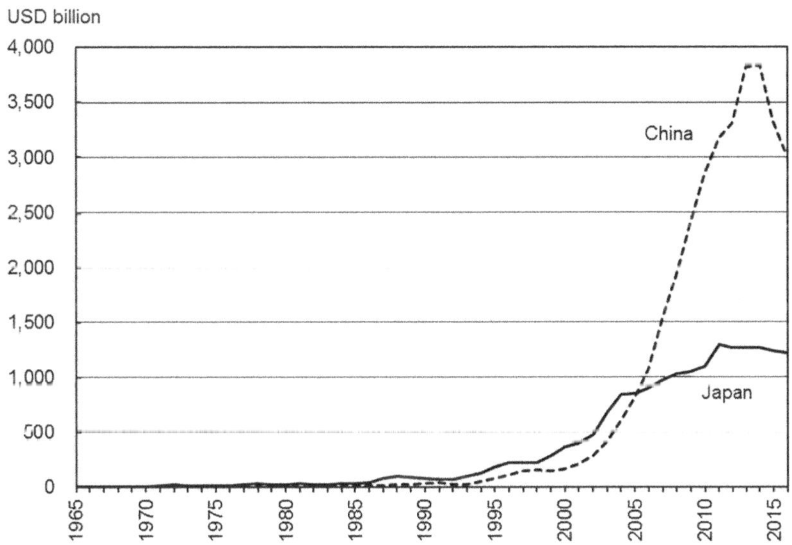

Figure 13.6 International reserves

Sources: Bank of Japan Time-series Data Search, and State Administration of Foreign Exchange, China.

has refrained from pushing up the dollar to keep the yen cheap in the currency market. This policy shift is reflected in Japan's international reserves which peaked at $1.296 trillion in 2011 and have fallen slowly since then. China dramatically overtook Japan as the largest collector of international reserves in the world in 2006 and continued to accumulate up to $3.843 trillion by 2014. But even China stopped purchasing dollars and began to sell them in the foreign exchange market in order to counter the recent declining pressure on RMB (Figure 13.6).

Unstoppable fiscal activism

Fiscal policy has been expansionary since the 1990s, although some say that it has not been expansionary enough relative to what they think is adequate. At the end of fiscal year 2015 (March 2016), outstanding government debt stood at 1,066 trillion yen amounting to twice GDP (Figure 13.7). This is the highest ratio among major industrial countries[2] although it stabilized, temporarily, in recent years thanks to relatively strong tax receipts. Budget deficit is bound to grow in the long run even with effort in spending cuts because fiscal expenditure is dominated by two mandatory and constantly increasing components, namely, servicing of past debts and social security payments, which respectively occupied 24.4 percent and 33.1 percent of total expenditure in fiscal year 2016. It is uncertain whether this public debt explosion can be slowed down and reversed in the future. Moreover, the above figure does not include short-term debt or contingency liabilities (amounts that are unknown at present but must be paid in the future for rescuing the bankrupted social security system, cleaning up the nuclear disaster, coping with natural calamities, etc.) International rating companies have downgraded Japanese government bonds in recent years.

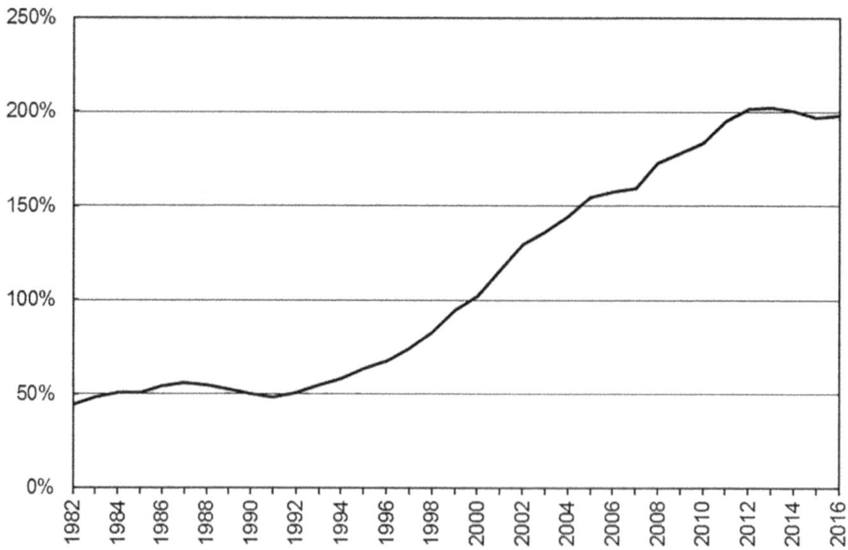

Figure 13.7 Government debt as percent of GDP

Sources: Ministry of Finance, and Cabinet Office.

The government is often torn between the need for fiscal consolidation and the wish for more macroeconomic stimuli. But most of the time, fiscal policy tended toward expansion because weak business situation at hand is politically more critical (for the next election) than restoring a sound budget in the distant future. There has always been a strong political pressure for additional fiscal stimuli to avoid a "deflationary spiral" (price deflation and output recession enforcing each other). Many contended that no reform was possible unless and until the economy improved. Others were comforted that Japanese government bonds were debt owed mostly to Japanese people, which was less worrisome than debt owed to foreigners.

But the effectiveness of fiscal policy under such circumstances is an open question. Opponents of fiscal activism countered that Japan had already tried fiscal stimuli many times since the early 1990s, but the economy had failed to recover strongly. They argued that old-fashioned fiscal spending driven by local politics and lobbyists that built expensive but underused highways, bridges, airports and Shinkansen (fast trains) would only benefit construction companies while national debt snowballed. Did Japan really need three giant bridges to span the Inland Sea? Did Kansai Region need three airports next to each other? Further fiscal stimuli, which would add to the already huge government debt, might actually lower growth due to greater pessimism over fiscal vulnerability and unsoundness. The current political system in which votes are secured by channeling fiscal spending to rural supporters should be ended, it is said.

There were attempts to cope with the fiscal time bomb. The Koizumi government (2001–6, Liberal Democratic Party) set limits on infrastructure and social welfare spending but succeeded in slowing down the speed of debt accumulation only for one year, in 2003. From 2009 to 2012, three consecutive governments of the Democratic Party of Japan cut "unnecessary" public projects randomly and arbitrarily but did not touch the social welfare spending which was the largest and most rigid part of public expenditure. The second and third governments of Abe Shinzo (2012–, Liberal Democratic Party) returned to monetary and fiscal activism (see below).

In 2012, the parliament passed a plan to raise the general consumption tax in steps but it was only partially implemented. The tax was raised from 5 to 8 percent in 2014 but the subsequent increase from 8 to 10 percent was put on hold (until 2019) due to weak business conditions. Welfare "reforms" are under way to increase people's payments and decrease their receipts, but it is questionable whether this is really a solution or mere acceptance of the worsening social welfare balance sheets. In 2014–15, business profits and corporate income tax receipt both rose thanks to the "success" of Abenomics, which slightly reduced the need to issue new government bonds. But this improvement may be temporary.

It is unclear what Japan's gigantic fiscal debt will bring in the future. The debate between fiscal activists and sound budget campaigners goes on. Innovative ideas, such as issuance of unredeemable public bonds or the Fiscal Theory of Price Level (don't worry about budget deficit, inflation will solve it later), are occasionally floated but their relevance to reality is in question. Joseph Dodge, who imposed a super-balanced budget on occupied Japan in 1949, or traditional IMF conditionality, would surely require Japan to tighten its budgetary belt despite short-term pain and protests. But Japan is not under US occupation or IMF financial rescue. Alternatively, hyperinflation or unilateral debt cancellation would instantly solve the problem, even at great costs to certain people, but such sweeping measures are difficult to propose, let alone adopt, in peace time. Meanwhile, domestic politics does not seem to generate any policy option to pay short-term cost first to achieve long-term gain later. Perhaps that is the crux of the problem.

Earthquakes

Japan, sitting on where four tectonic plates meet and shove each other on the earth's crust, is continuously hit by large and small earthquakes. In the last few decades two large quakes caused particularly serious human and physical damage.

On January 17, 1995, an active fault under the port city of Kobe moved to destroy urban dwellings and structures resulting in 6,437 fatalities, which were mostly due to collapsing houses. The physical damage of this earthquake was estimated at 9.9 trillion yen or 2.0 percent of GDP, and the recovery budget amounted to 3 trillion yen or 0.6 percent of GDP. As the damage was too big to be coped with by official hands alone, popular movement emerged to help natural disaster victims through NGOs and volunteering.

On March 11, 2011, a much greater, deeper and widely impacting earthquake occurred off the eastern coast of Japan, generating tsunami and killing 18,446 people due mainly to drowning. The estimated stock damage of this earthquake was 16.9 trillion yen or 3.6 percent of GDP, and the recovery budget for the first five years was 19 to 23 trillion yen or 4.0–4.9 percent of GDP. This did not include the costs related to the Fukushima nuclear accident. The handling of this earthquake by the Kan government (Democratic Party of Japan), including formulation of the reconstruction plan, response to the radiation problem, power shortage and future energy policy, was severely criticized as inept and haphazard.

The human and physical damage of these earthquakes was immense. In terms of economic growth, however, the impact of an earthquake is usually hard to detect from annual statistics. This is because the negative effect of lost production capacity is offset by the positive effect of increased private and public investment for recovery and reconstruction. Gross National Happiness certainly fell, but Gross Domestic Product did not show any visible sign of decline. In the case of the Great East Japan Earthquake, production fell temporarily and slightly in 2011 due to supply chain disruption and depressed national psychology, but recovered soon as vigorous reconstruction investments started. This even caused serious shortage of construction workers and materials. Global recession, yen appreciation and slowdown of Chinese or US economies will have much greater impacts on Japanese growth than natural catastrophes.

Aging, labor shortage and widening gaps

Japanese society is rapidly aging because old people live longer and young people are not eager to marry or have babies. Such trends are also visible in other countries, but Japan is the global leader in *koreika* (aging) and *shoshika* (producing fewer children). The Japanese population peaked around 2008 at 127 million, then began to decline gradually. Depopulation is expected to continue well into the future. The share of working-age population (aged 16 to 64) started to decline much earlier, peaking at 70 percent around 1995, then falling to about 60 percent at present. This means fewer workers must support more retired people through higher tax burden and social security contributions. A shrinking and aging population also means lackluster domestic demand, reduced saving, low growth and skyrocketing medical and pension bills. Japanese society, once based on communal spirit and intra-family care for the young and the old, no longer functions that way.

A related problem is *kasoka*, or accelerated decline and aging of population in rural areas to the extent that basic transport, medical and commercial services are no longer rendered. The problem of disappearing communities permeates in virtually all cities, towns and villages in rural Japan. This is caused by migration of young people to large cities for education and job opportunities, in addition to gradual passing away of remaining senior citizens. Revitalizing rural communities has become one of the top priorities of any Japanese administration.

Labor shortage has become apparent in recent years. The unemployment rate has steadily fallen from 5.1 percent in 2009 to 3.1 percent in 2016. Many businesses, especially small ones, find it difficult to recruit enough workers. Labor shortage is widespread in all sectors, and especially acute in such service industries as construction, transportation, food catering, elderly care and childcare. Scarcity of construction workers is aggravated by strong reconstruction demand in the aftermath of the Great East Japan Earthquake in 2011 and construction toward the Tokyo Olympics in 2020. Japan has traditionally accepted only a small number of foreign workers except those with highly professional skills or Japanese ethnic origin. This was largely because of the fear that a rapid increase in foreign workers may lead to social friction and problems such as crime and failure to integrate with Japanese society. However, the immigration policy now has to be reconsidered because labor shortage is a structural problem that is not likely to go away soon, and Japan must therefore rely heavily on foreign workers in the future.

Another serious problem is emerging social gaps. Japan in the 1960s attained high growth and income equalization simultaneously until most people felt that they belonged to the middle class (Chapter 11). After the bursting of the bubble, this happy memory was replaced by a sad combination of little growth and perceived inequality. Surveys conducted every three years by the Ministry of Health, Labor and Welfare show that income before tax and subsidies is rapidly becoming unequal, although there is no evidence of widening income gaps after income redistribution through tax and social welfare systems is taken into account. For income after redistribution, the Gini coefficient, which ranges from zero (perfect equality) to one (perfect inequality), declined slightly from 0.3812 in 2002 to 0.3759 in 2014. The Ministry interprets this as evidence of effective redistribution policies.[3]

Despite this, poverty is on the rise even after income redistribution. Japan's poverty ratio (relative definition counting the number of people below 50 percent of median income) increased during the last three decades from 12.0 percent in 1984 to 16.1 percent in 2014, which is second highest among advanced countries after the United States. Popular perception is that Japan is rapidly becoming an unequal society. In recent surveys, about 70 to 80 percent of respondents concur with this assessment.[4] In their view, this fact is most visible in wage gaps, followed by distinction between regular and non-regular workers (next paragraph), differentiated job opportunities, increase in low-income families and social service gaps between urban and rural areas. In Japan, inequality is associated mainly with increasing poverty rather than the existence of a very few extremely rich people (Tachibanaki, 2016).

Inequality in work places is most apparent in unequal treatment between regular workers who enjoy permanent status and non-regular workers such as part-timers and workers with short-term contracts. The ratio of non-regular workers has risen rapidly from about 20 percent in 1990 to 40 percent in 2014. The prolonged recession increased management's desire to cut labor cost and have an option to reduce workforce at times of slow business, as well as workers' reluctant acceptance of such inferior positions. Even if their job description is the same, non-regular workers receive lower wages, to the tune of only 63 percent of the wages of regular workers (Ministry of Health, Labor and Welfare survey, 2014), little or no benefits and promotion prospects, and job insecurity. Female workers and youths account for the bulk of non-regular workforce, who tend to be trapped in the second-rate status with little prospect of moving up to regular positions. This generates long-term problems such as the inability to marry for financial reasons, less production of children, low lifetime saving, continued poverty into old age and the next generation, and extreme hardship for single, divorced or widowed mothers. Even seemingly protected regular workers are forced to work hard to keep their position under strong cost-cutting pressure. Unpaid overwork is a common practice, often leading to job-caused illness and suicide.

In response, the Japanese government is promoting equality between regular and non-regular workers, urging wage increases and fewer working hours to company management, helping female labor to take up more jobs and high positions and, through all these, achieving a better work–life balance for Japanese workers.

Abenomics

After the relatively strong government of Koizumi Junichiro (2001–6), a series of weak and short-lived governments ensued, three by the long-ruling Liberal Democratic Party (LDP—Abe, Fukuda and Aso) and three by the Democratic Party of Japan (DPJ—Hatoyama, Kan and Noda). Japan had six prime ministers in just as many years. In 2009, people voted for untested DPJ to replace unimpressive LDP leaders by fresher faces, but new governments proved even worse than traditional ones. A hoped-for two-party regime in which LDP and DPJ would compete for power was not realized. Disappointed, in 2012, people voted back an LDP government led by Abe Shinzo, who held the top office earlier but had to resign due to illness. Fully recovered, Abe emerged as a vigorous and very powerful prime minister in his second and third term, introducing many initiatives and visiting a large number of countries. His energetic way, in stark contrast with incapacitated opposition parties, won the hearts of Japanese people even though they did not fully agree with many of his agendas. Abe was a conservative politician interested in boosting national pride, active engagement in regional security, opposing Chinese military advances and pursuing Japanese business interests at home and abroad. He began to yield strong and unilateral power over his party and central government in place of the collective and bottom-up decision making of the past. As of 2017, LDP, in coalition with Komeito Party, has absolute majority in both Houses,[5] which allows it to pass any law it pleases subject to time, popular sentiment and the absence of serious political scandals.

Abenomics was the most prominent economic initiative of his government. As soon as Abe came to power for the second time in December 2012, he launched the initiative for the purpose of ending deflation and reviving growth. Although Abenomics contained nothing really new, it was presented far more effectively than any other previous economic package. It consisted of three "Arrows"—aggressive monetary policy in "different dimension," flexible (i.e., active) fiscal policy and new growth strategy. In March 2013, Abe appointed Kuroda Haruhiko as Bank of Japan Governor who immediately began to execute the Monetary Arrow of Abenomics. Kuroda declared an inflation target of 2 percent, to be attained in two years, and promised to double monetary base and the central bank's government bond holding, also in two years. With this monetary expansion, the extremely high yen was also to be corrected. For the Fiscal Arrow of Abenomics, investment in infrastructure was increased under the slogan of revive economy first, consolidate budget later. To implement the Growth Arrow, the Japanese Economy Revitalization Headquarters and the Industrial Competitiveness Conference were established, and the Cabinet approved the Japan Revitalization Strategy featuring three Roadmaps and three Plans in June 2013. From then on, it became customary to add, adjust or otherwise revise the Growth Arrow of Abenomics annually around June.

Abenomics was enormously successful in its first several months in uplifting national psychology, pushing up the stock market and depreciating the yen. These collectively improved business sentiment and conditions. Corporate profits rose, tax revenue increased and unemployment started to fall. Abe naturally took full credit for these improvements. The Monetary Arrow of Abenomics was particularly praised by such foreign and domestic economists as Joseph Stiglitz, Paul Krugman, IMF Managing Director Christine Lagarde, US Fed Chairman Ben Bernanke, Takenaka Heizo, Hamada Koichi and Ito Takatoshi. However, there were also skeptics such as George Soros, Okina Kunio, Ueda Kazuo and Kono Ryutaro who pointed to future risks and uncertainties associated with such a bold monetary move as well as the problem of the broken monetary transmission mechanism (as mentioned previously).

One problem associated with inflation targeting was that the Bank of Japan was only a small part of factors that determined the inflation rate. Actual inflation rose somewhat, then fell back to the zero-to-negative range, missing the 2 percent target by a wide margin. The Bank of Japan extended the deadline beyond the second year, shifted to negative (rather than zero) interest rate policy, introduced a policy rule centered on long-term interest rates, then finally admitted that 2-percent inflation might be unrealistic for some time to come. Unmoving prices were blamed on the declining global oil price (which was actually good for the Japanese economy), the negative impact of (modest) consumption tax increase and uncertainty surrounding the growth potential of emerging economies.

Yet, most criticism of Abenomics was directed to the Growth Arrow. Macroeconomic policy is not an end in itself but a means to prepare a congenial environment for strong and sustained economic growth. The growth policy therefore should take center stage, but the Growth Arrow of Abenomics was ambiguous, spread-out and continuously shifting. The original version announced in June 2013 had three Roadmaps and three Plans, which branched out to twelve pillars, thirty-seven items and fifty-six sub-items. They were revised and expanded annually. Proposed actions were not unreasonable but too general and too many without prioritization or implementation details. Many coincided with initiatives frequently adopted by past governments. It may even be said that the Growth Arrow was just a long and evolving wish list whose execution depended on concrete projects of individual ministries that might or might not be proposed or approved. Line ministries rushed to come up with projects that were likely to be approved under the Growth Arrow, carrying such key words as women, childcare, rural area revitalization, foreign trainees, inbound tourism, overseas expansion of SMEs and so forth. However, these projects were not properly integrated or structured for achieving concrete targets. After several years of adjusting the Growth Arrow, the initial appeal of Abenomics as a Japan revival plan seems to have been lost.

The book comes to a close here, under this somewhat pessimistic tone, leaving the economic development of Japan as an unending story. After traveling a few centuries since the Edo period, with many twists and turns as well as successes and failures, Japan has reached a stage where obsession with material wealth—catching up with the West or competing with China—is no longer desirable or feasible. Yet mature Japan has many spiritual, communal and other non-material values that are unique but were mostly pushed aside in the race to high technology and income. Whether they can be reactivated to produce a new society is yet to be seen.

Box 13.1 The future of manufacturing SMEs

Small and medium enterprises (SMEs) in the manufacturing sector have been a great value creator in post-WW2 industrialization. While Japan's big-name car, electronics and machinery makers are globally well known, they heavily rely on the supply of materials and components produced by manufacturing SMEs. Such materials and components require precision, zero defects and on-time delivery, and contribute far more to the product value than final assembly. Japan has many industrial areas where manufacturing SMEs congregate such as Ota Ward of Tokyo, Nagoya and its surrounding areas in Aichi Prefecture, Higashi Osaka, Sakai, Kobe, Amagasaki, Kitakyushu, Suwa and Okaya, Ota and Isezaki, and so on. Some component manufacturers operate independently but many are organized as regular suppliers in a pyramidal keiretsu relationship led by a large parent company.

However, small manufacturers have been in trouble since the bursting of the asset bubble. From around 1990 to most recent observation (2012–13), manufacturing SMEs in Japan shrunk 44 percent in number of establishments, 36 percent in employment and 23 percent in output. Difference in these numbers implies that the average size of firms rose as smallest ones were eliminated or merged. This is a nationwide phenomenon replicated in virtually all industrial areas mentioned above. Multiple reasons are cited for this, including the prolonged post-bubble recession, severe pressure for cost reduction, exodus of large customer companies abroad, recurrent yen appreciation, aging and declining population, high corporate income tax, competition with emerging economies, labor shortage, global economic crises, and so on. Among these, the particularly unique problems facing Japanese manufacturing SMEs are declining orders in the domestic market and the lack of young workers who join and take over the factory. Many SMEs have closed because retiring owners could not find anyone to inherit the business.

For distressed SMEs, one way to survive and even to prosper is to go abroad. This is certainly not the first time Japanese manufacturers have gone abroad, but the previous waves of overseas investments were carried out mostly by globally well-known giants or their subsidiaries that were encouraged or forced to go with them. Most SMEs remaining in Japan then were passive producers receiving orders and blueprints from large customers and producing and delivering products promptly and in perfect quality. They had high skills and technology but little capacity for making dynamic strategies such as proposing and designing new products, seizing new customers and markets, finding international partners, recruiting foreign managers and engineers, utilizing IT and social networking services, registering and protecting intellectual properties, etc. SME owners spoke only Japanese and seldom travelled abroad. But after the global financial crisis of 2008 (which Japanese call the "Lehman Shock"), even such *machikoba* (small local factories) had to consider going abroad because orders for their products suddenly vanished. Even so, they had no knowledge or experience to succeed in unknown foreign markets. This situation was very different from manufacturing SMEs in Germany ("Hidden Champions"), China or Taiwan which were equipped with full corporate functions to forge ahead in global markets.

Traditionally, the Japanese government had been hesitant to promote overseas investment of manufacturing SMEs for fear of "hollowing out" of the Japanese industrial base. But seeing the enormous size and irreversibility of the Lehman Shock, it switched to actively supporting such investment. In 2010, the Minister of Economy, Trade and Industry began to host the Conference for Supporting Overseas Business Expansion of SMEs, which compiled and revised a policy guideline in 2011 and 2012, respectively. For the first time, the Japan International Cooperation Agency (responsible for development aid) and the Japan External Trade Organization (in charge of trade promotion) were also tasked with assisting Japanese manufacturing SMEs to venture abroad. Not only the central government but local governments, business organizations and NPOs were also mobilized to execute this policy. It soon became a major pillar in Japan's SME assistance package. Information dissemination, business consultation, matching with foreign partners and suppliers, business support abroad and negotiating and creating business ties with foreign provinces and cities are among the standard measures. Some institutions provide "hands-on" support, or customized and intensive support to overcome initial difficulties for a small number of carefully selected SMEs.

Not all manufacturing SMEs in distress are advised to go abroad. Even with official assistance, international business is a huge challenge for firms with little experience. Prior screening is necessary to pick eligible firms from those that are better off home or those that are truly hopeless. The most important criterion is whether the company boss has a strong will and a reasonable initial plan to start the process. When proper selection is made, there is a good chance that *machikoba* will grow into a larger and more dynamic enterprise in an entirely new environment. This means that Japanese manufacturing will prosper and develop in different soils and cultures. From the viewpoint of developing countries, arrival of high-precision Japanese SMEs is very welcome for learning skills and technology, offering gainful employment to youths and overcoming middle income traps. Vietnam and Thailand are the most popular destinations for Japanese manufacturing SMEs, and Indonesia is additionally popular among Japanese SMEs in the automotive sector. On the receiving side, domestic firms in these countries often crave partnering with Japanese SMEs that will help them with technology and marketing.

Let us look at a few actual cases. Firm A, a precision metalworking factory in Higashi Osaka, hired several *gino jisshusei* (technical intern trainees who stay in Japan for up to three years) from Vietnam starting in 2004. They were diligent and excellent workers. Soon they were hired as full timers. In 2014, the firm decided to build a branch factory in Ho Chi Minh City by dispatching its Vietnamese staff to their fatherland.

Firm B, a hand tool maker in Tokyo, invested in Vietnam in 1997 while also assisting other Japanese SMEs to come to Vietnam by offering business services and rental factory space. It expanded its own Vietnamese factory in 2008 and built a new rental factory complex nearby in 2014. A naturalized and highly experienced Vietnamese engineer was recruited from Gunma Prefecture to implement these expansions.

Firm C, a metal parts manufacturer in Nagoya, shares its unused factory space in Bangkok, Thailand with other manufacturing SMEs from Nagoya. It provides multiple and flexible support to Japanese SMEs coming to Bangkok, for example, through trading services, matching with local Thai suppliers and a branch office in Nagoya.

In all of these cases, human and inter-firm networking and government support programs contributed, with different intensity and effectiveness, to minimize initial investment cost and risks of overseas investment by Japanese manufacturing SMEs.

Notes

1 In April 1997, the Hashimoto Cabinet, backed by the Ministry of Finance's desire to restore fiscal soundness, raised the general consumption tax from 3 to 5 percent. The economy weakened immediately and the tax hike was blamed. However, it is strange that such a small tax increase had such a huge economic impact.

2 In 2015, the ratio of general government (central and local governments) gross debt to GDP of Japan was 248 percent, which was highest in the world (IMF World Economic Outlook Database, October 2016). The other countries whose public debt stock was greater than GDP were Greece (177 percent), Italy (133 percent), Portugal (129 percent), Cyprus (109 percent), Belgium (106 percent), United States (104 percent) and Singapore (103 percent).

3 The Ministry of Health, Labor and Welfare's data show that, before redistribution, the Gini coefficient rose significantly from 0.4983 (2002) to 0.5263 (2005), 0.5318 (2008), 0.5536 (2011) and 0.5704 (2014). But after redistribution, it was quite stable at 0.3812 (2002), 0.3873 (2005), 0.3758 (2008), 0.3791 (2011) and 0.3759 (2014).

4 In the survey conducted by the Yomiuri Newspaper in March 2007, for example, 81 percent felt that gaps were widening while 3 percent did not think so. Don't Knows and no response accounted for the remaining 16 percent.

5 As of this writing (April 2017), LDP holds 61.9 percent and Komeito holds 7.4 percent of 475 seats in the House of Representatives, and LDP has 47.1 percent and Komeito has 8.3 percent of 242 seats in the House of Councilors. The term of the House of Representatives is four years, with the last election taking place in December 2014. The term of the House of Councilors is six years with half elected every three years, with the last batch elected in July 2016.

QUESTIONS AND ANSWERS

Below are some of the questions raised by students in my class over the years, followed by my answers. Some questions were quite difficult to answer and compelled me to do additional research. I am not entirely confident whether all my answers can stand the scrutiny of the latest academic research. I list them nonetheless because questions raised by foreign students often throw new light on old questions that are too familiar to the Japanese. Many are on the Edo and Meiji period, partly because my students actually asked many questions about these early periods, and partly because of my uneven recording. It should also be noted that many of the class discussions have already been incorporated in the main text of this edition.

1 When did Japan feel it had finally caught up with the West?

It happened two times—around the 1910s, and around 1970.

The first time was when Japan felt that it finally joined the group of "First Class" nations. It won an (unexpected) victory against the Russian Empire in 1905, and the industrial revolution in light manufacturing was also completed, overtaking the British textile industry in the global market. Japan had also acquired two main colonies of Taiwan (1895) and Korea (1910) and secured certain territorial and economic interests in Northeast China. Renegotiations of unequal commercial treaties with the West had been made in steps until they were all corrected in 1911. The national goals of the Meiji period, to become a strong Westernized nation diplomatically, economically and militarily, were more or less realized. After WW1, Japan was regularly invited to major international conferences as one of the "Big Five" nations along with the United States, the United Kingdom, France and Italy.

The second time was when Japan grew very fast for a quarter century from the devastation of war defeat and largely caught up with the United States and Western European nations in per capita income. By around 1970, modern infrastructure such as the Tokyo Tower, highways and fast trains had been built, the Olympic Games were held in Tokyo in 1964, the first time ever in Asia, and such modern industries as steel, automobile and electronics had attained—or were attaining global competitiveness.

2 Has Japan ever been a socialist economy?

Japan has never been a socialist economy in the ownership sense. That is to say, in all periods, production was undertaken mostly by individuals, families or private

 DOI: 10.4324/9781315444048-15

firms. The government did not organize farmers and workers into collective units in any significant way. Even during the wartime of 1937–45, the government chose to control and direct private companies toward the war effort without nationalizing them.

But in the sense of economic management, the above-mentioned wartime was a period of rigid planning based on physical inputs and outputs. The period of recovery from the war damage in 1945–49 was also characterized by continued official planning and directives, although black markets emerged and prospered at the same time. Japan was a planned economy from 1937 to 1949 although ownership remained private. This clearly shows separability of ownership and the allocative mechanism.

During the high growth era of the 1950s and 1960s, the Japanese government was guiding the private sector in a milder form, which was neither free market nor socialist planning.

3 In world history, kings and emperors usually did not last very long. Political upheavals could easily end their rule, bringing in another dynasty or empire. Why has Japan's imperial family lasted so long?

According to the oldest official record of Japanese history (*Kojiki*, or Ancient Chronicle, 712), Japanese islands were created and inhabited by a group of gods who descended from heaven, and their progeny became the imperial family. The Meiji government determined that transformation from god to human in the imperial family occurred on February 11, 660 BC, when Jimmu, the first human emperor, assumed power. In 1940, the war government celebrated the 2,600th anniversary of this event. Apart from the legend, however, we do not know the exact date or circumstances of the rise of the imperial family, whose consolidation of power occurred in the seventh century AD.

During the war years in the late 1930s and up to 1945, schools taught that the Japanese imperial family was an unbroken divine lineage from time immemorial. This bestowed superiority on the Japanese people who were ruled by such an auspicious family. But even counting from the seventh century, it must be admitted that continuation of the same ruling family for more than thirteen centuries is very unique in world history. Some argue that the imperial family is not really of one lineage because of the family feud in the fourteenth century, but we are mainly interested in its political, not genetic, continuity. The emperor had real political power in the eighth century, but his power declined quickly in the subsequent centuries. Why was the Japanese monarchy never abolished by warlords or shogun?

The first samurai leader who came to national power was appointed by the emperor in 1192 with the official title of *Seii Tashogun* (Great General Who Conquers Foreign Enemies). This approval procedure was a political convenience, but it was followed by all subsequent top samurai leaders with the same honorary title. For a new military leader who was challenged by his competitors and needed legitimization of his rule, the use of imperial authority was extremely useful. For him, there was no need to topple the emperor who resided in Kyoto, composed poems, performed rituals and was militarily impotent. Once the tradition began in which a new political leader had to be formally appointed to Seii Taishogun by the emperor, it became firmly entrenched. The political cost of ousting the emperor was far greater than the cost of operating under his nominal authority. The Meiji government also resorted to this political practice when it wanted to consolidate power.

Another important factor is that Japan was never invaded or occupied by foreigners except by the Americans during 1945–52. This means that no external force had the chance to wipe out the imperial family. Although the Americans first considered the possibility of judging and executing the emperor as a war criminal, they decided not to, being afraid of nationwide riots that such action might trigger. The same political consideration was at play.

4 What was the system of land ownership in the Edo period? Were farmers permitted to own land?

Under the pre-modern political system of the Edo period, which was a kind of feudalism, the shogun gave land to daimyos to govern in exchange for their loyalty. Farmers were considered to be part of the land and were not allowed to move, and no land sale or rental was officially permitted. Under such a system, the modern concept of land ownership is difficult to apply. However, Tanaka Keiichi, an Edo scholar, says that the prohibition of land title transfers was ineffective. Farmers actually bought and sold land without any punishment and some even left the village to avoid repression or in search of better life. I am sure such practices did exist but how widespread it was remains an open question. Officially, all land directly or indirectly (through hans) belonged to the shogun. But within each han, the daimyo had the right to govern and tax his land. Moreover, each village had autonomy as long as it paid rice taxes. In such a society, it is difficult to say precisely who owned the land.

5 Why could the bakufu suppress military uprisings by hans?

Tokugawa Ieyasu, the first shogun, was a very clever man. To end the warring years, a number of institutions were installed at the beginning of the Edo period making a revolt against the central power virtually impossible. For example, a heavy financial burden was imposed on daimyos through obligatory residence in Edo every other year, assignment of public works and ad hoc taxation. Meanwhile, daimyo's wives and children were to always reside in Edo as potential hostages. Strict bans and restrictions were imposed on travel, shipbuilding, type of weaponry, construction of castles and bridges, and so on. Powerful hans were given land away from Edo, and Tokugawa families and friendly hans (former followers of Tokugawa Ieyasu) were given locations of military importance. Moreover, the physical sizes and locations of hans were changed at the bakufu's will at any time, and mutual surveillance and checks were forced on daimyos. All samurai leaders and their retainers were given positions in a complicated ranking system where upper samurai had absolute authority over lower ones. Under this system, any sign of disobedience led to the termination of the daimyo's reign and his family.

6 Why was only the Dutch language used for Western studies by Edo scholars?

Because the Netherlands was the only Western country that the bakufu granted the right to trade with Japan (the other officially permitted trading partner was China). For this reason, all technical and medical books imported from the West were in Dutch. Studying the Dutch language was equivalent to learning Western technology. Among Western countries, the bakufu allowed only the Netherlands to trade with Japan because the Dutch were Protestant. Catholic countries such as Spain and Portugal sent aggressive missions to convert the Japanese to Christianity, which was disliked by Japanese rulers. Meanwhile, the Dutch were more interested in commercial profit than religious activity. The Dutch also seem to have made up the story that the Spaniards and the Portuguese were planning to invade Japan or seize gold and silver mines in Japan.

7 I understand that Edo society was a conservative class society, but was there any mobility among the classes through marriage or any other means?

Officially and in principle, no class mobility was allowed. Distinction between the ruling class (samurai) and all others was especially strict while differences among the ruled—farmers, craftsmen and merchants—were less so. In reality, however, there were certainly cases of poor and lordless samurai becoming farmers, and rich merchants with merits or large donations being upgraded to samurai. Despite such records, there are no reliable statistics that prove the frequency of such transition at the national level.

8 Was dissatisfaction with unequal land distribution one of the main reasons for farmers' uprising?

No, that was not the main reason. From the mid-seventeenth century onwards, the main reasons for farmers' revolts (called *ikki*) included protestation against a heavy tax burden, corrupt officials, han's policy and bakufu's policy. The typical actions in uprisings included direct appeal to the government (which was illegal and punishable), collective abandonment of land to escape to another area, and attacks on the residences of targeted officials. Some researchers insist that farmers' uprisings in the Edo period were well planned and followed pre-set rules and procedure, and participants were highly disciplined. They were not spontaneous violence without leaders. Toward the end of the Edo period, as the number of poor and landless peasants increased, many uprisings against rich merchants and rural landlords occurred. Their houses were attacked and destroyed.

9 Was Japan linguistically unified in the Edo period?

We can say yes by the standard of today's developing countries. Although there were different dialects and nuances in pronunciation, which made oral communication across different regions sometimes difficult, these were all variations of the same Japanese language. Grammar and written language were uniform across all regions. The important thing is that, through the use of one language, Japanese national identity had been firmly established. In fact, this was true even before the Edo period. To put it differently, linguistic differences did not cause social division or ethnic conflict in Japan. However, it must also be pointed out that there were ethnic minorities who did not integrate into the Japanese society. For example, the Ainu (indigenous) people in Hokkaido and the Okinawa people in the southwestern islands spoke different languages and had separate cultures. There were also a small number of hunters living in mountains who did not mingle with the Japanese majority. These people were not counted as Japanese then.

10 What is Confucianism?

There were many ancient Chinese philosophers, but the most famous ones are Confucius (551–479 BC) and Lao-tse (sixth century BC? His existence is not proven). Their ideas are called Confucianism and Taoism, respectively. They both taught how humans should live and behave, but had quite different orientations. Confucius taught virtue and discipline in social life including how to properly perform rituals and ceremonies, respect parents and serve your lord, and how kings and emperors should rule. Meanwhile, Lao-tse emphasized natural experience and alignment with the universe. He instructed how to achieve things without effort, feel the mystery of being, perceive the world without leaving the house and so forth. These two saints had enormous impacts on East Asian societies such as China, Korea, Japan and Vietnam for the next 2,500 years.

Confucius wanted to become an advisor to a truly wise king, but he never found one. All his life, he traveled with his disciples and taught them through discussion. This method is similar to that of Buddha, Jesus and Socrates. The disciples wrote down his words in *Lun-yu* (Rongo in Japanese pronunciation) which became the best-selling textbook and a subject of serious research (the meaning of his terse words is often unclear) for a long time. My favorite lines from Lun-yu go like this: "Learning without thinking is useless, thinking without learning is precarious"; "Clever words and superficial smiles carry little virtue"; "You shall always remember the ages of your parents. One, for celebrating. Two, for fearing." Confucianism was introduced in Japan in the fourth or fifth century AD, but it remained unpopular until the Edo bakufu reactivated it as an official doctrine. Its teachings were suitable for maintaining social order in a class society.

11 How was the relationship between Japan and Korea during the Edo period?

Toward the end of the warring period, in 1592–93 and 1597–98, the army of Toyotomi Hideyoshi, then the supreme military commander of Japan, twice invaded and devastated Korea but failed to occupy it due to Chinese military intervention and declining morale of Japanese samurai who did not clearly see the purpose of the campaign. Tokugawa Ieyasu, the first Edo shogun, tried to mend the strained bilateral relations by ordering Tsushima Han, situated on two islands between the two countries, to negotiate with the Korean government. This resulted in commercial trade between Korea and Tsushima Han as well as an agreement to exchange official letters and receive Korean envoys to Japan. The bakufu wanted to maintain stable ties with Korea for national security reasons. Perhaps the reasons on the Korean side were similar.

Korean missions to Japan were diplomatic and symbolic ones, expressing political goodwill on the occasions of assumption of power by a new shogun or the birth of a shogun's son. Korea was not one of the two countries permitted to trade with Japan. Even though gifts were exchanged, they did not amount to very much in Japan's total trade. Twelve such missions were dispatched from Korea to Japan throughout the Edo period with decreasing frequency. Japanese people watched with great curiosity the passing foreign mission of several hundred people as it paraded from Shimonoseki to Edo via the Inland Sea and over land. However, reciprocal missions from Japan to Korea were not sent (there were missions only from Tsushima Han).

12 Tell us more about the outcast class in the Edo period.

There were two types of outcast people in the Edo period: *hinin* (literally, non-human) and *eta* (meaning unclean). These discriminatory words existed from long ago, but the bakufu institutionalized certain people at the bottom of the society by giving them organization and functions.

The hinin were beggars who lived in designated districts in urban areas. They were usually organized and policed by managers who were internally elected or officially appointed. There were also unorganized hinin as well. Some mobility existed between the hinin and normal people. For example, the latter could become beggars through poverty.

The eta were people whose profession was to process dead animals such as horses and cattle, and supply raw materials for the leather industry. They were also forced to perform criminal executions. These were considered unclean jobs. However, eta people were also engaged in other professions including farming. The eta were also organized by managers at the han level.

Discrimination against these people continued even after the Edo period. To eliminate unjustified prejudice, *Zenkoku Suiheisha* (the National Level Society) was created in 1922 and *Buraku Kaiho Domei* (the League for Liberating Discriminated People) was organized in 1955. Legally, of course, the present Japanese constitution and laws guarantee equal rights to all. But even today, we cannot say that prejudice against the formerly discriminated has been eradicated completely. The movement for ending social discrimination continues.

13 By the early Meiji period, why did Japan feel that it no longer faced the risk of colonization?

When Japan was forced by the West to open its ports (1853–54), the possibility of colonization was considered real. But by Meiji Restoration (1868), Japan worried less about military invasion by Western powers. Instead, the national goal of catching up fast with the West had emerged. What happened during these fifteen or so years? It is difficult to answer succinctly, but the following factors might have been at play.

First, despite social confusion, Japan retained national unity and policy autonomy. A devastating civil war was avoided, and the internal war turned out to be short and small-scale. The state machinery continued to function after the change of government. Second, Japan was importing and absorbing Western technology very rapidly, and military and economic capabilities were being enhanced. Seeing this, Westerners became mainly interested in securing commercial interests rather than using military means to occupy and colonize Japan. At any rate, Japan was too far from their homelands to mobilize large-scale forces, and Americans were busy with their own Civil War.

There was also rivalry among the Western powers in Japan, especially between the British and the French, who tried to intervene and influence domestic politics. This prevented the dominance of any single foreign country and benefited the Japanese side.

14 How many foreign advisors were employed in the Meiji period? Even though their salaries were very high, can we say that their productivity was also high?

In the Meiji period, officially or privately employed foreigners numbered in the hundreds in any year, but their composition changed over time. In the first ten years of Meiji (1868–77), most foreign advisors were hired by the government and numbered between 300 and 600 in any year. Subsequently, the number of officially contracted foreigners declined sharply while the number of privately hired ones increased. Nearly half of those hired privately were teachers and professors at academic institutions, many of whom were English teachers at private universities. By nationality, the British dominated followed by the French and the Germans. There were also a large number of Americans, but most of them were professors and teachers. There were very few American engineers.

Here are some statistics in the Report on the Outline of the Ministry of Industry compiled in 1931. In early Meiji (around 1872), Yokosuka Shipyard employed twenty-eight foreigners (all French), the Railroad Agency had eighty (mostly British), the National Mint had twenty (mostly British) and Ikuno Mine had fifteen (all French). These four state-run bodies alone accounted for 143 foreigners. But not all were top notch engineers with advanced technology. They included factory operators, accountants, secretaries and doctors as well.

It is reasonable to believe that these foreigners were worth the money. But it is difficult to precisely measure their labor productivity since their task was to bring something entirely new to Japan. Without British help, Japan could not have laid its first railroad. Does this mean their productivity was infinite? Can we measure the contribution of any new industry to growth when the economy is propelled by many other factors? The return on foreign advisors also depended on how quickly the Japanese side could take over the new enterprise. Had the Japanese never learned, new industries would have forever depended on foreign management and instructions, which would have been very costly. In reality, this did not happen.

15 Tell us about schools that taught practical engineering.

Establishment of *Koto Kogyo Gakko* (High-level Industrial Schools) to supply mid-range industrial instructors and factory supervisors was proposed by Gottfried Wagener, a German engineer hired by the Meiji government, and Tejima Seiichi, a Ministry of Education official. *Tokyo Shokko Gakko* (Tokyo Craftsmen School) was set up by the Ministry of Education in 1881. It recruited students among high school graduates aged 16–17 through nationwide examination, except those with good past grades who were accepted without examination. Mechanical engineering and chemical engineering were offered with more courses added later. The name of this school changed several times, including *Tokyo Kogyo Gakko* (Tokyo Industrial School).

Unlike *Kobu Daigakko* (Institute of Technology) where foreign instructors taught top engineers mainly for the government, all teachers at Tokyo Kogyo Gakko were Japanese except Mr. Wagener who taught ceramics and glass making. Most Japanese teachers came from the Faculty of Science of Tokyo University. The school faced administrative and financial troubles initially, but operation stabilized around 1890 as Mr. Tejima took over the school. Tokyo Kogyo Gakko became the leading institute for producing industrial instructors, factory managers, engineers and entrepreneurs (education of industrial instructors was later delegated to another institution). After its campus near Asakusa was destroyed by the Great Kanto Earthquake in 1923, the school relocated to O-okayama (Meguro-ku, Tokyo). It is now the Tokyo Institute of Technology.

Besides Tokyo, publicly run *Kogyo Gakko* (Industrial Schools) were established in Osaka (1901), Kyoto (1902), Nagoya (1905), Kumamoto (1906), Sendai (1906), Yonezawa (1910) and Akita (mining course only, 1910) with a total of eight schools during the Meiji period. After Meiji, twenty-three more Kogyo Gakko were created. After WW2, most of these schools were transformed into faculties of engineering of national universities. Japan also has private industrial schools but most of them were established after WW2.

16 In what respect was the Meiji Constitution ambiguous?

Here are some translated excerpts from the Constitution of the Empire of Japan promulgated in 1889. Underlined parts were controversial or subject to different interpretations.

Article 1. The Empire of Japan shall be reigned over and governed by a line of Emperors unbroken for ages eternal.

Article 3. The Emperor is sacred and inviolable.

Article 4. The Emperor is the head of the Empire, combining in Himself the rights of sovereignty, and exercises them, <u>according to the provisions of the present Constitution</u>.

Article 5. The Emperor exercises the legislative power <u>with the consent of</u> the Imperial Diet [Parliament].

Article 55. The <u>respective</u> Ministers of State shall give their advice to the Emperor, and be responsible for it.

Article 3 may look like deification of the emperor which is unique to Japan, but it is in fact a direct copy from a typical European constitution. This line was inserted on the advice of Karl Friedrich Hermann Roesler, a German legal advisor to the Meiji government. It means the ministers, and not the emperor, bear the responsibility for the consequences of any policy.

The intention of the original drafters of the Meiji Constitution, especially Ito Hirobumi, was to place the emperor within the state mechanism and under this constitution, as Article 4 makes it clear. But conservative members of the Privy Council, a body created to review the constitution draft, demanded that the underlined part in Article 4 should be deleted, which Ito strongly resisted. He argued successfully that there would be no constitutional government if the emperor was placed outside its framework. However, much later in the 1930s, Ito's interpretation and its developed form, *Tenno Kikan Setsu* (The Organ Theory of the Emperor), were criticized by the military and rightwing groups. As a result, the emperor was elevated above the state and the constitution.

Article 5 says that the parliament must give "consent" to the Emperor's legislative decision. In the Japanese original, the term *shonin* (approve) was first proposed but it was replaced by a weaker term, *kyosan* (humbly support).

The problem with Article 55 was that it was unclear whether individual ministers or the cabinet as a whole were to advise the emperor, especially on military matters. If a joint cabinet decision was required, the Minister of Army or Navy must discuss the issue with other ministers, especially the Ministers of Finance and Foreign Affairs. This would certainly put a damper on any proposed military action for fiscal or diplomatic reasons. If not, he could advise the emperor directly and independently.

The Meiji Constitution also said little about the precise relationship between the legislative and executive powers. This permitted adoption of a party cabinet (a government formed by the political party that had the largest parliamentary seats) as well as *chozen naikaku* (government of appointed generals and bureaucrats that included no elected representatives). Other strong political players in prewar Japan, such as *genro* (old politicians with past merits) and the Privy Council itself, which later became a permanent advisory organ for the emperor, were not even mentioned in the constitution. As a result, the Japanese government was run through competition among many groups with the exact role of each undefined.

17 How did Meiji Japan mobilize investment capital?

There were super businessmen such as Shibusawa Eiichi and Godai Tomoatsu who introduced the Western system of joint stock companies and encouraged their rich friends to invest in stocks. Shibusawa also used his First "National" (actually private) Bank to finance working capital of burgeoning firms. Prominent business leaders such as these contributed to the establishment of many large companies. In addition, expansion of foreign demand for silk and tea and domestic demand for rice, along with their rising prices, enriched rural Japan permitting self-financing of industries by well-to-do farmers, landlords and merchants. From the late 1880s, Japan experienced waves of "company booms" during which many modern joint stock companies in textile and railways were created. All of the above were methods of mobilizing domestic savings. There was very little foreign participation in the capital of these companies. In fact, foreigners' investment in Japanese enterprises (foreign direct investment, or FDI) was prohibited until the commercial law was revised in 1899. Even then, policy and popular opinion remained hostile to FDI.

According to the estimates by Teranishi Juro (Chapter 6), savings mobilization within the domestic private business sector, including creation of joint stock companies and self-financing, seemed to have played the largest role. Moreover, resource transfer from agriculture to industry through the fiscal system (i.e., the land tax) cannot be ignored. While Teranishi's dataset does not cover years before 1900, savings mobilization through the land tax must have been significant in the early Meiji period.

18 It is not easy for my country to issue foreign bonds. Why could the central and local governments of Meiji Japan issue them in global financial markets?

Because Japan joined the International Gold Standard, a world monetary system that no longer exists. During most of the nineteenth century and up to 1914 (outbreak of WW1), the world was on a gold standard orchestrated by the United Kingdom. The period of 1879–1913 was called the Classical Gold Standard (or International Gold Standard) because all major Western countries participated in it. Under this system, each central bank was obliged to fix the value of its currency in gold, and freely exchange paper money with gold upon request. This meant that exchange rates were also fixed. As long as these obligations were honored, paper money of any country was as good as gold. Trade was liberalized and capital was highly mobile. National economies operated under the same financial mechanism led by London. Prices and interest rates converged globally. For thirty-five years, there was no realignment of exchange rates among major countries.

Japan joined this system in 1897 with gold reserves received from China as war reparation. Even though Japan was only a "developing" country then, its money was accorded with high trust in the global market, allowing its central and local governments to issue foreign bonds denominated in sterling or dollar in world financial centers with little risk premium. American railroad bonds were also popular among British investors. Today, there is no such institutional backing of developing country monies. Their confidence must be secured by political stability, good policy and sufficient foreign exchange reserves.

19 Import substitution failed in many countries. Why did Meiji Japan succeed in the import substitution of cotton textile industry?

High capacity to absorb new technology, the existence of innovative business leaders, the growing supply of Japanese engineers and appropriate official support were all important (Chapters 4 and 5). In addition, market discipline imposed by a low uniform tariff of 5 percent may have been a factor. This made high protection impossible and forced manufacturers to improve competitiveness rather than lobby government. But simply listing these conditions cannot explain why they existed in

Meiji Japan. A government that can effectively manage commercial rents and stimulate industries, together with a very dynamic private sector, are not the features commonly seen in developing countries today. For a possible explanation of these dual strengths of Meiji Japan, see the Umesao Hypothesis in Chapter 1.

20 Can we say that wars with China (1894–95) and with Russia (1904–5) accelerated Japanese industrialization?

As explained in Chapter 6, these two wars had the effect of increasing the economic size of the government. After each war, government, including both central and local governments, became eager to promote industries and build infrastructure. Meanwhile, military spending was not held back after these wars. Such aggressive public spending stimulated domestic businesses in the short run. Whether it also contributed to the long-term sound economic development of Japan is an open question. Fiscal activism produced macroeconomic instabilities such as balance-of-payment pressure and the loss of gold reserves. It was strong foreign demand associated with WW1 (1914-18), rather than the wars with China and Russia, that had an enormous impact on Japanese business activities (Chapter 7).

21 Please tell us about inflation in the Meiji period.

Japan's prewar overall price index is available only from 1901. But we can use the price of rice as a proxy to study the general trends in the earlier period. Inflation and monetary confusion, which started after ports were opened to trade with the West in 1859 (not shown in Figure A.1) was ended by Finance Minister Matsukata's deliberate deflation policy in the early 1880s. While Matsukata Deflation was the longest (three years) and proportionately largest deflation in the Meiji period, other smaller and shorter (usually one year) deflation episodes can be detected as well. Throughout Meiji, the general trend in the rice price was upward. From 1873 to 1912, the average annual increase was 4 percent. After Japan joined the international gold standard in 1897, also thanks to Matsukata's initiative, the yen was fixed to the pound, dollar and other major currencies, and Japanese inflation began to trace global inflation, which was low.

22 What happened to factories damaged by the Great Kanto Earthquake of 1923?

Before the earthquake, key industrial areas of Tokyo were Honjo, Fukagawa, Asakusa, Kanda, Shiba and Kyobashi on the central and eastern coasts (Figure A.2). Large textile mills and their component suppliers congregated, and steel mills, shipbuilders and fertilizer plants were also located. These areas were seriously affected by the earthquake. Honjo recovered strongly but Fukagawa, severely damaged by fire, did not. Oji, which featured textile mills, continued to grow with a stable supply of power from Oji Electric Company.

After the Great Kanto Earthquake, Tokyo's main industrial activities shifted toward southern coastal areas. Omori and Kamata emerged as new industrial areas.

Additional industrial areas were formed by land fill in Keihin Area (between Tokyo and Yokohama). Large producers including Asahi Glass, Asano Shipbuilding, Asano Cement, Ajinomoto, Nippon Cable, Fuji Electric, Tokyo Electric Power, Nisshin Flour, Mitsubishi Oil and Meiji Confectionery gathered in this area during the Taisho Period.

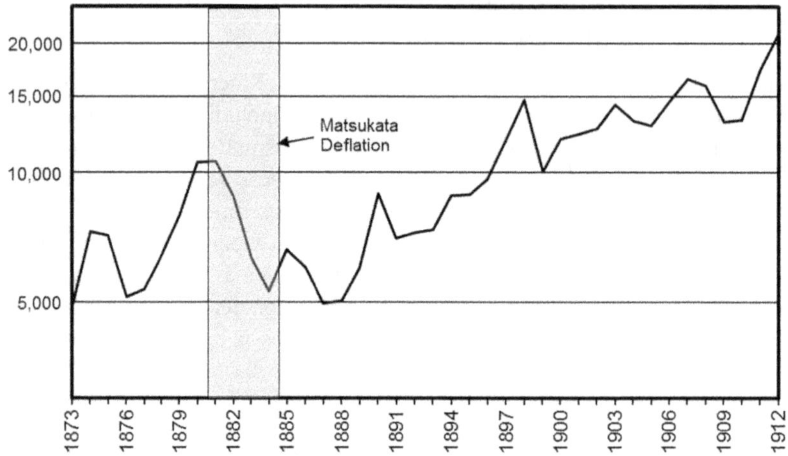

Figure A.1 Rice price in semi-log scale (Yen/koku)

Source: Management and Coordination Agency, *Historical Statistics of Japan*, Vol. 4, 1988. A koku is about 150 kilograms.

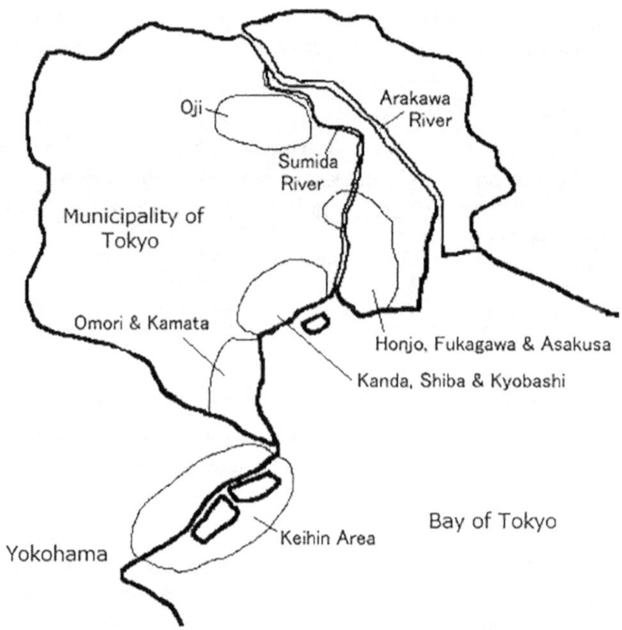

Figure A.2 Tokyo's industrial areas in the Taisho period

23 Please explain the Security Maintenance Law.

This was a law to crack down on people, groups, associations or political parties that denied the National Regime (i.e., sovereignty of the emperor) or private property ownership. It was enacted in 1925 and revised (strengthened) in 1928 and 1941 until it was finally abolished in 1945. The death penalty was introduced in the 1928 revision. The definition of illegal activities in this law was so ambiguous that anyone whom the government considered undesirable could be arrested. Targeted subjects included (underground) Communist Party members, Koreans protesting against Japanese rule, certain religious groups and lawyers defending arrested socialists.

Between 1925 and 1945, over 70,000 persons were arrested by this law, and 10 percent of them were persecuted. Instead of executing socialists, the authorities preferred to convert them into avid nationalists with "Japanese spirit," and they had developed a highly elaborate method for persuasion and conversion.

In Japan, no one was sentenced to death by this law. Richard Sorge, a German national, and Ozaki Hotsumi were charged with spying for the Soviet Union and sentenced to death, but this was in combination with other laws and not by this law alone. However, after WW2, the Japan Communist Party indicated that, while no one was legally sentenced to death by this law, 194 persons died during investigation involving torture and mistreatment, and an additional 1,503 persons died in jail. In Korea, then a Japanese colony, over 23,000 persons were arrested and 45 persons were executed by this law. Application of the law was more severe in Korea than in Japan.

24 Who were the members of the Privy Council that rejected the proposed imperial edict at the time of the banking crisis in 1927?

The Privy Council (*Sumitsuin* in Japanese) was originally established in 1888 to deliberate on the draft of the Meiji Constitution (see Question 16 above). After the constitution was promulgated, it became a permanent advisory body to the emperor. Members were chosen from a group of *genkun* (old politicians who had merits in establishing the Meiji government) and "experienced" statesmen. The members were generally conservative and disliked the idea of government run by political parties. They also supported strong military stance against China and criticized Shidehara Diplomacy which tried to restrain military intervention in China.

On April 14, 1927, the government submitted an imperial edict draft, which permitted the Bank of Japan to rescue the Bank of Taiwan to contain the banking crisis, to the Privy Council for review. The Council's deliberation committee noted several "inconsistencies" in the draft edict and advised its rejection. The edict was subsequently voted down in the general session of the Privy Council. This was because the members of the Council objected to Shidehara Diplomacy of the incumbent government.

One of the characteristics of Japan's prewar politics was the multiplicity and ambiguity of authority for making important decisions, which included the power to start and end a war. The constitution clearly stipulated that the sovereignty rested with the emperor, but he was not responsible for policy consequences. All responsibility was borne by his advisors. The government, either the entire cabinet or individual ministers, were to advise the emperor on policy matters. The military often believed that it had the exclusive right to make military decisions and advise the emperor on military issues. The Privy Council also advised the emperor. In addition, as democracy grew, elected officials and political parties also claimed authority in making decisions. Such decentralization of power in prewar Japan was in sharp contrast to the case of Nazi Germany where Hitler alone had supreme power.

25 What happened to the Bank of Taiwan after its closure in April 1927? Was it liquidated?

No, the Bank of Taiwan survived the 1927 financial crisis. As discussed in Chapter 8, the government passed the law to cover the loss up to 2 million yen incurred by the Bank of Japan. Taxpayers' money was injected into the Bank of Japan by as early as June 1928 to cancel the bad bills held by the Bank of Taiwan. This money, in the main, was used to repay the Bank of Taiwan's interbank "call" (short-term) loans to other commercial banks. As a consequence, the entire financial market was greatly eased. The Bank of Taiwan even expanded its business during the wartime, extending loans to China and Southeast Asia. After Japan's war defeat, it was finally abolished by the order of the US occupation forces.

26 What did political parties do to prevent the takeover of power by the military in the 1930s?

Up until political parties were emasculated in 1937 and finally dissolved in 1940, major parties in the 1930s were the Seiyukai and the Minsei Party, plus a number of small but emerging social democrats such as the Social Mass Party. It must first be noted that these parties did not always fight with rising militarism, as positions held by individual statesmen shifted across time and factions. Even so, we can say on average that they constituted an important force to restrain militarism. The Seiyukai aligned frequently with the army to pursue its partisan interest, but there were also groups within it that tried to cooperate with the Minsei Party to oppose militarism. The Minsei Party was far more consistent in challenging the military's undemocratic ways, but it too failed to amass sufficient power internally and with other parties to form strong enough opposition. Social democrats were naturally against wars, but they too were sometimes attracted to the military's argument that rich capitalists must be punished and the life of poor farmers and workers should be elevated. On the military side, not all commanders and officers were "militaristic" as some endorsed democratic rules while others completely ignored them. Political developments in the 1930s were quite complex (Chapter 9).

In 1934–36, two strategies were proposed to cope with the rise of militarism. The first was establishment of a special temporary mechanism with the participation of all stakeholders (including the military) to supersede normal legislative and/or executive functions until the emergency was overcome. The second was a merger or coalition of the Seiyukai and the Minsei Party to create a super dominant government. The first idea was adopted as the Cabinet Council which, however, was unable to stop militarism. Only its secretariat office survived and was later transformed into the powerful Planning Board to execute war. The second idea was not implemented due to feuds among politicians and party factions. Meanwhile, some statesmen bravely and openly criticized the military in parliamentary sessions. Anti-military speeches by Saito Takao (Minsei Party) in 1935, 1936, 1938 and 1940, and by Hamada Kunimatsu (Seiyukai) in 1937, are particularly famous examples. These can be heard on recorded tapes.

27 Was the Pacific War unavoidable?

This is a big question. Each reader should form his or her opinion after reading this book or attending my lectures. There may not be a simple and uniform answer.

The Pacific War (1941–1945), a total war with the West and especially the United States, was the final stage of Japan's economic and territorial expansion toward neighboring Asia that began in the Meiji period. Japan's interest was mainly directed first to Korea, then its adjacent areas in China (Manchuria or Northeast China). Wars with Qing Dynasty China (1894–95) and with the Russian Empire (1904–5) were fought to secure these areas. In the 1930s, as the Japanese army stationed in China started to ignore and act independently from the Tokyo government, conflict expanded to entire Manchuria as well as Northern and Central regions of Coastal China. In 1937 this aggression ignited a total war with China. As the war prolonged, Japan turned to Southeast Asia to obtain more food, energy and mineral resources. The Japanese military advanced to North Vietnam in 1940 and South Vietnam in 1941, which angered the United States enormously. It immediately imposed an oil embargo on Japan. The Japanese government and military chose to declare war against the United States, with no clear winning strategy, before Japan's oil reserves ran out. With the Pearl Harbor attack in December 1941, the Pacific War began.

In this long and advancing story of outward expansion, it is difficult to locate only one date in which Japan made the wrong and irreversible decision. Any nation with rising military and economic power tends to behave aggressively. Mistakes had been accumulated since the Meiji period. It is even harder to argue what concrete action could have saved Japan from the disastrous course. Some say the Manchurian Incident of 1931 was critical. Others point to 1941, but this may have been too late for turning back. Between 1931 and 1941, Japan seemed gradually pushed and pulled toward a world war without clear diplomatic thinking or long-term planning.

28 My country stagnated after the shock approach was taken to stop inflation after the collapse of the Soviet Union. Wasn't Japan lucky because the Dodge Line austerity measures in 1949 were followed by an external demand increase from the Korean War?

You are quite right. As I discussed in class (Chapter 10), many were fearful of severe recession as a result of abrupt ending of recovery spending and production subsidies by the order of Joseph Dodge, an economic expert dispatched by Washington. The Japanese economy began to shrink as these measures were taken. But the Korean War that broke out in June 1950 suddenly increased US demand for Japanese military and civilian goods, more than offsetting the negative effect of the shock approach. It is sad that the Japanese economy was rescued, not once but twice, by a foreign war in the twentieth century—this time and at the time of WW1. Today, no developing country can expect such timely demand compensation from abroad so it must carefully choose the size and speed of belt-tightening measures to cope with domestic economic crisis.

29 When the bubble economy was forming in the late 1980s, were Japanese people and policy makers aware of it?

They were not clearly aware that an asset bubble was forming. Although many people felt something strange was going on, few analysts said that the economic upswing was only temporary and very dangerous. The Ministry of Finance tried to prop up the stock market whenever it started to fall. The Bank of Japan should perhaps bear the main responsibility for fueling the stock and land markets, but it was politically difficult to tighten monetary policy and end the good time that everyone was enjoying. While asset prices were soaring, consumer prices remained stable. Only after the bubble collapsed, did everyone know it was a bubble. This is almost always the case with any bubble around the world and across ages.

30 What did the Bank of Japan do after the Great East Japan Earthquake in 2011?

Despite the physical damage to financial institutions, "the settlement system and financial institutions, including the Bank of Japan, continued to operate reliably after the quake and maintained normal functions. This was mainly thanks to the great effort made by financial institutions in the affected area to restart operation and respond to the needs of depositors and enterprises. Moreover, cumulative past improvements on emergency response operations made by the settlement system and financial institutions also contributed to minimize the damage" (Report of the Bank of Japan's Bureau of Settlement Mechanism, June 2011).

The Bank of Japan set up the Emergency Response Headquarters fifteen minutes after the quake hit on March 11, 2011. It supplied extra cash to financial institutions in affected areas. The computerized interbank settlement and transaction system (BOJ Net) continued to operate normally. Twenty-nine commercial bill exchanges (about half) in affected areas closed immediately but all except three reopened within ten days. Tax and pension payment services at damaged financial institutions were provided temporarily by the Bank of Japan branches. Paper notes damaged by the earthquake and tsunami were exchanged. The central bank and government also requested financial institutions to allow depositors to withdraw money with minimum identification requirement even if they had lost bankbooks. The number of inoperative financial institution branches in affected areas were 310 (among about 2,700 in all) on March 16, which was reduced to seventy-two by June 21.

Unlike the time of the Great Kanto Earthquake in 1923, the central bank did not indiscriminately re-discount commercial bills to supply liquidity in affected areas. The financial system continued to operate more or less normally despite the serious damage inflicted by the earthquake and tsunami.

BIBLIOGRAPHY

Abe, Takeshi (1990), "*Men Kogyo*" (Cotton Industry), in S. Nishikawa and T. Abe, eds, *Nihon Keizaishi 4: Sangyoka no Jidai 1* (Japanese Economic History vol. 4: The Age of Industrialization 1), Tokyo, Iwanami Shoten, pp. 163–212.

Ando, Yoshio, ed. (1979), *Kindai Nihon Keizaishi Yoran* (Databook on Modern Japanese Economy), 2nd edn, Tokyo, University of Tokyo Press.

Arisawa, Hiromi, ed. (1967), *Nihon Sangyo Hyakunenshi* (One Hundred Year History of Japanese Industries) 1 and 2, Nikkei Shinsho, Nihon Keizai Shimbunsha.

Arisawa, Hiromi (1989), *Sengo Keizai o Kataru: Showashi eno Shogen* (A Commentary on the Postwar Economy: A Testimony to the History of Showa), Tokyo, Tokyo University Press.

Arisawa, Hiromi, ed. (1994), *Nihon Sangyoshi* 1 (History of Japanese Industries vol.1), Tokyo, Nikkei Bunko.

Arisawa, Hiromi, ed. (1994), *Showa Keizaishi* 1 (Economic History of the Showa Period 1), Tokyo, Nikkei Bunko.

Banno, Junji (2001), *Democracy in Pre-War Japan: Concepts of Government, 1871–1937: Collected Essays*, Translated by Andrew Fraser, London and New York, Routledge.

Banno, Junji (2004), *Showashi no Ketteiteki Shunkan* (Decisive Moments in the History of Showa), Tokyo, Chikuma Shinsho.

Banno, Junji (2006), *Kindai Nihon Seijishi* (Political History of Modern Japan), Tokyo, Iwanami Shoten.

Banno, Junji (2007), *Mikan no Meiji Ishin* (Unfinished Meiji Restoration), Tokyo, Chikuma Shinsho.

Banno, Junji (2008), *Nihon Kensei Shi* (History of Japanese Constitution Politics), Tokyo, University of Tokyo Press.

Banno, Junji (2013), *Kindai Nihon to Asia: Meiji Shiso no Jitsuzo* (Modern Japan and Asia: the True Content of Meiji Philosophy), Tokyo, Chikuma Gakugei Bunko.

Banno, Junji and Kenichi Ohno (2010a), *Meiji Ishin 1858–1881* (Meiji Restoration 1858–1881), Tokyo, Kodansha Shinsho.

Banno, Junji and Kenichi Ohno (2010b), "The Flexible Structure of Politics in Meiji Japan," Developmental Leadership Program Research Paper 07, April.

Bytheway, Simon J. (2005), *Nihon Keizai to Gaikoku Shihon 1858–1939* (Japanese Economy and Foreign Capital 1858–1939), Tokyo, Tosui Shobo

Chang, Ha-joon (2002), *Kicking Away the Ladder: Development Strategy in Historical Perspective*, London, Anthem Press.

Dore, Ronald P. (1984), *Education in Tokugawa Japan*, Center for Japanese Studies, Ann Arbor, MI, University of Michigan.

Editorial Committee of the Biography of Marquis Inoue Kaoru (1933), *Seigai Inoue Ko Den* (Biography of Marquis Inoue), vol. 2, Tokyo, Naigai Shoseki.

Editorial Committee of the Essays of Inoue Junnnosuke (1935), *Essays of Inoue Junnosuke*, vol. 1, pp. 573–574.

Francks, Penelope (2015), *Japanese Economic Development: Theory and Practice*, Abingdon, Routledge.

Fujimoto, Takahiro (2004), *Nihon no Monozukuri Tetsugaku* (Japanese Philosophy of Manufacturing), Tokyo, Nihon Keizai Shimbunsha.

Fujimoto, Takahiro, Akira Takeishi and Yaichi Aoshima, eds (2001), *Business Architecture: Seihin, Soshiki, Process no Senryakuteki Sekkei* (Business Architecture: Strategic Design of Products, Organizations and Processes), Tokyo, Yuhikaku.

Fujimoto, Takahiro and Junjiro Shintaku, eds (2005), *Chugoku Seizogyo no Architecture Bunseki* (Architectural Analysis of Chinese Manufacturing Industries), Tokyo, Toyo Keizai Shimposha.

Fukuzawa, Yukichi (1962), *Bunmeiron no Gairyaku* (Outline of Civilization), Tokyo, Iwanami Shoten, (reprint, originally 1875).

GRIPS Development Forum, ed. (2009), *Introducing Kaizen in Africa*, produced for the Ethiopian Government in the course of Ethiopia–Japan Industrial Policy Dialogue.

GRIPS Development Forum, ed. (2016), *Ethiopia Sangyo Seisaku Taiwa Kirokushu: Ethiopia ni okeru Seisaku Taiwa to Seisaku Chosa* (Records of Ethiopia-Japan Industrial Policy Dialogue: Policy Dialogue and Policy Research in Ethiopia), vol. 1, GRIPS Development Forum.

Hanai, Shunsuke (2000), "*Keikogyo no Shihon Chikuseki*" (Capital Accumulation of Light Manufacturing), ch. 3 in K. Ishii, A. Hara, and H. Takeda, eds, *Nihon Keizaishi 2: Sangyo Kakumei Ki* (Japanese Economic History 2: Industrial Revolution), Tokyo, University of Tokyo Press.

Hara, Akira (1994), *Nihon Keizaishi* (Japanese Economic History), Tokyo, University of the Air Press, (revised in 1999).

Hara, Yonosuke (1996), *Asia Dynamism: Shihonshugi no Network to Hatten no Chiikisei* (Asia Dynamism: Capitalist Networks and Regional Characteristics of Development), Tokyo, NTT Publishing.

Hayami, Akira and Matao Miyamoto, eds (1988), *Nihon Keizaishi 1: Keizai Shakai no Seiritsu 17–18 Seiki*, (Japanese Economic History vol. 1: Establishment of Economic Society 17th–18th Centuries), Tokyo, Iwanami Shoten.

Honda Soichiro Study Group, eds (1998), *The Analects of Honda Soichiro*, Tokyo, Shogakukan.

Iijima, Manji (1949), *History of Japanese Textile Spinning Industry*, Tokyo, Sogensha.

Inada, Masatsugu (1960), *Meiji Kempo Seiritsushi* (The History of Formulation of the Meiji Constitution), vol. 1, Tokyo, Yuhikaku.

Inoki, Masamichi (1995), *Gunkoku Nihon no Kobo: Nisshin Senso kara Nitchu Senso e* (The Rise and the Fall of the Japanese Militarist State: From the Japan–Qing War to the Japan–China War), Tokyo, Chuko Shinsho.

Institute of Japanese Management History, ed. (1971), *Godai Tomoatsu Denki Shiryo* (Biographical Documents of Godai Tomoatsu), vol. 1, Tokyo, Toyo Keizai Shimposha.

Irokawa, Daikichi (1970), *Meiji no Bunka* (The Culture of Meiji), Tokyo, Iwanami Shoten.

Ishii, Kanji, Akira Hara and Haruhito Takeda, eds (2000a), *Nihon Keizaishi 1, Bakumatsu Ishin Ki* (Japanese Economic History 1: End of Bakufu and Meiji Restoration), Tokyo, University of Tokyo Press.

Ishii, Kanji, Akira Hara and Haruhito Takeda, eds (2000b), *Nihon Keizaishi 2, Sangyo Kakumei Ki* (Japanese Economic History 2: Industrial Revolution), Tokyo, University of Tokyo Press.

Itagaki, Taisuke, ed. (1957), *Jiyutoshi* (History of the Liberal Party), vol. 1, Tokyo, Iwanami Shoten.

Ito, Motoshige, Kazuharu Kiyono, Masahiro Okuno and Kotaro Suzumura (1988), *Sangyo Seisaku no Keizai Bunseki* (Economic Analysis of Industrial Policy), Tokyo, University of Tokyo Press.

Ito, Osamu (2007), "*Senji Sengo no Zaisei to Kinyu*" (Fiscal and Financial Policies during the War and Postwar Periods), ch. 3, in K. Ishii, A. Hara and H. Takeda, eds, *Nihon Keizaishi 4, Senji Sengo Ki* (Economic History of Japan vol. 4: War and Postwar Periods), University of Tokyo Press, pp. 141–189.

Ito, Takatoshi (1992), *The Japanese Economy*, Cambridge, MA, MIT Press.

Japan Historical Document Society (1967), *Kido Takayoshi Nikki* (The Diary of Kido Takayoshi), vol. 3, Tokyo, University of Tokyo Press.

Japan Historical Document Society (1969), *Okubo Toshimichi Bunsho* (Documents of Okubo Toshimichi), vol.7, Tokyo, University of Tokyo Press.

Japan International Cooperation Agency (JICA) (1995), Country Study for Japan's Official Development Assistance to the Socialist Republic of Vietnam (Committee Report), March.

Japan International Cooperation Agency (JICA) and Japan Bank for International Cooperation (JBIC) (2008), *Report of the Stocktaking Work on the Economic Development in Africa and the Asian Growth Experience*, May.

Johnson, Chalmers (1982), *MITI and the Japanese Miracle: The Growth of Industrial Policy, 1925–1975*, Stanford, CA, Stanford University Press.

Kamiyama, Tsuneo (2000), "*Zaisei Seisaku to Kinyu Kozo*" (Fiscal Policy and Financial Structure), in K. Ishii, A. Hara, and H. Takeda, eds, *Nihon Keizaishi 2, Sangyo Kakumei Ki* (Japanese Economic History 2: Industrial Revolution), Tokyo, University of Tokyo Press, pp. 61–109.

Kaneda, Tatsuo (1992), *Kyrgyzstan Keizai Saisei no Michi: Chiteki Shien no Kokoromi* (The Path to the Recovery of the Kyrgyzstan Economy: An Attempt in Intellectual Assistance), JIIA Paper No.1, Japan Institute of International Affairs.

Kawakatsu, Heita (1991), *Nihon Bunmei to Kindai Seiyo: Sakoku Saiko* (Japanese Civilization and Modern West: Rethinking the Closed Door Policy), Tokyo, NHK Books.

Keynes, John Maynard (1936), *The General Theory of Employment, Interest and Money*, London, Macmillan.

Kikkawa, Takeo (2002), "*Zaibatsu no Conzern-ka to Infrastructure Kinou*" (Conzernization of Zaibatsu and their Infrastructure Functions," ch. 3, in K. Ishii, A. Hara and H. Takeda eds, *Japanese Economic History vol. 3: Inter-war Period*, Tokyo, Tokyo University Press.

Kikuchi, Tsuyoshi (2014), "*Chukaigata Gijutsu Iten ni kansuru Kosatsu: 3 Dankai Model no Kochiku to Tekiyo*" (A Study on Intermediary Technology Transfer: Construction and Application of the Three Step Model," Doctoral Dissertation, Tokyo, Takushoku University, March.

Koichi Emi, and Yuichi Shionoya (1971), *Capital Formation*, Long-term Economic Statistics vol. 4, Tokyo, Toyokeizai Shimposha.

Komiya, Ryutaro (1988), Masahiro Okuno, and Kotaro Suzumura, eds, *Industrial Policy of Japan*, San Diego, CA, Academic Press.

Komiya, Ryutaro (1994), *Boeki Kuroji Akaji no Keizaigaku: Nichibei Masatsu no Orokasa* (Economics of Trade Surplus and Deficit: The Folly of the Japan-US Friction), Tokyo, Toyo Keizai Shimposha.

Komiya, Ryutaro and Miyako Suda (1983), *Gendai Kokusai Kinyu Ron: Riron, Rekisi, Seisaku* (Modern International Finance: Theory, History and Policy), in two volumes, Tokyo, Nihon Keizai Shimbunsha.

Kosai, Yutaka (1995), *En no Sengoshi* (The Postwar History of the Yen), Tokyo, NHK Ningendaigaku Textbook.

Kosai, Yutaka and Juro Teranishi, eds (1993), *Sengo Nihon no Keizai Kaikaku: Shijo to Seifu* (Economic Reforms of Postwar Japan: Market and Government), Tokyo, University of Tokyo Press.

Maddison, Angus (2003), *The World Economy: Historical Statistics*, Paris, OECD Development Centre.

Maegawa, Keiji (1998), "*The Continuity of Cultures and Civilization: An Introduction to the Concept of Translative Adaptation*," in K. Ohno and I. Ohno, eds, *Japanese Views on Economic Development: Diverse Paths to the Market*, London and New York, Routledge, pp. 166–177.

Maegawa, Keiji (2004), *Glocalization no Jinruigaku: Kokusai Bunka, Kaihatsu, Imin* (The Anthropology of Glocalization: International Cultures, Development, Migration), Tokyo, Shinyosha.

Management and Coordination Agency (1987–88), *Historical Statistics of Japan*, five volumes, Japan Statistical Association.

Maruyama, Masao (1961), *Nihon no Shiso* (Japanese Thought), Tokyo, Iwanami Shinsho.

Matsumoto, Takanori and Miyako Okuda (1997), "*Senzenki Nihon ni okeru Zairai Sangyo no Zenkoku Tenkai: Eigyozei Deta ni yoru Suryoteki Bunseki*" (Nationwide Development of Indigenous Industries in Prewar Japan: Quantitative Analysis Using Sales Tax Data), in T. Nakamura, ed.,

Nihon no Keizai Hatten to Zairai Sangyo (Japanese Economic Development and Indigenous Industries), Tokyo, Yamakawa Shuppansha, pp. 11–68.

McKinnon, Ronald I., and Kenichi Ohno (1997), *Dollar and Yen: Resolving Economic Conflict between the United States and Japan*, Cambridge, MA, MIT Press (also available in Japanese translation from Nihon Keizai Shimbunsha, 1998).

Minami, Ryoshin (1986), *The Economic Development of Japan*, Basingstoke, Macmillan.

Miyamoto, Matao (1999), *Nihon no Kindai 11: Kigyokatachi no Chosen* (Modern Age of Japan vol. 11: Challenges of Entrepreneurs), Tokyo, Chuo Koron Shinsha.

Miyamoto, Matao and Masahito Uemura (1988), "*Tokugawa Keizai no Junkan Kozo*" (Circulation Structure of Tokugawa Economy) in A. Hayami and M. Miyamoto, eds, *Nihon Keizaishi 1, Keizai Shakai no Seiritsu 17–18 Seiki*, (Japanese Economic History vol. 1: Establishment of Economic Society 17th–18th Centuries), Tokyo, Iwanami Shoten, pp. 271–324.

Miyamoto, Matao, Takeshi Abe, Masaru Udagawa, Minoru Sawai and Takeo Kikkawa (1995), *Nihon Keieishi: Nihongata Kigyo Keiei no Hatten, Edo kara Heisei e* (History of Japanese Management: Development of the Japanese Management Model from Edo to Heisei), Tokyo, Yuhikaku.

Miyazaki, Yasusada (1697), *Nogyo Zensho* (Encyclopedia of Agriculture).

Miyoshi, Yukio, ed. (1986), *Soseki Bunmei Ronshu* (Soseki's Writings on Civilization), Tokyo, Iwanami Bunko.

Murakami, Katsuhiko (2000), "*Boeki no Kakudai to Shihon no Yushutsunyu*" (Trade Expansion and Capital Export and Import), in K. Ishii, A. Hara, and H. Takeda, eds, *Nihon Keizaishi 2, Sangyo Kakumei Ki* (Japanese Economic History 2: Industrial Revolution), Tokyo, University of Tokyo Press, pp. 1–59.

Murakami, Yasusuke (1984), *Shin Chukan Taishu no Jidai* (The Age of New Middle Mass), Tokyo, Chuo Koronsha.

Nakamura, Masanori (1982), *Showa no Kyoko: Daifukyo to Shinobiyoru Fascism* (Showa Crisis: Depression and Approaching Fascism), Tokyo, Shogakukan.

Nakamura, Takafusa (1989), "*Gaisetsu: 1937–54*" (Overview: 1937–54), in T. Nakamura, ed., Nihon Keizaishi 7, Keikakuka to Minshuka (Japanese Economic History vol. 7: Planning and Democratization), Tokyo, Iwanami Shoten.

Nakamura, Takafusa (1994), *Showa Kyoko to Keizai Seisaku* (Showa Depression and Economic Policy), Tokyo, Kodansha Gakujutsu Bunko.

Nakamura, Takafusa (1997), "*Joron: Zairai Sangyo no Bunseki Shikaku*" (Introduction: An Analytical Framework of Indigenous Industries), in T. Nakamura, ed., *Nihon no Keizai Hatten to Zairai Sangyo* (Japanese Economic Development and Indigenous Industries), Tokyo, Yamakawa Shuppansha.

Nakamura, Takafusa and Konosuke Odaka, eds (1989), *Nihon Keizaishi 6, Nijukozo* (Japanese Economic History vol. 6: The Dual Structure), Tokyo, Iwanami Shoten.

Nakamura, Takafusa, ed. (1989), *Nihon Keizaishi 7, Keikakuka to Minshuka* (Japanese Economic History vol. 7: Planning and Democratization), Tokyo, Iwanami Shoten.

Nakamura, Takafusa, ed. (1997), *Nihon no Keizai Hatten to Zairai Sangyo* (Japanese Economic Development and Indigenous Industries), Tokyo, Yamakawa Shuppansha.

Nishikawa, Shunsaku and Masatoshi Amano (1989), "*Shohan no Sangyo to Keizai Seisaku*" (Industries and Economic Policies of Hans), in H. Shimbo and O. Saito, eds, *Nihon Keizaishi 2, Kindai Seicho no Taido* (Japanese Economic History 2: The Dawn of Modern Development), Tokyo, Iwanami Shoten, 173–217.

Nishikawa, Shunsaku and Takeshi Abe, eds (1990), *Nihon Keizaishi 4, Sangyoka no Jidai 1* (Japanese Economic History vol. 4: The Age of Industrialization 1), Tokyo, Iwanami Shoten.

Nishikawa, Shunsaku and Yuzo Yamamoto, eds (1990), *Nihon Keizaishi 5, Sangyoka no Jidai 2* (Japanese Economic History vol. 5: The Age of Industrialization 2), Tokyo, Iwanami Shoten.

Noguchi, Yukio (1995), *1940 nen Taisei: Saraba Senji Keizai* (The 1940 Regime: A Farewell to the Wartime Economy), Tokyo, Toyo Keizai Shimposha.

Odaka, Konosuke (1989), "*Niju Kozo*" (Dual Structure), in T. Nakamura and K. Odaka, eds, *Nihon Keizaishi 6, Niju Kozo* (Japanese Economic History vol. 6: The Dual Structure), Tokyo, Iwanami Shoten.

Odaka, Konosuke (1990), "*Sangyo no Ninaite*" (Workforce and Work Systems), in S. Nishikawa and T. Abe, eds, *Nihon Keizaishi 4, Sangyoka no Jidai 1* (Japanese Economic History vol. 4: The Age of Industrialization 1), Tokyo, Iwanami Shoten, pp. 303–350.

Odaka, Konosuke (1999), "The Dual Structure of the Japanese Economy," ch.3, in T. Nakamura and K. Odaka eds, *The Economic History of Japan, 1914–1955: A Dual Structure*, Oxford, Oxford University Press, pp. 111–136.

Odaka, Konosuke (2000), *Shokunin no Sekai, Kojo no Sekai, Shinban* (The World of Craftsmen and the World of Factories, New Edition), Tokyo, NTT Publishing.

Ohkawa, Takmatsu, and Yoshihiko Yamamoto (1979), *Patterns of Japanese Economic Development: A Quantitative Appraisal*, New Haven, CT and London, Yale University Press.

Ohno, Kenichi (2002), "*Nihon Keizai, Mikuro karano Saisei o*" (Renewal of Japan's Economy Begins from Microeconomic Cleanup), *Nihon Keizai Shimbun*, December 31.

Ohno, Kenichi (2003), *East Asian Growth and Japanese Aid Strategy*, GRIPS.

Ohno, Kenichi (2004), "Designing a Comprehensive and Realistic Industrial Strategy," Vietnam Development Forum Discussion Paper, No.1, June.

Ohno, Kenichi (2006), *The Economic Development of Japan: The Path Traveled by Japan as a Developing Country*, GRIPS Development Forum (translation available in Japanese, Vietnamese, Chinese, Arabic, Russian and Persian).

Ohno, Kenichi (2013), *Learning to Industrialize: From Given Growth to Policy-aided Value Creation*, London and New York, Routledge.

Ohno, Kenichi and Izumi Ohno, eds (1998), *Japanese Views on Economic Development: Diverse Paths to the Market*, London and New York, Routledge.

Ohno, Kenichi and Kojiro Sakurai (1997), *Higashi Asia no Kaihatsu Keizaigaku* (Development Economics of East Asia), Tokyo, Yuhikaku.

Ohno, Kenichi and Nguyen Van Thuong, eds (2005), *Improving Industrial Policy Formulation*, Vietnam Development Forum, Hanoi, The Publishing House of Political Theory.

Oishi, Shinzaburo (1977), *Edo Jidai* (The Edo Period), Tokyo, Chuko Shinsho.

Okazaki, Tetsuji (1997), *Kogyoka no Kiseki: Keizai Taikoku Zenshi* (The Road to Industrialization: Prehistory of the Economic Giant), Tokyo, Yomiuri Shimbunsha.

Okazaki, Tetsuji (1999), *Edo no Sijo Keizai: Rekishiseido Bunseki kara Mita Kabunakama* (The Market Economy of Edo: Trade Cartels from the Viewpoint of Historical Institutional Analysis), Tokyo, Kodansha Sensho Metier.

Okazaki, Tetsuji and Masahiro Okuno, eds (1993), *Gendai Nihon Keizai System no Genryu* (The Source of the Modern Japanese Economic System), Tokyo, Nihon Keizai Shimbunsha.

Okimoto, Daniel I. (1989), *Between MITI and the Market*, Stanford, CA, Stanford University Press.

Ota, Hiroko (2010), *Kaikaku Gyakuso* (Reform in Reverse), Tokyo, Nihon Keizai Shimbun Shuppansha.

Oyama, Azusa, ed. (1966), *Yamagata Aritomo Ikensho* (The Policy Documents of Yamagata Aritomo), Tokyo, Hara Shobo.

Ranis, Gustav (1969), "The Financing of Japanese Economic Development," in K. Ohkawa et al., eds, *Agriculture and Economic Growth: Japan's Experience*, Tokyo, University of Tokyo Press, pp. 37–57.

Rosovsky, Henry (1961), *Capital Formation in Japan: 1868–1940*, New York, Free Press of Glencoe.

Saburo Okita, ed. (1992), *Postwar Reconstruction of the Japanese Economy*, Tokyo, University of Tokyo Press,

Saito, Osamu (1985), *Proto-kogyoka no Jidai: Seiyo to Nihon no Hikakushi* (The Age of Proto-Industrialization: Western Europe and Japan in Historical Comparison), Tokyo, Nihon Hyoronsha.

Saito, Osamu and Masayuki Tanimoto (1989), "*Zairai Sangyo no Saihensei*" (Restructuring of Indigenous Industries), in M. Umemura and Y. Yamamoto, eds, *Nihon Keizaishi 3, Kaiko to Ishin*

(Japanese Economic History vol. 3: Opening of Ports and Meiji Restoration), Tokyo, Iwanami Shoten, pp. 223–283.

Sawai, Minoru (1990), "*Kikai Kogyo*" (Machinery Industry), in S. Nishikawa and T. Abe, eds, *Nihon Keizaishi 4, Sangyoka no Jidai 1* (Japanese Economic History vol. 4: The Age of Industrialization 1), Tokyo, Iwanami Shoten, pp. 213–253.

Shiba, Ryotaro (1993–2000), *Kono Kuni no Katachi 1–6* (The Shape of This Nation, vols. 1–6), originally published in *Bungei Shunju* from 1986 to 1996, republished in Bunshun Bunko in six volumes, 1990–1996 in hard cover and 1993–2000 in paperbacks.

Shibusawa, Eiichi (1994), *The Autobiography of Shibusawa Eiichi: From Peasant to Entrepreneur*, translated by Teruko Craig, Tokyo, University of Tokyo Press.

Shimbo, Hiroshi and Osamu Saito, eds (1989), *Nihon Keizaishi 2, Kindai Seicho no Taido* (Japanese Economic History vol. 2: The Dawn of Modern Development), Tokyo, Iwanami Shoten.

Shimizu, Yoji (2007), "*Sengo Kiki to Keizai Fukko 1: Shokuryo Kiki to Nogyo Fukko*" (Postwar Crisis and Economic Recovery Part 1: Food Crisis and Agricultural Recovery), ch. 6, in K. Ishii, A. Hara and H. Takeda, eds, *Socio-Economic History of Modern Japan vol. 4: War and Occupation*, Tokyo, University of Tokyo Press, 311–356.

Sonobe, Tetsushi and Keijiro Otsuka (2004), *Sangyo Hatten no Roots to Senryaku: Nicchutai no Keiken ni Manabu* (Roots and Strategies of Industrial Development: Lessons from the East Asian Experience), Tokyo, Chisen Shokan.

Special Survey Committee of the Ministry of Foreign Affairs (1992), *Postwar Reconstruction of the Japanese Economy*, compiled by Saburo Okita, Tokyo, University of Tokyo Press (the original report in Japanese, *Nihon Keizai Saiken no Kihon Mondai* (Basic Problems in Rebuilding the Japanese Economy), was published in September 1946).

Statistics Bureau of Management and Coordination Agency (1988), *Historical Statistics of Japan Vol. 3*, pp. 240–241 and p. 289.

Sugihara, Kaoru (1996), *Ajiakan Boeki no Keisei to Kozo* (Formation and Structure of Intra-Asia Trade), Kyoto: Minerva Shobo.

Suzuki, Jun (2000), "*Jukogyo Kozangyo no Shihon Chikuseki*" (Capital Accumulation of Heavy Industry and Mining), in K. Ishii, A. Hara and H. Takeda, eds, *Nihon Keizaishi 2: Sangyo Kakumei Ki* (Japanese Economic History 2: Industrial Revolution), ch. 4, Tokyo, University of Tokyo Press, pp. 199–247.

Tachibanaki, Toshiaki (2016), *21 Seiki Nihon no Kakusa* (Income Gaps of 21st Century Japan), Tokyo, Iwanami Shoten.

Takahashi, Kamekichi, and Sunao Morigaki (1968), *Showa Kinyu Kyoko Shi* (History of Showa Financial Crisis), Tokyo, Seimeikai Shinsho (revised and reprinted in Kodansha Gakujutsu Bunko, 1993).

Takamura, Naosuke (1966), "Shokusan Kogyo" (Industrialization Policy), in Mitsusada Inoue et al. eds, *Nihon Rekishi Taikei* (Comprehensive Japanese History), vol. 13, Tokyo, Yamakawa Shuppansha, pp. 438–439.

Tanaka, Keiichi (2000), *Hyakusho no Edo Jidai* (The Edo Period of Farmers), Tokyo, Chikuma Shinsho.

Teranishi, Juro (1990), "*Kinyu no Kindaika to Sangyoka*" (Modernization of Finance and Industrialization), in S. Nishikawa and Y. Yamamoto, eds, *Nihon Keizaishi 5, Sangyoka no Jidai 2* (Japanese Economic History vol. 5: The Age of Industrialization 2), Tokyo, Iwanami Shoten, pp. 37–84.

Tominaga, Kenichi (1990), *Nihon no Kindaika to Shakai Hendo: Tuebingen Kogi* (The Modernization of Japan and Social Change: A Lecture at Tuebingen), Tokyo, Kodansha Gakujutsu Bunko.

Toriumi, Yasushi (1996), *Nihon no Kindai: Kokumin Kokka no Keisei Hatten to Zasetsu* (Modern Japan: The Formation, Development and Collapse of the Nation State), University of the Air Press.

Uchida, Hoshimi (1990), "*Gijutsu Iten*" (Technology Transfer), ch. 3, in N. Shunsaku, and T. Abe, eds, *Nihon Keizaishi 4, Sangyoka no Jidai 1* (Japanese Economic History vol. 4: The Age of Industrialization 1), Tokyo, Iwanami Shoten (unofficial English translation available from the GRIPS Development Forum, 2011), pp. 255–302.

Umemura, Mataji and Yuzo Yamamoto, eds (1989), *Nihon Keizaishi 3, Kaiko to Ishin* (Japanese Economic History vol. 3: Opening of Ports and Meiji Restoration), Tokyo, Iwanami Shoten.

Umesao, Tadao (1986), *Nihon towa Nanika: Kindai Nihon Bunmei no Keisei to Hatten* (What is Japan? Formation and Development of Modern Japanese Civilization), Tokyo, NHK Books.

Umesao, Tadao (2003), *An Ecological View of History: Japanese Civilization in the World Context*, Melbourne, Vic., Trans Pacific Press (Japanese original published by Chuo Koronsha, 1957).

Umetani, Noboru (1968), *Hired Foreign Advisors*, vol. 1, Tokyo, Kajima Research Institute Publishing House.

United Nations Conference on Trade and Development (UNCTAD) (2004), *Least Development Countries Report 2004*.

Waseda University Institute of Social Sciences, ed. (1958), *Okuma Bunsho* (Documents of Okuma), vol. 3, Tokyo, Waseda University.

Watanabe, Toshio (1995), *Shinseiki Asia no Kousou* (The Design of Asia in the New Century), Tokyo, Chikuma Shinsho (excerpted English translation available in K. Ohno and I. Ohno, eds, *Japanese Views on Economic Development: Diverse Paths to the Market*, Routledge, 1998).

Yamamoto, Yoshihiko, ed. (2002), *Kiyosawa Kiyoshi Hyoronshu* (Collected Essays of Kiyosawa Kiyoshi), Tokyo, Iwanami Shoten.

Yoshikawa, Hiroshi (1997), *Kodo Seicho: Nihon o Kaeta 6000 Nichi* (The High Growth Period: 6000 Days that Changed Japan), Tokyo, Yomiuri Shimbunsha.

Yoshino, Sakuzo (1975), "*Kensei no Hongi o Toite sono Yushu no Bi o Nasu no Michi o Ronzu*" (Discourse on the Principle of Constitutional Government and the Way to Fully Develop its Potentiality), in Y. Oka, ed., *Yoshino Sakuzo Hyoronshu* (Collected Essays of Yoshino Sakuzo), Iwanami Bunko (initially published in *Chuo Koron*, January 1916), pp. 10–131.

Yoshitomi, Masaru (1998), *Nihon Keizai no Shinjitsu: Tsusetsu o Koete* (The Truth of the Japanese Economy: Beyond Popular Views), Tokyo, Toyo Keizai Shimposha.

Yukio, Miyoshi, ed. (1986), *Soseki's Writings on Civilization*, Tokyo, Iwanami Bunko.

INDEX

Figures and tables, which are separate from the main discussion in the text, are indicated by page numbers in *italics*. Boxes are indicated in **bold**.

For Product Safety Concerns and Information please contact our EU representative GPSR@taylorandfrancis.com
Taylor & Francis Verlag GmbH, Kaufingerstraße 24, 80331 München, Germany

www.ingramcontent.com/pod-product-compliance
Lightning Source LLC
LaVergne TN
LVHW080809011026
849160LV00015B/1580
9781138215429